CURRICULUM AND IDEOLOGY

"This book undertakes a comprehensive and critical review of contemporary curriculum reforms in Ireland and sets them in their cultural, political and global contexts. It contains contributions by some of the best scholars of curriculum change and should be of great interest to policy-makers and educationalists in and beyond Irish shores. This book will challenge the thinking of anyone who naïvely assumes that globalisation is shaping the curriculum in uniform rather than diverse ways." — *John Elliott, Professorial Fellow, Centre for Applied Research in Education, University of East Anglia*

"Sugrue calls for a changed national debate about curriculum, teaching and learning by surfacing *signposts* and *silences* in conversations about Irish education reforms. This volume takes a 'glocal' perspective, situating the Irish reforms in the context of a global reform movement. Sugrue and collaborators make a critical contribution by surfacing elements that shape Irish education in fundamental ways, but are seldom part of the dialogue. The assembled papers present a compelling case for a 'new beginning' to deliberations that can foster curriculum transformation in Ireland and make a valuable addition to both the Irish and international education reform communities." — *Milbrey McLaughlin, David Jacks Professor, Education and Public Policy, Stanford University*

"These outstanding essays both focus and brace the mind with their challenging analyses of the most pressing issues that face state education authorities in all Western countries. They will be of particular interest to all those who deal with policy and the administration of education in Ireland, but they also offer many insights about the current debates that affect education in all modern states. The essays provide keen analyses of power relationships at international and national levels but also bring the same keenness to discussions of detailed curriculum implications. This is an exemplary set of essays: coherent, challenging, and providing valuable suggestions for the best way forward." — *Professor Kieran Egan, Canada Chair of Education, Simon Frazer University, California*

"This book is about Ireland and its recent curriculum reforms; that makes it important enough. But it also sets out those changes against a clearly analysed and well written account of globalisation. In doing so, it offers a framework for an examination of the purposes of curriculum more generally. Ciaran Sugrue's book certainly rewards a detailed read." — *Professor Ann Edwards, Faculty of Education, University of Birmingham*

CURRICULUM AND IDEOLOGY

Irish Experiences, International Perspectives

Edited by
Ciaran Sugrue

The Liffey Press

Published by
The Liffey Press Ltd
Ashbrook House, 10 Main Street
Raheny, Dublin 5, Ireland
www.theliffeypress.com

A catalogue record of this book is
available from the British Library.

ISBN 1-904148-43-3

Printed in Spain by GraphyCems

CONTENTS

Acknowledgements .... *vii*

Notes on Contributors .... *xi*

Foreword .... *xv*

Introduction 1

SECTION ONE
CHANGE FORCES: INTERNATIONAL PERSPECTIVES

1   **Change Processes and Historical Periods:**
     An International Perspective 19
     Ivor F. Goodson

2   **Towards a Curriculum for Lifelong Learning** 35
     Malcolm Skilbeck

SECTION TWO
SECONDARY CURRICULUM REFORMS: IRISH PERSPECTIVES

3   **Politics and Partnership in Curriculum Planning in**
     Ireland 67
     Gary Granville

4   **Cultural and Political Contexts of Irish Post-Primary**
     Curriculum: Influences, Interests and Issues 101
     Jim Gleeson

5   Secondary School Curriculum Reforms in Northern
       Ireland: A Critical Analysis 141
       Alex McEwen

                         SECTION THREE
       PRIMARY CURRICULUM REVISIONS: IRISH PERSPECTIVES

6   Whose Curriculum Is It Anyway? Power, Politics and
       Possibilities in the Construction of the Revised
       Primary Curriculum 167
       Ciaran Sugrue

7   Making the Irish: Identity and Citizenship in the
       Primary Curriculum 209
       Fionnuala Waldron

8   The Primary Curriculum in Northern Ireland:
       Aping Big Brother or Finding its own Voice? 239
       Margaret Reynolds

                          SECTION FOUR
       IRISH EXPERIENCES: INTERNATIONAL PERSPECTIVES

9   Signposts and Silences: Situating the Local within the
       Global 269
       Ciaran Sugrue and Jim Gleeson

ACKNOWLEDGEMENTS

One of the more inevitable consequences of being editor of a book is the accumulation of various debts of gratitude in the process. It is one of the more pleasurable aspects of the work to acknowledge the various and varied contributions that make this work possible. First and foremost, I am very grateful to my colleagues, locally and internationally, who readily agreed to contribute individual chapters. I would like to thank my colleague Fionnuala Waldron in particular for reasons that she will know and understand. I am very grateful also to Jim Gleeson for his collaboration on the concluding chapter, his friendship and good advice. Sincere gratitude to Ivor Goodson also whose periodic inquiries as to the status of the manuscript provided important impetus to the work when enthusiasm for the project was waning!

I am particularly grateful to David Givens of The Liffey Press for taking on the project of publishing this volume and to Brian Langan for the efficient, expeditious and masterful manner in which he transformed the manuscript into a "polished" book. Such skills and expertise are often the more invisible aspects of academic publishing, without which we would be the poorer.

A very sincere expression of gratitude is extended to the Research Committee of St Patrick's College, Drumcondra. Its generous financial support towards the publication of the text is part of its ongoing institutional strategy for, and commitment to, the cultivation of a strong and vibrant research culture within the College, and contribution to a national literature on education that fosters and promotes fresh ferment. Mo bhuíochas don gcoiste is don Choláiste.

I would like to acknowledge a deep debt of gratitude to Siobhán Nolan for her patience, skill and expertise in compiling the final version of the manuscript and for her careful husbanding and transformation of the various iterations of the chapters.

Finally, I continue to benefit from the unselfish and unstinting support of my partner Joan who has always been an enthusiastic supporter of my various writing projects. Her own teaching experience and sense of professionalism, through our ongoing conversations, provide an important reality check for my more fanciful theorising! As a token of my appreciation for her affection, loyalty and support, this book is dedicated to her.

For Joan, from whom I continue to learn
about the curriculum of Life, Love and Living

NOTES ON CONTRIBUTORS

Jim Gleeson has taught in vocational schools in Dublin and his native Tipperary. He is a lecturer in Education in the Department of Education and Professional Studies at the University of Limerick and was Head of that Department from 1991 to 1995. He was Project Leader of the SPIRAL 2 Transition Project at Shannon Curriculum Development Centre during the 1980s and has conducted curriculum evaluations in areas as diverse as transition from school to adult and working life, European Studies, gender equality and Exploring Masculinities. He was NCCA Education Officer for the Leaving Certificate Applied programme and has recently led the Irish part of an OECD-wide study on ICT and School Improvement. His doctoral thesis on the topic of "Post-Primary Curriculum and Practice in the Republic of Ireland: Fragmentation, Contestation and Partnership", submitted to the University of East Anglia, reflects his deep interest in education and curriculum policy matters.

Ivor F. Goodson holds a Chair in Education at the School of Education and Professional Development at the University of East Anglia, Norwich, Norfolk, UK. He has been Director of three research units, where he has directed a wide range of research projects on computer education, teachers' lives and careers, case histories of school and curriculum, environmental education and racial ethnocultural minority teaching. He is currently co-director of a large study of US and Canadian schools funded by the Spencer Foundation. He is author of more than thirty books, some of the most recent of which are: *Life History Research in Educational Settings: Learning from Lives* (with Pat Sikes) and *Professional Knowledge, Professional Lives: Studies of Education and Teaching* (2003). His books have been translated in Spain, Norway, Sweden, Finland, Portugal, Germany and Brazil, and most recently, Japan and China. He is the founding editor of *The Journal of Education Policy*, and editor of several book series for Falmer Press and Open University Press.

Gary Granville is Professor of Education at the National College of Art and Design, Dublin. He was Assistant Chief Executive of the National Council for Curriculum and Assessment (NCCA) for the first decade of its existence. He has also been a second-level teacher, a curriculum project leader in the Curriculum Development Unit, based in Trinity College, Dublin and a lecturer in education at NUI, Maynooth. He is currently a member of the Higher Education Authority and of a number of national curriculum committees.

Alex McEwen is a former Professor of Education at the Graduate School of Education, Queen's University Belfast. His area of expertise is the Sociology of Education. He has published extensively in this area and his book *Public Policy in a Divided Society: Schooling, Culture and Identity in Northern Ireland* (Ashgate, 1999) is a testament to his scholarly endeavours.

Margaret Reynolds graduated with a B.Ed degree in 1975 from St Mary's University College, Belfast and worked in the primary education sector in Belfast schools for fifteen years before taking up a post as senior lecturer in education in Stranmillis University College, Belfast. There she taught philosophy of education and professional studies. In August 2000 Margaret was appointed to the position of Head of Education and Curriculum Studies at St Mary's University College and in June 2001 became Director of the Faculty of Education in St Mary's. Her research interests are professional ethics, teacher education, values education and education for inclusion.

Malcolm Skilbeck is Emeritus Professor of Education at Deakin University, Australia. Previous positions he held include Vice-Chancellor and Principal at Deakin University, Professor of Curriculum Studies at the Institute of Education, London University, Director of Studies, Schools Council for Curriculum and Examinations for England and Wales, London, Foundation Director, Australian Curriculum Development Centre, Canberra and Professor and Dean of Education, University of Ulster, Coleraine. In his very active "retirement" he is a consultant and writer. Among his most recent publications of particular relevance to an Irish audience are: *The University Challenged: A Review of International Trends and Issues with Particular Reference to Ireland* (Higher Education Authority, 2002); *Access and Equity in Higher Education: An International Perspective on Issues and Strategies* (Higher Education Authority, 2000); *Redefining Tertiary Education* (OECD, 1998 (senior author)); *The Vocational Quest – New Directions in Education and Training* (Routledge, 1994 (senior author)) and *Curriculum Reform* (OECD, 1990).

Ciaran Sugrue is a Senior Lecturer and Director of Postgraduate Studies in Education at St Patrick's College, Dublin City University, where he has worked in teacher education for the past twenty years. He is General Editor of *Irish Educational Studies*, the journal of the Educational Studies Association of Ireland, and a member of the editorial boards of several international educational journals. He is currently Chairperson of the International Study Association for Teachers and Teaching (ISATT). His research interests are wide-ranging and include school leadership, educational change and policy, teacher professional development, teacher education in developing countries, as well as qualitative research theory and practice. He has published numerous book chapters and journal articles nationally and internationally on these topics. His most recent book (edited with Chris Day) is *Developing Teachers and Teaching Practice: International Research Perspectives* (Routledge/Falmer, 2003) while his forthcoming book *Passionate Principalship* is also being published by Routledge/Falmer.

Fionnuala Waldron is a member of the Education Department of St Patrick's College, Drumcondra where she specialises in Curriculum History. She taught at primary level for many years and was involved in developing history programmes currently in use in many Irish primary schools. Her research interests include equality and education, history education, textbooks and ideology and the social and political history of Dublin in the late nineteenth century.

FOREWORD

As I read *Curriculum and Ideology*, I was reminded of the recent visit to our campus of the celebrated linguist and political analyst, Noam Chomsky, who delivered a forceful denunciation of US foreign policy in the Middle East. A few days later an article appeared in the *Hartford Courant* that not only took issue with Chomsky but reprimanded the State of Connecticut for permitting a public university to squander taxpayers' money on such a venture. Independent analysis and critique, it was clear, served no public good.

Happily, this is not the frame of reference adopted in *Curriculum and Ideology* and consequently we are treated to a timely, multifaceted, and critical analysis of persistent issues affecting the school curriculum in Ireland. Here, curriculum is seen as a matter of ongoing discussion and revision rather than one upon which we may seek convenient closure without undue consideration of its ever-changing social, moral and intellectual underpinnings. This is a public service of no mean proportion for which one may be grateful. Governments, of course, and agencies such as the DES that are charged with carrying out their wishes, are responsible and held accountable for maintaining basic services in education as in other spheres. One would be foolhardy not to recognise the constraints and expectations under which they work. In the case of education in Ireland, carrying out these responsibilities often led to a partnership approach. While this may have aided the maintenance of stability and consistency, it sometimes siphoned off to the margins the open discussion of issues revolving around changing social and economic circumstances, values, and preferences.

Curriculum and Ideology serves as a counterbalance to this. It emphasises the necessity of attending to the underlying yet crucial moral, social, and political determinants of curriculum decision-making, the justifications entailed, the impact of hidden power structures and their implications for teaching and learning. These are matters that can easily go unrecognised or unattended in a public debate preoccupied, for example, by a points system. In this, the work presented here exemplifies the role of scholarly discourse in education and may even serve to earn it legitimacy in the public eye. In this, too, the contributions in *Curriculum and Ideology* stand in marked contrast to their absence in an earlier era where one rarely encountered the kind of independent and scholarly discussion of curriculum and policy in Irish education found here.

Between them the various authors focus on issues of curriculum at the primary and the post-primary levels both in the Republic of Ireland and in Northern Ireland. A consideration of the limitations of externally imposed change and the implications of the ideal of lifelong learning sets the international context. In addition, the literature upon which the work as a whole draws is taken from the worldwide scholarship that has shaped research and writing in curriculum over the past quarter of a century. As a consequence, not only is the work found here rich and varied but it signals an advance in the scholarly study of curriculum in the Irish context. This is not to say that there has not been important indigenous scholarship in recent decades upon which it builds, that the pinnacle has been reached, or that the work is complete, for it never is. That such serious and well-informed scholarly discussion is now conducted and is so well focused on uniquely Irish curriculum questions, however, is an occasion for celebration in itself, even as it points to new avenues for further exploration.

Professor D.G. Mulcahy
School of Education
Central Connecticut State University

INTRODUCTION

Ciaran Sugrue

In contemporary Ireland, the signs, sounds and symbols of conspicuous consumption, market forces and materialistic secularism abound; they have been described recently as "turbo-capitalism". Some of my friends from abroad jovially relate how they have encouraged colleagues and friends to visit Dublin soon, before its McDonaldisation "make-over" is complete and it is indistinguishable from the homogenised "shopping mall culture" evident elsewhere. The more local home-grown version of this phenomenon is now frequently related by suggesting that you can drink a pint of Guinness in any major European city, and further afield, in a factory (re-)produced "virtual" Irish pub, probably exported from County Monaghan, even if "the pint" does not taste the same without the influence of Liffey water! Academics refer to this phenomenon as "globalisation" (Wells et al., 1998; Beck, 2000) and identify it as part of the "postmodern condition" (Hargreaves, 1994).

What, you may ask, has this got to do with curriculum change in Ireland? More than you might think. Allow me to explain.

If the term globalisation had not quite entered vernacular language prior to September 11th, 2001, news agencies such as Sky and CNN, networks with a "global reach" as well as national and local broadcasting corporations, have certainly repeated it often enough since to ensure saturation. The US President has

frequently referred to the "global reach of terrorism" as part justification for declaring "war on terrorism". It appears to have come
as a shock to many North Americans that technological developments such as internet facilities with global reach are accessible to
all with a PC or miniaturised equivalent, that globalising tendencies can work in both directions: from the centre to the periphery
and back again.

While "globalisation" may be a contested and problematic
term, its core ingredients are "economic activity, political relations, information, communications and technology" (Hargreaves,
1994, p. 47). The Irish Government-sponsored IT 2000 initiative is
an obvious example of this phenomenon that may be "read" as
being either benign or malign. The proliferation of PCs and ISDN
lines in schools may be understood in a self-congratulatory
manner as evidence of our increasing prosperity, investment in
education and of providing unlimited access to information.
Alternatively, the pervasive presence of ICTs in schools may be
seen as a vocationalisation of curriculum, teaching and learning
where the acquisition of skills, frequently at the expense of more
holistic and humanistic values, is premised on preparing students
for the workplace in a concerted effort to improve market share
and competitive advantage; classrooms become "safe simula-
tions" of workplace collaboration (Hargreaves, 1994).

In using the term globalisation to describe a "complicated set
of economic, political and cultural factors", Wells and her colleagues readily recognise that it "signifies the diminishing of economic borders and the simultaneous increase in international
exchange and transnational interaction" (1998, p. 323). The presence in Dublin, for example, of the International Financial Services
Centre, multinational corporations, telesales and marketing facilities, as well as a plethora of franchised fast food outlets, are all
manifestations of this phenomenon, even if they are more readily
recognisable as contributing to Ireland's economic miracle, the
success story of Europe (EU). The marketing of and purchasing by
Irish citizens of holiday homes in destinations with preferred
climates such as Spain, Portugal and Florida, provide further

evidence of increasing prosperity (for some) and the relative ease with which national borders are traversed both financially and personally. There are benefits in the other direction also with significant increases in tourist revenues, some of which accrue from the niche marketing of golfing holidays, etc. The market rules and Ireland's open economy is vulnerable to these global forces; Ireland Inc. has been "deregulated".

There is a growing realisation among many commentators that the term McDonaldisation is no longer an adequate descriptor of this global phenomenon. Rather, as Beck (2000) suggests, the paradoxical consequence of globalisation is that the local has increased in significance. Consequently, he coined the term "glocal" as a means of capturing the nexus between the global and the local, rather redolent of Joyce's description of his native city, Dublin, as "lugly", simultaneously lovely and ugly. While regional accents (and identities?), and local "characters" may be in retreat or decline respectively, massaged beyond recognition by MTV and other homogenising influences that abhor idiosyncrasy, *Ballykissangel* became a cultural export, a packaged version of Irish identity. At a time of rapid urbanisation and consequent dislocation, we can romanticise nostalgically about the "global village" and hanker after lost community by re-inventing set-dancing and card-playing in the comfort of the local community centre, and in our centrally heated homes in "neighbourless neighbourhoods", as a means of cocooning ourselves and our identities against the fracturing and rupturing of old certainties (Barber, 1996).

As neo-liberal economic thinking, a version of nineteenth-century *laissez-faire* economics, has increasingly gained the high ground within this new world order, particularly since the fall of the Berlin wall, educational systems too have been deregulated internationally. While public sector facilities and services generally are being privatised, decentralisation has become a new educational policy orthodoxy, with opting out, vouchers, tax breaks and charter schools being used in several jurisdictions, but notably in England, the US and Canada, as a means of deregulating public schooling. While such manifestations of deregulation may not be as evident or virulent in the Irish context, they are present nevertheless. In the secondary sector, for example, those who can afford it are choosing in increasing numbers to spend time in new private sector schools, what have become known pejoratively as "grind" schools. Smyth's (1998) recent study indicates that more than 50 per cent of secondary school pupils do not attend their nearest (neighbourhood) school. At primary level, with the growing popularity of Scoileanna lán Ghaelacha (Irish medium) and the smaller but expanding multi-denominational and inter-denominational sectors, choice is being exercised by a significant number of parents in contrast with the more heterogeneous local national school. Meanwhile, in both sectors, the practice of levying a "voluntary contribution" on parents as a tithe towards various school activities and programmes provides more general evidence of the pervasiveness of a privatisation mindset. It is particularly ironic in the Irish context that, in 1995, when the Celtic Tiger's roar was being heralded and feted across the globe and embraced at home, we were simultaneously (re-)visiting the causes and consequences of the 1845 famine that were exacerbated significantly by a "market rules" mindset with devastating consequences for our peasant ancestors.

Many of these recent manifestations resonate strongly with Jonathan's description of Classical liberalism as "a collection of atomistic individuals whose rational self-interested choices lead to optimal social efficiency" (1990, p. 117–18). And yet, two major lessons emanating from the smouldering rubbled ruins of "Ground Zero" are both poignant and pertinent. Fire-fighters and police became heroes and Rudy Giuliani their mascot; there was a re-awakening of the importance of the public sector and a new (short-lived?) respect for, and recognition of, the vital services provided by this sector and its workers. At national level, the de-regulated airline industry rediscovered the importance of Government and sought financial respite, refuge and protection from the state — tacit acceptance that unfettered competition may be optimally efficient but also fragile and precarious. Ground Zero, therefore, becomes a massive metaphor of the postmodern where the local and the global collide.

Classrooms, schools, regional and national education structures, policies and curricula are another canvas on which these competing and conflicting forces play out to shape the minds, hearts and hands of the rising generation as they begin to shape and are shaped by an emerging world order. Riley attests to this when she states:

> For three consecutive years, opinion polls in the US have placed education as the top national issue (*USA Today*, 1999). "Education, Education, Education" has been the personal mantra of UK Prime Minister Tony Blair. These responses are not unique; governments across the globe are engaged in the education reform business, motivated by a range of concerns. (2000, p. 29)

In Ireland, too, the decade of the 1990s in particular has played host to unprecedented education reform efforts. While primary and secondary curricula have been revised, every sector, from early childhood to adult education, tertiary and further education, has been touched (if not transformed) by reports, policies, new structures and legislation, and the process continues unabated. Hargreaves argues that responses to such crossroads encounters between the local and global have led some "to resurrect old cultural certainties or impose new ones through centralised control of curriculum and assessment" (1994, p. 54). What are the defining contours and fault lines of recent educational reform efforts in Ireland?

This book responds to this question by recording compass readings on both continuities and changes in primary and secondary curriculum reform efforts over the past two decades and it signals signposts for the future from close critical scrutiny of the terrain. A child of the "glocal", the book situates national reform efforts within the larger canvas of global forces and its structure and content reflect this connectedness. Its focus is local and national but its reach is international: it includes contributions by recognised international scholars on the global forces of educational change and their impact on and consequences for the reshaping of curricula and schooling, as well as the authoritative voices of Irish educators located both north and south of the border.

The mantra of the reform trajectory in Ireland is "partnership", an approach that is hailed as significantly different from more adversarial, ideologically driven, top-down efforts that characterise reforms elsewhere. The foreword to the Government's *White Paper on Education, Charting Our Education Future*, is worth quoting at some length in this regard. It states:

> For the past three years there has been intense debate on the most appropriate framework for the future development of education in Ireland. The extent and depth of the dialogue is arguably unprecedented in our history. The debate has also been characterized by a number of unique and innovative features, specifically the National Education Convention in October 1993 [see Coolahan, 1994] and the subsequent Roundtable discussions on intermediate education structures and school governance, in 1994. These initiatives involved, for the first time, structured multi-lateral dialogue among all of the major partners in education on crucial issues affecting the development of education. They contributed substantively to enhanced mutual understanding and, I hope, have facilitated a more robust consensus in support of key changes. (Bhreathnach, 1995, p. *ix*)

The former Minister continues that the White Paper "reflects a widespread desire among all of the partners in education to take stock of the achievements and trends in educational provision and to chart future directions" (p. *ix*). But partnership too carries overtones of contented consensus that provides protective immunity through pragmatism from the gusting winds of change. Despite the depth of dialogue, therefore, more deeply embedded education structures have remained remarkably resistant to change. It is necessary therefore, particularly, in relation to curriculum reform, to delve even deeper into the substance and process of reform to identify continuities as well as changes wrought through partnership, to explore the very notion of partnership and the extent to which it has promoted more inclusive participation and more democratic decision-making. The quest north of the border is similar. To what extent are recent and ongoing international and local efforts to transform the political, cultural and social life of the province reflected in curricula and schooling? Has Northern Ireland shed some of its dependency on "big brother" across the Irish sea and begun to carve its own trajectory from its troubled history or are old and well-established hierarchies and divisions being re-invented by the imposition of prescriptive policy perspectives emanating from the centre?

While seeking answers to these questions, the book serves four important purposes. First, it situates national policies within international, global discourses on educational change, school restructuring, and curriculum reform; it reinterprets local reform efforts in light of these larger currents of debate and ferment. Second, it seeks to shed a "dependency culture" (Coolahan, 1994) frequently articulated in frustrated annoyance by graduate students in education when they ask: "Why are we so often expected to read research from other countries that frequently does not 'fit' our context and educational history?" This book, then, is a modest contribution to a small but growing literature that is "home-grown" rather than imported. Third, it has frequently been suggested that there is a lack of policy-related research in Ireland, a criticism made by the OECD in 1991, and reiterated on many occasions subsequently by policymakers themselves. The analysis conducted in Sections Two to Four of this text will be of considerable interest to policymakers and those in leadership positions across the education landscape. Fourth, many of the contributors to this text regard "partnership" as problematic and contested and seek to have their voices heard as a contribution to more critical debate. Collectively, the various chapters are a signal to, and potential catalysts for, others to raise their voices, to enter into a more broadly based and inclusive dialogue about the present and future direction of Irish education, identities and citizenship. These issues are central to the work of schools and crucial to the future of Irish society. The individual and collective challenge is

to reinvent identities, citizenship and society while simultaneously we position ourselves within, and are positioned by, forces
encountered and spaces occupied on the global–local landscape.
School curricula are important sites on which this process of construction is enacted.

The book is in four sections. Section One includes two chapters
that provide international perspectives on change forces and their
consequences for national systems as local and national policy elites grapple with international rhetorics of reform. Some readers
may wish to begin with these over-arching perspectives, depending on how comfortable they feel with "big ideas" in a relatively
abstract format. However, for readers who prefer to begin by con-
necting with the more local, the familiar, depending on their location in primary or secondary schooling or teacher education, they
could begin to engage with Sections Two and Three. Section Two
includes two chapters on secondary curriculum reform in the Irish
Republic while the third is a contribution on secondary reform in
Northern Ireland. Section Three has an identical structure, shifting
the focus on to the primary curriculum. Readers may choose initial engagement by reading any one of these chapters. At that
point, it may be more profitable to read the over-arching chapters
in Section One, before reading the chapter in Section Four which
identifies signposts for the future that are grounded in the analyses in Sections Two and Three while connected to the global influences discussed in some detail in Chapters One and Two. This
concluding chapter also identifies deeply embedded systemic silences that require critical analysis as an integral element of the
reform process. This approach is intended to encourage more
readers to engage with and enter into the dialogue of reform
while finding their voices and becoming players in the reshaping
of the field of education and its curricular agendas.

In Chapter One, Ivor Goodson provides a timely wake-up call.
His penetrating and foreshadowing analysis indicates that the
press of postmodern conditions is inclined to induce a collective
amnesia and that we ignore the lessons of history at our peril, lessons no less significant in education than in other fields. His

critique of the dominance of new management values underscores the fragility of current conditions. Despite global rhetorics, each enclave, each locality, each system of education and each school must work out its own future amidst conflicting and contradictory change forces. There is greater need than ever before to bring a historical perspective to bear, so that continuity as well as change, security and uncertainty are finely balanced in the process of school and curriculum change. He develops a cogent argument that indicates the extent to which change in recent times has been externally mandated rather than internally inspired. This has resulted in personal conflict and, in some contexts, profound deprofessionalisation and alienation. Sustainable change, he argues, needs to take greater cognisance of the embedded traditions and routines of teaching and schooling, to recognise the subjectivities of teachers as being at the heart of the educational enterprise rather than corporatist reform mandates that are often ill-conceived while being enforced by legislation and other accountability mechanisms.

In Chapter Two, Malcolm Skilbeck brings global perspectives to bear on what ought to count as a curriculum appropriate for the twenty-first century that would promote greater equity and inclusion as well as lifelong learning for all. While lifelong learning may be a new generative principle, its consequences for teaching, learning and curricula are, as yet, poorly understood. He seeks to articulate this new horizon as a means of re-conceptualising education, its agents and agencies. Skilbeck suggests that this challenge is rather redolent of tensions encountered a century earlier when demands for universal education were resisted by those who sought to retain an elite curriculum for the few. He argues persuasively that interdependency wrought by global forces results in the lives of the "haves" and "have-nots" being inextricably linked. Curricula, therefore, should address more explicitly issues of equity, access and inclusion. As part of this agenda, he says, civic, social and cultural education must shed its more nationalistic tendencies; it must connect with and attend to individuals' needs and interests while striving also to connect personal concerns with global trends in a manner that cultivates curiosity, concern and compassion as well as respect for and tolerance of difference and diversity. Such a curriculum, tailored to individuals' learning needs and trajectories, is likely to be delivered in a flexible, adaptable, rigorous and engaging manner. This requirement poses a considerable challenge to prominent school structures, curricula, timetabling and other routines. However, taking up this challenge is a necessity to complete the groundwork for lifelong learning; without it, the dream remains an aspiration, an illusion without substance. Educators must lead the charge as a matter of some urgency — an additional challenge to emerging forms of professionalism. Learning how to learn and learning across the lifespan need to be more than mere slogans; they need to be inscribed into the structures, content and pedagogy of all learning opportunities.

In Chapter Three, Gary Granville lifts the veil on the structures and processes of post-primary curriculum reform initiatives at national level during the past two decades. He provides a number of theoretical tools to deconstruct these reforms, from a structural, human resource, political and symbolic perspective. From his privileged position as both insider and outsider throughout much of that period, he charts the evolution of a significant national statutory body, from its more radical pioneering days to its recent evolution as a more permanent and powerful player on the national educational landscape. This should be compulsory reading for secondary teachers in particular, to gain insight into the manner in which their lives and work are shaped by various competing interests and forces. His penetrating analysis raises crucially important questions that continue to require critical scrutiny and attention: the limits of a social partnership model of curriculum change and the emergence of possible alternatives, as well as the necessity to hold to account this emerging and expanding elite as it becomes more established and evolves its own more distinct culture. His contribution, though critical of aspects of the NCCA's work, seeks also to record its significance in altering the educational landscape to a significant degree.

In Chapter Four, Jim Gleeson situates post-primary curriculum reform within its wider socio-cultural and economic context. In doing so, he is highly critical of a persistent essentialism and indicates also the extent to which rhetoric and reality often diverge significantly in public life generally and in curriculum reform in particular. Gleeson's critical gaze indicates the manner in which various power-brokers within the system have sought to present curriculum change in a value-neutral manner, thus perpetuating an uncontested, unproblematic understanding of curriculum, behind which underlying tensions regarding power and control have been fought over and maintained for several decades. Maintaining the status quo in curriculum terms while focusing on more technical aspects of the system such as examinations has promoted and maintained, he argues, a "cosy consensus" among the most powerful brokers in the system, with the result that curriculum matters have been relegated to a lower division of priority. Consequently, he argues, curriculum reform has tended to be a series of quick fixes while structures, power and control have remained remarkably consistent and curriculum studies as a discipline continues to be marginal to teacher preparation. In conclusion he speculates on the nature as well as the future of partnerships as they have been practised and looks to a new more permanent NCCA elite for leadership beyond consensualism that is more likely to open up silent areas of the terrain for debate and public scrutiny.

In Chapter Five, Alex McEwen provides a wide-ranging critique of the underpinnings of the traditions of a liberal curriculum (at secondary level in Northern Ireland) and its attendant means of assessing pupils' progress. His insightful comments indicate how curriculum, as part of state apparatus and ideology, can also become a tool in a sectarian conflict that segregates and stratifies through its content and assessment procedures, thus perpetuating existing employment patterns and social class structures. He argues that there continues to be considerable emphasis on content knowledge, and the perpetuation of a liberal curriculum places emphasis on the individual when the marketplace is said to be seeking a collaborative workforce. He concludes that, faced with twenty-first-century challenges of globalisation and attendant loss of old certainties, students remain poorly equipped — to meet the challenges of constructing identities, to engage with meaningful participation in public life, and for participation in a largely de-regulated economic sphere.

In Chapter Six, Ciaran Sugrue provides a detailed analysis of the power relations that operated between the various competing interests in the education system during the past twenty years, but particularly during the decade of the 1990s as the revised primary curriculum was being framed and developed. This criti-cal analysis reveals that, through the power exercised by the pri-mary teachers union (INTO), the rhetoric of progressive or child-centred education was rearticulated and rehabilitated but in modified form, with greater emphasis on the necessity for speci-fied objectives and more systematic use of assessment. The chap-ter indicates that, in the absence of a body of research evidence concerning actual practice in Irish primary classrooms, there was a persistent tendency to condemn structural inadequacies in the system — lack of resources, facilities and relatively high pupil–teacher ratios — while a discourse on teaching and learning was silenced. The analysis suggests also that the period was marked by the emergence of a new policy elite, while the new statutory status of the NCCA provides it with an opportunity to develop its own distinctive culture separate from undue influence by teach-ers' unions. The chapter concludes that there is a very definite evi-dence deficit in the system regarding the processes of teaching and learning rather than their outcomes, and collectively the NCCA and a more focused inspectorate is likely to address this gap in the system, in partnership with the research and teacher education communities.

In Chapter Seven, Fionnuala Waldron provides a very timely deconstruction of Irish identity and citizenship as some distance is put between us and more essentialist, relatively uncontested if not entirely hegemonic, versions of Irishness. Hers is a penetrating analysis of the lineage of these important concerns as they have been represented and constructed within the primary school curriculum, particularly during the past thirty years. Waldron draws on a wide-ranging literature as a means of framing a more narrowly focused analysis of the revised primary curriculum, particularly the documentation on History, Geography, and Social, Personal and Health Education (SPHE). Her argument, as well as the perspective she develops, indicate that precisely because the documents are freed from the imprisoning heroic "foundational" myths of the past, a hugely heavy burden is placed on teachers to enable learners to create identities that are at once local, rooted in time and place, while being conscious also of an interdependence, and of a sense of citizenship that is action-oriented rather than being acquiescent in the face of the status quo. She is optimistic about the possibilities for a more transformative agenda for schools while recognising also that aspects of the documentation and its accompanying rhetorics are evidence of continuing "domestication".

In Chapter Eight, Margaret Reynolds interrogates dominant influences on the primary curriculum in Northern Ireland, and indicates a growing instrumentalism where assessment procedures in tandem with an emphasis on behavioural objectives diminish the importance of the individual and downplay the importance of values. Consequently, she argues, the instrumental values of the marketplace predominate, and she expresses considerable unease with a doctrine of what is measurable being regarded as important to the exclusion of more enduring educational aims. Nevertheless, she expresses cautious confidence that more independence of mind is evident in recent critiques of approaches to curricula in the Province, thus giving rise to some optimism that Northern Ireland can be the author of its own future while shedding its more traditional dependence on policy mandarins located on the "mainland". She detects embryonic evidence of coalitions of interest around values, pedagogy and assessment that will give greater autonomy to practitioners and challenge initial teacher education to move beyond preoccupation with competencies to more holistic understandings of the processes of teaching and learning.

In Chapter Nine, Ciaran Sugrue and Jim Gleeson identify key concerns that emerge from the analysis provided in the foregoing chapters. Additionally, systemic silences are exposed and subjected to critical scrutiny. The emergent signposts, as well as the systemic silences, are situated within more global rhetorics of social movements and the increasing necessity for lifelong learning. We argue that existing structures within the NCCA are deeply redolent of systemic structures in teacher education that were determined in the nineteenth century, and their perpetuation is inimical to the best interests of learners, particularly the more vulnerable. Current structures, despite a rhetoric of partnership, perpetuate artificial divisions, particularly during the period of compulsory schooling, that are anachronistic in the twenty-first century. In an Ireland that is increasingly closer to Boston than Berlin it is necessary, we argue, to prepare students adequately for the knowledge society and not merely for the knowledge economy. Towards this end, education for citizenship and cosmopolitan identity in an interdependent world is vital, while rediscovering the moral mission of teaching is necessary also as part of the process of developing more sophisticated kinds of teacher professionalism. These are the various change forces that make partnership a contested ideology and the conclusions indicate clearly why curriculum reform in Ireland needs to be more "glocal" than parochial, more self-conscious and reflexive when dealing with its limitations, and more determined to engage and get to grips with international rhetorics, as well as actively seek to reinvent and reinvest in the public sphere and the common good. This is the larger canvas on which curriculum ideology, policy, practice and reform are likely to be contested.

References

Barber, B. R. (1996), *Jihad Vs. McWorld*, New York: Ballantine Books.

Beck, U. (2000), *What Is Globalization?* Cambridge: Polity Press.

Bhreathnach, N. (1995), Foreword, in Government of Ireland, *Charting Our Education Future. White Paper On Education* (pp. *ix–x*), Dublin: Government Publications.

Coolahan, J. (ed.) (1994), *Report on the National Education Convention*, Dublin: The National Education Convention Secretariat.

Hargreaves, A. (1994), *Changing Teachers, Changing Times*, London: Cassell.

Ireland, Government of (1995), *Charting Our Education Future White Paper on Education*, Dublin: Government Publications.

Jonathan, R. (1990), "State Education Service or Prisoner's Dilemma: The 'Hidden Hand' as Source of Education Policy", *British Journal of Educational Studies*, Vol. 38, No. 2, pp. 116–32.

Riley, K. (2000), "Leadership, Learning and Systemic Reform", *Journal of Educational Change*, Vol. 1, No. 1, pp. 29–55.

Smyth, E. (1999), *Do Schools Differ? Academic and Personal Development among Pupils in the Second-Level Sector*, Dublin: Oak Tree Press in association with The Economic and Social Research Institute.

Wells, A.S., Carnochan, S., Slayton, J., Allen, R.E. and Vasudeva, A. (1998), "Globalization and Educational Change", in Hargeaves, A., Lieberman, A., Fullan, M. and Hopkins, D. (eds.), *International Handbook of Educational Change*, Dordrecht/Boston/London: Kluwer, Part One, pp. 322–48.

SECTION ONE

CHANGE FORCES:
INTERNATIONAL PERSPECTIVES

Chapter 1

CHANGE PROCESSES AND HISTORICAL PERIODS: AN INTERNATIONAL PERSPECTIVE

Ivor F. Goodson

INTRODUCTION

Most recent school restructuring initiatives internationally have combined a series of features. They have adopted a posture of "optimistic newness": an amnesia which focuses on the spontaneous creation of solutions, of new "change forces". Above all, they have shown an almost wilful disregard of previous change efforts and of the embedded contexts and frames of schooling which are historically sedimented.

In some ways, it may be sensible to view "change" and "reform" as themselves aspects of culture. They represent, in a sense, cultures of disavowal and denial. They wish for the "end of history", and proclaim that end by denying the forces of history: "change forces", not "historical forces"; new standards, not old human agency.

A good example of such a proclamation of newness was the British National Curriculum, which applies to England and Wales, announced as a major new initiative of a triumphalist Thatcher government in 1987. Educational theorists often uncritically accepted this ideology of newness. Much of the curriculum theory at the time adopted the "new" triumphalist tone and sought to construct new "guides" as to how to "implement" this new panacea. It was thought "inappropriate" to provide a more analytical and historical approach. The work of Bob Moon is a classic example of such "implementationist myopia". I warned at the time:

> As the study of the National Curriculum confirms it is easy to be beguiled by the frantic activity in the foreground. To be drawn into the contemporary foreground is to run the danger of ignoring the continuities in the background. Being drawn into the frenetic foreground curriculum study and curriculum theory can forego much of their potential to provide independent scholarship. (Goodson, 1995, Preface, p. *xvii*)

In fact, the National Curriculum produced a wide range of problems, from teacher discontentment, through to a debilitating narrowing of curriculum opportunities and growing student disaffection. It is generally accepted that centralised prescription only goes so far and that restoring some professional autonomy to teachers is necessary for morale and emergent forms of professionalism. The Government is now trying to loosen the hold of the National Curriculum and develop again broader curriculum opportunities to try to reverse teacher and student disaffection. As the fate of the National Curriculum confirmed, independent scholarship does not equal left-wing "carping criticism". It is what it pronounces: "independent scholarship", providing analytical advice that might save huge sums of money being wasted on ill-conceived and under-prepared new initiatives. Governments would do well to retain independent advisory forces in the face of the global spin-doctors they will increasingly confront. Educational changes of course are subject to similar global forces.

As we shall find, history does not "end" and change forces will, in the end, have to negotiate with other historical forces. It would be better to begin such negotiation from the earliest stages in defining change theory, not leave it until the changes are themselves subverted and inverted in the melting pot of human actions.

INTERROGATING CHANGE THEORY

In historical terms, it is not at all surprising that "change forces" and pervasive restructuring initiatives should be sweeping the world at the moment. Since 1989, we have seen a seismic shift in the world in terms of the dominant political ideologies. Beyond the triumphalist "end of history" line peddled by camp followers lies the belief that American democratic and business values have now vanquished all alternative political and economic systems. Behind this ideological shift is, of course, a massive technological transformation, which many believe puts us within a "third industrial revolution". Such huge transformations, quite understandably, lead to a passing belief that history is now irrelevant, suspended, over.

But in the everyday world of social life and social institutions, this glib dismissal of history does not stand scrutiny for a moment. Can the situations in Kosovo, Rwanda or Northern Ireland really transcend history? In the end, won't the change forces, with all their smart bombs and surveillance technology, nonetheless have to confront human and historical fabric? The answer, of course, is inevitably that transformational change forces will have to confront existing patterns of life and understanding. This will also be the case with regard to change forces in our schools. Schools are great collectivising and socialising areas where our social memory is deeply embedded. Restructuring schools may not prove a great deal simpler than restructuring Kosovo.

John Meyer et al. (1992) talked about school reforms as "world movements" that sweep across the global arena: invented in one country, they are rapidly taken up by political elites and powerful interest groups in each country. But what then becomes clear is that these world movements of school reform "embed" themselves in national school systems in very different ways. The national school systems are *refractors* of world change forces. Our task is to understand this process of social refraction, for only then can we develop a change theory that is sensitive to the circumstances, albeit deeply changed circumstances, of schooling.

In his book, *Fluctuating Fortunes*, Vogel (1988) documented the changing cycles of power of global business. In periods of high business power, schooling tends to be driven towards business values. These periods move educational policy and economic policy into close harmony. At such times, educational questions tend to be driven hard by vocational questions; issues of competitiveness and economic efficiency are widely promoted. But the educational and the economic are, of course, not synonymous. Sometimes they can be performed in harmony, but at other times they lead in very different directions if the educational needs of school students are scrutinised in their own right. At times, when business power is held in balance by other forces, the "internal" professional power of educator groups can emerge as a major defining force.

Such a period began in the years after the Second World War. This period of "cold war" between political ideologies set capitalist business values against systems of Communist production. In the west, egalitarian social policies were pursued and public education systems were heavily promoted as vehicles of common purpose and social good. Business values and the private sector lived in "mixed economies" where public sectors provided a good deal of the "public services" of national systems.

In this period, which lasted well into the 1970s — even into the 1990s in some countries (e.g. Canada) — educators were seen as having large amounts of professional autonomy. Much educational change was, at this time, left to internal educational experts, to initiate and define.

In these historical circumstances of substantial professional autonomy, change theory looked for the sources of initiation and promotion of change to the educator groups "internal to the school systems". In conceptualising curriculum change in the 1970s, I developed a model which scrutinised the "internal affairs" of change and set this against the "external relations" of change.

INTERNAL EDUCATIONAL CHANGE

One example of the internal patterns of change that predominated in the 1960s and 1970s were the models of curriculum change that were developed in a range of work that I conducted at that time. For instance, the model of school subject change, which provided a four-stage evolutionary pattern, was defined in Goodson (1995) in the following way:

1. *Invention* may come about from the activities or ideas of educators; sometimes as a response to "climates of opinion" or pupil demands or resistance or from inventions in the "outside world":

   > The ideas necessary for creation . . . are usually available over a relatively prolonged period of time in several places. Only a few of these inventions will lead to further action. (Ben-David and Collins, 1966)

2. *Promotion* by educator groups internal to the educational system. Inventions will be taken up where and when persons become interested in the new idea, not only as intellectual content but also as a means of establishing a new intellectual identity and particularly a new occupational role. Hence, subjects with low status, poor career patterns and even with actual survival problems may readily embrace and promote new inventions such as environmental studies. Conversely, high-status subjects may ignore quite major opportunities as they are already satisfactorily resourced and provide existing desirable careers. The response of science groups to "technology" or (possibly) contemporary mathematics groups to "computer studies" are cases in point. Promotion of invention arises from a perception of the possibility of basic improvements in occupational role and status.

3. *Legislation.* The promotion of new inventions, if successful, leads to the establishment of new categories or subjects. Whilst promotion is initially primarily internally generated, it has to develop external relations with sustaining "constituen-

cies". This will be a major stage in ensuring that new categories or subjects are fully accepted, established and institutionalised. And further, that having been established, they can be sustained and supported over time. Legislation is associated with the development and maintenance of those discourses or legitimating rhetorics which provide automatic support for correctly labelled activity.

4. *Mythologisation*. Once automatic support has been achieved for a subject or category, a fairly wide range of activities can be undertaken. The limits are any activities which threaten the legitimated rhetoric and hence constituency support. The subject at this point is mythological. It represents essentially a licence that has been granted (or perhaps a "patent" or "monopoly rights"), with the full force of the law and establishment behind it. At this point when the subject has been successfully "invented", the process of invention and of establishment is completed. (Goodson, 1995, pp. 193–4)

It is possible to restate this model of school subject change as a more general educational change model. Hence:

1. Invention might be seen as change formulation;

2. Promotion as change implementation;

3. Legislation as policy establishment;

4. Mythologisation as established or permanent change.

But the most important conclusion from studying these patterns of change in the 1960s and 1970s is to evidence how internally generated change works its way towards external legitimation. Of course, it is true that such internally generated change exists in externally contrived climates of opinion, but the important point is that the invention and generation of the change idea begins internally and then works for external legitimation. As we have seen, during the period following the Second World War, and well into the 1970s and 1980s, public service provision was left largely in the hands of professional groups. In this sense, education was left in the hands of teachers and educationalists to initiate and promote educational change. Whilst occasionally these changes were responses to external stimuli, by and large, the development of external opinion came in the later stages of change establishment. Educational change was, therefore, defined, instigated and promoted internally, and then went on to sustain and win external support in order to ensure establishment and legislation.

EXTERNAL RELATIONS OF CHANGE

Until the late 1970s, internally generated change remained the lynchpin of the change theory that was subsequently codified and written. Since the triumph of western corporatism in 1989, it is important to revisit the assumption that change is internally generated and analyse the kinds of patterns of educational change which now prevail.

I recently argued that internal change agents faced a "crisis of positionality" (Goodson, 1999). This crisis of positionality prevails where the balance of change forces is substantially inverted. Now change can be seen as invented and originating within external constituencies. In this situation, internal change agents find themselves responding to, not initiating, changes. Thus, instead of being progressive change agents, they often take up the role of conservative respondents to the externally initiated change. Since educational change is not in line with their own defined missions, it is often seen as alien, unwelcome and hostile. The crisis of positionality for internal change agents is, then, that the progressive internal change agent can become the conservative, resistant and reluctant change agent of external wishes.

For these reasons, above all, change theory now has to develop a finer sense of history. Where change was the internal mission of educators and external relations were developed later, educational goodwill and a sense of purpose and passion might be assumed. Now the educator groups are less initiating agents or partners, and more deliverers of externally defined purposes.

For this reason, Andy Hargreaves and I have been working on a new multi-site project examining change in American and Canadian schools. Our primary concern has been to analyse and historically compare the changing *conditions of change*. Our methodology has, as a result, been both historical and ethnographic (see Hargreaves, 1994; Goodson, 1995).

In the schools we are studying, we have developed a historical archive of the changes and reforms that have been attempted within the school. We have begun to see how educational change follows a series of cycles, not unlike that of the economy. Indeed, we begin to see how, just as Kondratiev (1984) argued, economic change often went in long- as well as short-wave cycles — so too does educational change.

In these cycles, the powers of internal professional groups and external constituencies oscillate quite markedly and, in doing so, affect the change forces and associated change theories that we analyse and define.

Let me provide an example: Durant School in an industrial city in upper New York State was initiated and promoted by internal educator groups in the late 1960s. One group was concerned to establish an urban learning environment of a broadly progressive character and began to build up a new educational infrastructure in the city centre. A student clientele was attracted as the educators defined and promoted their educational mission. In due course, a loose coalition of like-minded schools grew up and ideas and materials were exchanged. The change forces, then, had some of the features of a social movement. In the later stages, the school began to negotiate with external constituencies — parents, local business, school boards — and, in due course, became a member, albeit a radical one, of the local school system.

More recently, though, the patterns of change have begun to alter radically towards the pattern of inversion noted earlier. Now the school primarily responds to change developed by external groups. For instance, in the sponsorship of new buildings and resources, the role of local business (e.g. Citibank) has been central. There, the consent and collaboration of local business interests have begun to influence school policy. Moreover, local business groups have been hugely influential in pushing for new educational "standards" and in initiating and promoting major educational changes. "Schools without walls" has followed progressive practice in stressing course work and project work as a way of assessing student achievement. The school is now challenged by the new mandate pushed by the school board commissioners to have students sit the Regents' examination. This will transform the context and control of the school's curriculum and, in doing so, change the teaching/ learning milieu. In the new change dispensation, change is externally mandated and only then internally negotiated.

In the contemporary conditions of change, combining ethnographic and historical methods of inquiry provides us with the database to develop new contextually sensitive change theory. This new theory allows us to arbitrate between the changing balance of external relations and internal affairs in contemporary historical circumstances. I have recently defined a reformulated change model which is based on the evidence gathered in our recent research projects (Goodson, 2001):

- *Change formulation*. Educational changes are discussed in a variety of external arenas including business groups, associated think-tanks, new pressure groups like "Standards Mean Business", and a variety of relatively newly formed parental groups. Often these changes resemble world movements that can be traced back to the World Bank and the International Monetary Fund (Torres, 2000). Much of the change is driven by a belief in marketisation of education and the delivery of educational services to parental "consumers" who are free to choose and to bargain over their provision (Kenway, 1993; Whitty, 1997; Robertson, 1998).

- *Change promotion* is handled in a similar fashion by external groups with varied internal involvement. As Reid (1984) has written:

  external forces and structures emerge, not merely as sources of ideas, promptings, inducements and constraints, but as defin-

ers and carriers of the categories of content, role and activity to
which the practice of schools must approximate in order to at-
tract support and legitimization. (p. 68)

- *Change legislation* provides the legal inducement for schools
to follow externally mandated changes. In some countries,
schools are evaluated by examination results (which are published in league tables). Measures also exist or are under way
to link teachers' pay to teachers' performance in terms of students' examination or test results (Menter et al., 1997). Such
legislation leads to a new regime of schooling, but allows
teachers to make some of their own responses in terms of
pedagogy and professionalism. Overall, school change policy
and curricula and assessment policy is thereby legislated, but
some areas of professional autonomy and associated arenas
for change can still be carved out. In certain countries and regions (for example, Scandinavia), this is leading to progressive
decentralisation and a push for new professional autonomy.
Again, the world movements for change are historically refracted by national systems.

- *Change establishment*. Whilst external change has been established systematically and legally, the power resides mostly in
the new *categorical* understandings of how schools operate —
delivering mandated curriculum, being assessed and inspected,
responding to choice and consumer demands (Hargreaves, et
al., 2001). Much of the marketisation of schools is taken for
granted now in many countries and, in that sense, has
achieved mythological status (Goodson, 2001, pp. 51–2).

CHANGE VERSUS CONTINUITY:
EXTERNAL VERSUS INTERNAL

In the contemporary conditions of change, educational change
forces are mainly driven by external constituencies. These external
forces have essentially followed the seismic shifts of the decade
since 1989 in promoting globalisation and marketisation. In the
triumphalist period of the 1990s, this appeared to be the end of

the story, or "the end of history" in Fukuyama's (1993) felicitous phrase. As our combined ethnographic and historical work focuses on the longer cycles of change, it becomes clear that, in fact, the apparent triumph of markets and globalisation in schooling is likely to be a temporary phase. Schools themselves are major repositories of institutionalised practices, social memories, and the procedures and professionalisms that have been historically constructed and embedded over many centuries. Hence, the apparent triumphalist externally mandated changes confront what might be called the contextual inertia of the existing school system. The changes which will actually emanate will come from a collision between externally mandated change forces and the existing historical context of schooling.

Already, the optimism of externally mandated change in many western countries can be seen to be weakening in the face of the continuity of school practice. In many countries, there is a moral panic because so much financial and political capital has been expended on educational reform for such little apparent result that a delicate game of "blaming and shaming" is often played out. The teachers are blamed, or the pupils are blamed, or the families are blamed: what is seldom blamed is the poorly articulated external change programme.

To analyse *change sustainability*, we have to understand the *conditions of change*, and to do this we have to develop our historical and ethnographic studies. That is why this chapter argues so consistently for a sense of history in our analyses — not out of some obscure scholarly belief, but because, quite simply, we cannot pursue *change sustainability* without such understandings. Without context sensitivity, the new change forces may be shipwrecked in the collision with the hard sedimentary rocks of existing school context. Externally mandated change forces are all very well as triumphalist symbolic action pronouncing the new world order, but unless they develop context sensitivity, the triumph may be short-lived and unsustainable. In this sense, a more historical understanding of change theory is a deeply pragmatic project.

I have argued recently, in The Lawrence Stenhouse Lecture at the British Educational Research Association, that one of the problems of new market triumphalism is *overreach* in a number of areas. Most notably, the new marketeers have, I believe, overreached themselves in the attempt to direct and diminish professional agents, whether they are doctors, social workers or teachers. Professional groups are vital agents in delivering professional services, and their missions need to be sensitively and seriously negotiated and defined. Triumphalist overreach leads to systematic professional under-performance, when change forces act with external force but internal ignorance.

Again, let me provide an example. Lessons from history are instructive but must be read with the warning that past historical experiences are, themselves, embedded in different political and social contexts. Nonetheless, the example comes from an early period of triumphalism in English schooling. The British State had recently developed a national system of "state schools" and, in the period 1892–95, began to demand that teachers were prescribed a syllabus and paid according to their success in teaching it. It was, in short, an instance of controlling schools and teachers as a "symbolic action", to show who was boss and to insist on a particular and closely defined form of schooling. E.G.A. Holmes (1912) has given his contemporary opinion of what happened, and it illuminates some of the dangers of external change forces acting with internal context insensitivity:

> The State, in prescribing a syllabus, which was to be followed, in all the subjects of instruction, by all the schools in the country, without regard to local or personal considerations, was guilty of one capital offence. It did all the thinking for the teacher. It told him in precise detail what he was to do each year in each "Standard", how he was to handle each subject, and how far he was to go in it; what width of ground he was to cover; what amount of knowledge, what degree of accuracy was required for a "pass". In other words, it provided him with his ideals, his general conceptions, his more immediate aims, his schemes of work; and if it did not control his meth-

ods in all their details, it gave him (by implication) hints and suggestions with regard to these on which he was not slow to act; for it told him that the work done in each class and each subject would be tested at the end of each year by a careful examination of each individual child; and it was inevitable that in his endeavour to adapt his teaching to the type of question by which his experience of the yearly examination led him to expect, he should gradually deliver himself, mind and soul, into the hands of the officials of the Department — the officials at Whitehall who framed the yearly syllabus, and the officials in the various districts who examined on it.

What the Department did to the teacher, it compelled him to do to the child. The teacher who is the slave of another's will, cannot carry out his instructions except by making his pupils the slaves of his own will. The teacher, who has been deprived by his superiors of freedom, initiative, and responsibility, cannot carry out his instructions except by depriving his pupils of the same vital qualities. The teacher, who in response to the deadly pressure of a cast-iron system, has become a creature of habit and routine, cannot carry out his instructions except by making his pupils as helpless and puppet-like as himself. But it is not only because mechanical obedience is fatal, in the long run, to mental and spiritual growth that the regulation of elementary or any other grade of education by a uniform syllabus is to be deprecated. It is also because a uniform syllabus is, in the nature of things, a bad syllabus. (pp. 103–4)

In the event, payment by results was rapidly abandoned, but interestingly enough, given the historical amnesia of educational policy, the British Government is again promoting payment by results, as are some states and districts in the US. In the nineteenth-century episode, in due course, a more sensitive balance between external prescription and internal expertise was negotiated. As some of the current initiatives began to founder, I suspect the same renegotiation will take place as "external" change theory begins to confront the challenge of sustainability and generalisability. Already, in some countries, we can see how overreach has led to a progressive handing back of professional power to internal practitioners and educationists.

In England, for instance, the Private Finance Initiative has allowed private sector entrepreneurs to build and lease schools and provide a range of associated services. They have, however, been reluctant to enter the professional terrain of teaching and learning. Here, new funding for developing "pedagogy" and internal expertise is becoming available. Hence, in this new discussion, a good deal of professional power to initiate change is left to internal agents. Once again, change theory will need to concentrate on those changes that are being internally generated, as well as externally mandated. I believe we shall, once again, see "bottom-up" change, internal to the school, generating new agendas of change for a time, maybe alongside top-down externally mandated change. Those different models and sequences of change will now be tested for their crucial capacity to sustain and generalise school change.

For this reason, in the last section, I want to revisit our models of school change to point to a few lessons from past change initiatives.

CONCLUSIONS AND COMPLEXITIES

The moving matrix of change models and theories has taken us from a confident belief in professionally generated internal change to triumphantly proclaimed externally mandated change. The move is now well-enough established for us to begin to interrogate externally mandated change for its capacity to sustain new reforms. The acid test is *the sustainability of change*.

The key lacuna in externally mandated change is the link to teachers' professional beliefs and to teachers' own personal missions. In the previous model of change, this was built in as an integral part of the model; in the externally mandated model, it is merely *assumed*.

All the evidence that is now gathering shows this assumption to be patently false. The personal and professional commitment that must exist at the heart of any new changes and reforms is absent. Not only is it neutrally absent, it is in fact positively absent in the sense that there is a mixture of profound indifference and active hostility to so many changes and reforms: profound indifference, in the sense that many teachers report a moving of their centre of gravity towards personal and social missions *outside* their professional life; active hostility, because so many changes seem ill-conceived, professionally naïve and against the heart and spirit of professional belief.

References

Ben-David, T. and Collins, R. (1966), "Social Factors in the Origins of a New Science: The Case of Psychology", *American Sociological Review*, Vol. 31, No. 4, August.

Fukuyama, F. (1993), *The End of History and the Last Man*, London: Penguin Books.

Goodson, I.F. (2001), "Social Histories of Educational Change", *Journal of Educational Change*, Vol. 2, No. 1, pp. 45–63.

Goodson, I.F. (1999), "The Educational Researcher as a Public Intellectual", *British Educational Research Journal*, Vol. 25, No. 3, pp. 277–97.

Goodson, I.F. (1995), *The Making of Curriculum: Collected Essays* (2nd ed.) London and Washington, DC: Falmer Press.

Hargreaves, A. (1994), *Changing Teachers, Changing Times: Teachers' Work and Culture in the Postmodern Age*, London: Cassell; New York: Teachers College Press.

Hargreaves, A., Earl, L., Moore, S. and Manning, S. (2001), *Learning to Change: Teaching Beyond Subjects and Standards*, San Francisco: Jossey-Bass.

Holmes, E.G.A. (1912), *What Is and What Might Be*, London: Constable.

Kenway, J. (1993), *Economizing Education: The Post-Fordist Directions*, Geelong, Victoria: Deakin University Press.

Kondratiev, N.D. (1984), *The Long Wave Cycle* (translated by Guy Daniels), New York: Richardson & Snyder.

Menter, I., Muschamp, Y., Nicholls, P., Ozga, J. and Pollard, A. (1997), *Work and Identity in the Primary School: A Post-Fordist Analysis*, Buckingham, UK: Open University Press.

Meyer, J.W., Kamens, D.H. and Benavot, A. (1992), *School Knowledge for the Masses*, London and Washington, DC: Falmer Press.

Reid, W.A. (1984), "Curricular Topics as Institutional Categories: Implications for Theory and Research in the History and Sociology of School Subjects", in Goodson, I.F. and Ball, S.J. (eds.), *Defining the Curriculum: Histories and Ethnographies*, pp. 67–75. London and Philadelphia: Falmer Press.

Robertson, H.-J. (1998), *No More Teachers, No More Books: The Commercialization of Canada's Schools*, Toronto, Ontario: McClelland and Stewart Inc.

Torres, R.M. (2000), *One Decade of Education for All: The Challenge Ahead [Una Decada de Educacion para Todos: La Tasrea Pendiente]*, FUM-TEP, Montevideo; Editorial Popular, Madrid; Editorial Laboratorio Educativo, Caracas; IIPE UNESCO, Buenos Aires; Artmed Editoria, Porto Alegre.

Vogel, D. (1988), *Fluctuating Fortunes: The Political Power of Business in America*, New York: Basic Books.

Whitty, G. (1997), "Marketization, the State, and the Re-formation of the Teaching Profession", in Halsey, A.H., Lauder, H., Brown, P. and Wells, A.S. (eds.), *Education: Culture, Economy, Society*, New York: Oxford University Press.

Chapter 2

TOWARDS A CURRICULUM FOR LIFELONG LEARNING

Malcolm Skilbeck

INTRODUCTION[*]

Throughout the centuries, educational thinkers have looked to school reform as a means not only of enhancing individual growth and development but of promoting social transformation. More conservative voices have expressed caution about root-and-branch reform. In expressing scepticism about the capacity of the school to change fundamentally, they have wanted schools to focus on inducting children into society as it is by equipping them with basic competences and inculcating virtues which, if not universal in the conduct of adults, are still held up as desirable. Hence the notion of an education based on the 3Rs with moral and perhaps also physical training. It is as well to recall that in most countries until well into the twentieth century, basic schooling was all that most children received, secondary and technical education being reserved for a small minority.

The conservative, minimalist position was often explicitly stated in legislation, regulations and programmes for the establishment in the nineteenth century of state systems of "public

[*] I should like to acknowledge the help of Helen Connell with this chapter.

instruction". The reformers have had either to attack the narrowness of purpose and the drudgery of practice, or to set up alternatives, as for example in the progressive education movement which
developed strongholds in the US, Australasia, Japan and a number
of European countries in the early decades of the twentieth century
(Connell, 1980). Thus the minimalist model of the purpose of the
school, while often dominant in practice, has never been able to ex-
clude wider aspirations and alternative views. Indeed, as schooling
has become universal, extending over many years from early
childhood to early adulthood, the broader goals proclaimed by reformers and critics in the past have gained the ascendancy.

Contemporary school systems, notably in the industrialised
countries but increasingly worldwide, have greatly broadened in
scope, they are diverse in respect of types of school or streams
(technical, academic, scientific, humanistic, etc.) and in curricula.
These developments of the school from a minimalist to a maxi-
malist institution reflect vastly increased rates of participation into
late adolescence and early adulthood. The complexities of societies and economies require highly skilled people in a great variety
of fields on the one hand and, on the other, generate difficult
problems for communities, families and children which the school
among other agencies is expected to ameliorate.

Whereas, historically, there have often been great divergences
between conservatives and reformers, minimalists and maximal-
ists, they share a common belief — that it is the cycle of schooling
now extending from early childhood into tertiary institutions for
adults that is the primary, essential vehicle for education. By some
people, it is well understood that there are educational vehicles
other than the school, in the generic sense used here — for example, self-education, informal study circles, and employment-based
training. But it is only very recently that there has been a wider
realisation that some fundamental conditions have changed and
that the conventions of schooling no longer suffice. A wider education vision is beginning to emerge. Two factors stand out: the
growth of training and re-training in the workplace to keep pace
with changing knowledge and an increasingly competitive

international environment; and the advent of the new communication and information technologies which demand new skills while opening opportunity for the extension and application of knowledge on a global scale. Together, these two are the source of innovations which, while they will not eclipse the schooling model, will, over time, lead to a reconceptualisation of the school and a realignment of school-type institutions and processes within a much larger, more varied framework of educational opportunity and action. Other factors are also at play: the demands and opportunities of social and civic life, and the perceived need for active personal interests to be cultivated into old age. Together these factors are generating new, more varied forms of education extending over the life-cycle.

The shorthand expression for this realignment is lifelong learning. It is the purpose of this chapter to consider the nature of some of the changes, the gathering momentum lifelong learning is bringing in its train, and the challenges posed to educational policy-makers and practitioners alike.

SCHOOLING OR LIFELONG LEARNING?

With the recent emergence or resurfacing of the concept of lifelong learning as both a vision for the future of society and an instrument of national policy, it has become necessary to reshape our ideas about the education processes and to rethink the structures, resources, institutions, agencies and other arrangements that sustain them. Unless this happens at all stages from preschool to tertiary education and beyond, we shall not succeed in transforming declarations that are being heard on all sides about the need for lifelong learning into practical strategies and action programmes. In some countries, this is beginning to happen, through a mix of policy frameworks and an emerging industry of research reports, analytic studies, conferences and books and journals (Aspin et al., 2001). But we still have a long road to travel before lifelong learning becomes as familiar in practical terms as schooling is today.

The title of a major international report, *Lifelong Learning for All*, provides one clue as to the new directions that are emerging, namely universalism and inclusiveness (OECD, 1996). Traditionally education in a full, extended sense from childhood into adulthood has been for the few, not the many. Tertiary education is rapidly becoming the norm in several countries, as more young people complete schooling and move onto tertiary study, while opportunities for adults to return to learning are increasing. By contrast, in many poorer countries of the world and in the regions where violence and disorder rule, only a small minority receive more than rudimentary schooling (Skilbeck, 2000). Education in a formal, structured sense has been and often still is selective and discriminating, even in the most developed, economically advanced and stable countries, where it continues in some sense to be a process of choosing and rejecting. Through a variety of devices people are screened out as well as screened in. Failure at school or very low attainment levels and adult illiteracy are, it seems, endemic and resistant to the most vigorous reform efforts. In spite of impressive achievements in the establishment and expansion of national systems of education, large numbers of young people continue to leave school poorly educated, dissatisfied and hostile to learning in school terms.

Countries vary in the education attainment of their populations, as measured by levels of completion of stages of formal study. Completion of upper secondary education is now seen as a standard to which countries aspire for young people, even if in practical terms only the most economically advanced are at present able to achieve this goal. But this is relatively recent and, in the adult population overall across the OECD membership, not only are there major disparities, in all countries attainment levels of adults fall short. Thus the higher rates of completion of younger people are to be contrasted with the very large pool of adults whose levels of formal study are extremely modest.

The lifelong learning movement is predicated on optimistic expectations: that all shall have not just the opportunity provided by universal schooling, but should build successful foundations

and continue active learning throughout life. While it is not assumed that the adult population will be "schooled" through formal education institutions and processes, there is a growing determination that learning should become pervasive throughout
life and this includes those who are already beyond school-
leaving age. Thus, a second clue to the new directions that are being taken or are foreshadowed is the shift from "education", with
its connotations of providers and providing institutions, to "learning", which is what people must increasingly do for themselves,
albeit with assistance and guidance.

"Learning" is also being given a much broader connotation
than hitherto: for example, learning from experience, from life,
through quite diverse activities. Desirable as this more open approach is, it does raise some issues, especially for policy-makers
who must specify educational conditions and requirements for
legislative, regulative and financial purposes and for institutions
that need to design programmes and assess performance. "Lifelong learning", because it is such an amorphous concept, is resistant to clear-cut categorisation and precise structuring. There is a
tendency to narrow the concept to employment-related training
and retraining, but this addresses only one aspect of learning
throughout life.

The expression "lifelong learners" has become commonplace;
but there is no comparable shift in terminology to denote facilita-
tors of lifelong learning. The terms "teachers" and "teaching" are
inadequate where learning is self-directed, on-the-job, experiential. Nor is there anything resembling a shorthand term for the
diverse settings or places of lifelong learning, comparable to
"school" or "college". Our language reflects and conveys a sense
that schooling and formal procedures for supplying something
("learning") are what education is about, and teachers are the
agents of learning. These terms of course refer to people and institutions responsible for some segment of the educative process, but
are not all-embracing. We lack a language to express in any adequate way the directions and procedures for learning which is
lifelong, experiential and inclusive of all people. We need a richer,

multi-faceted concept of education: education for all through varied processes of lifelong learning, fostered, facilitated and supported by many different kinds of people and agencies.

The explanation for the current shortcomings and lacunae in our terminology, for our rather fragmentary and disjointed conceptual mapping and for the lack of clearly defined and articulated policies is to be found largely in the recency of many of the developments and continuing vagueness about roles and responsibilities. It is also to be found in part in our intellectually lazy habit of equating education and learning with schooling, in the generic sense of institutional provision and formal requirements (attendance, courses of study, examinations).

We must also acknowledge that, for anything other than schooling, there is a relative dearth of well-attested alternative structures, frameworks and role models. Until very recently, there have been few conceptual and empirical inquiries into just what is meant by learning over the lifecycle — as distinct from a long-established philosophical and research tradition of inquiries and studies of schools, colleges, universities and the activities of students and teachers in these institutional settings. For each of these types of institutions and agencies, there are now declarations of intent, and sometimes policies and programmes in place that are relevant to lifelong learning. "Preparing undergraduates as lifelong learners" or "new programmes for adult education" or "laying the basis for lifelong learning in the school" are becoming familiar expressions, at least in the literature. But these are parts or aspects. They are not the whole picture. In neither structural nor institutional terms are we really clear about the frameworks or pathways needed for a continuing trajectory, society-wide, of learning lifelong, as distinct from somewhere on the way (school, college, adult institute, etc.).

We are thus still at a very early evolutionary stage whereby models of learning derived from schooling become transformed into models of learning over the life-cycle. Front-end models of learning (e.g. primary schooling, vocational preparation for working life) have yet to be built systematically and comprehensively

into continuing processes of development that foster skill formation, depth of knowledge, conceptual development, practical capability, reconstruction of experience, reflection and inquiry, and
so on throughout life and for all people. There are too many administrative divisions, institutional barriers, blocked pathways
and other structural inhibitions, to say nothing of the mental sets
and the organisational cultures which govern the teaching profession, standing in the way of smooth transition from "schooling" to
"lifelong learning". Whereas for the long-established models of
compulsory or basic schooling, initial and continuing vocational
training, and university and other tertiary level studies, we have a
well-established (if still contentious) apparatus of definite (if
changing) institutional structures, forms of curriculum organisation, administrative procedures, financial arrangements and categories of trained personnel, there is no comparable definiteness or
clarity in relation to lifelong learning.

Thus our education modelling is still restricted to a kit whose
parts fit the needs of children and young adults (but only up to a
point) while they only very partially serve adult needs extending
into old age. For basic education, the no-longer-disputed requirement of compulsory attendance and widely accepted principles of
school organisation, curriculum, teaching, testing and examining
and so forth set goals and standards and provide an authoritative
(if contested) basis for resourcing and for evaluating performance.
For tertiary education there are many comparable structures and
understandings. Even for rates of participation beyond the compulsory years of schooling, there is an evolving climate of public
policy which gives rise to predictions of mass and universal participation. But these predictions still refer to provision in formal
education institutions, such as the proportion of an age group that
can be expected to complete upper secondary schooling, or vocational programmes, and undertake some kind of recognisable tertiary level study over the lifespan. Implicit is the belief that this
study will have as its base some kind of tertiary level institution.

Indeed, tertiary institutions have a major role to play in continuing adult education but to play this role they will have to

change quite substantially. Moreover, there are many other community agencies and arrangements with roles to play in lifelong learning, the employment sector not least. National education statistics and their international counterparts do not, as a rule, capture the so-called "informal" sector and cannot at present serve as indicators of the nature of learning outside the school/college/ university, or of the level of participation. Lack of clarity about missions, roles, responsibilities, weak partnerships and limited, cluttered pathways are among the problems to be addressed in developing effective strategies of lifelong learning for all. Our understanding of what is happening, and of what is needed, will remain poor while these problems persist. There are, however, signs of progress.

It is the transformation in the final third of the twentieth century of a number of national systems of tertiary education from elite, to mass, and now universal systems that provides one new, vital link of the learning chain. So long as the tertiary sector was for a minority, screening out rather than drawing in the populace at large, continuing learning was a policy backwater, treated as an outgrowth of the largely voluntary sector of adult education and well outside the policy mainstream. It is the new policy climate in tertiary education, including growing links with the enterprise sector and a wide range of community organisations, that gives a lead into a model for lifelong learning. On the one hand, the outward-looking community-oriented service university or college is a model that is in principle feasible and practical, and, on the other, could enable many of the unresolved conceptual, resource and other practical difficulties of implementation to be addressed.

These difficulties require close attention if policy making is to move beyond the present stage of declaration of intent and the outlining of a broad, loose agenda for future action. A conceptual mapping exercise is required to find ways of distinguishing *any* kind of experience involving a changed perception, or mental or physical act from *learning which has educational value*. In other words, for analytic and public policy purposes what is to count as learning and education over the lifecycle and therefore what is to be fostered, encouraged, funded, evaluated and by whom?

No less important is the need to reach clearer and more definite views about just how embracing is the term "all" and, by implication, what kinds of learning opportunities and arrangements, society-wide and at all age levels, are needed, and how and by whom are they to be made. Schooling, at least in socially and economically developed countries, is an extended process for all children and young people to the ages of 15–16 and beyond. Legal requirements, financial provision and a culture of expectation sustain this, even if, in practice, "all" may mean effective participation and successful learning by no more than seventy or eighty per cent of the target population. But for most adults, learning which satisfies educational criteria — of depth, systematic engagement with content and issues, reflectiveness, critical inquiry and continuing development of skills, competence, insight and understanding — if it takes place at all, is voluntary, episodic and often self-financed. From a society perspective, lifelong education at the adult stage lacks structure, coherence and order. Policy-making in several countries is beginning to remedy these deficiencies but implementation is far short of what is needed to make lifelong learning a reality for all people (Hasan, 2001).

In order to address this issue, we need to clarify the arguments for lifelong learning as a domain of inclusive public policy — and not merely of private preference and individual choice, to consider the basis on which such policy should be deemed "for all" and not just for select groups, as is the case at present, and to map out strategies of realisation and attainment which take account of the totality of education provision, formal and informal, from early childhood into old age. Enthusiasm for lifelong learning needs to be tempered by realisation of the scale of the task and the time and resources required.

WHY LIFELONG LEARNING IS A PUBLIC POLICY ISSUE

As a generalisation, the justification for public policy initiatives aimed at opening up lifelong learning opportunities is twofold. First, changing socio-economic-cultural environments world-wide point up the increasing role of knowledge in all its forms as the prime mover of growth and prosperity. Individuals benefit from investment in the continued enhancement of knowledge and capability, but on a much larger scale so does the whole society. Second, the wider, more equitable diffusion of the benefits of growth, or shared prosperity, is a tenet of democratic governance and participation; active, responsible citizenship requires knowledge and competence, commitment and a civic ethic, all of which require regular refreshment.

These claims justify the extension of public education policy to embrace learning over the life-cycle but why should this learning not be confined to cadres of self-financing professionals and other specialists in the economic and civic domains? The arguments for inclusiveness or universalism are a mixture of (a) socio-economic perceptions about the pervasiveness of new knowledge touching all aspects of life; (b) the need in a knowledge society for greater depth of understanding, engagement with issues and all-round capability (personal, professional, socio-cultural) in the population at large; and (c) democratic values, alluded to above, which posit equity and opportunities for all people, not just cadres of experts, to be participants in the active society. It is from this array of socio-economic changes, perceptions and values that a new philosophy of lifelong learning for all has emerged (Aspin and Chapman, 2001). But as to what that might entail for policy and for the design, content, organisation and delivery of educational programmes and the extension of educational opportunity, many questions remain. Key amongst these is the nature of the partnerships and other associations for shared responsibility in the design, resourcing and provision of study programmes and facilities that need to be developed. These involve the state, the private and voluntary sectors, individuals and employers, formal education institutions, professional bodies and community groups and agencies. There is already a complex, diverse informal sector particularly active in adult education. For the formal sector, a key issue is the relationship between lifelong learning and the enormous growth of tertiary education in recent decades in industrialised countries.

In the words of the editors of a new *International Handbook*, lifelong learning, is "a concept whose time has come" (Aspin et al., 2001, p. *xviii*). But are we ready for it? The emerging climate of opinion internationally is reflected in both the numerous and varied activities of a multitude of providing agencies and institutions and in the formulation of national policies. International agencies, such as UNESCO and the OECD, have issued strong statements and orchestrated conferences, meetings and declarations as well as publishing or supporting major studies. OECD Education Ministers in 1996 agreed that strategies for lifelong learning need "a wholehearted commitment to new system-wide goals, standards and approaches, adapted to the culture and circumstances of each country" through: strengthening the foundations for learning throughout life; promoting coherent links between learning and work; rethinking the roles and responsibilities of all partners, including government; creating incentives for individuals, employers, and education and training providers to invest in lifelong learning. Hasan (2001) documented recent initiatives in some twelve industrialised countries; Atchoarena and Hite (2001) surveyed lifelong learning policies and challenges in the low-development African context (Delors, 1996; OECD, 1996; Hasan, 2001). The contrasts, in practical opportunities, provision and resources between the OECD countries and the developing world is stark but aspirations towards extended, inclusive education over the life-cycle are shared.

It is necessary to temper this acknowledgement of dramatic, far-reaching shifts in our understanding of the scope and nature of education and of what is required for the future with the realisation that the action agenda has yet to be constructed in depth and detail. The time has come not only to extend the boundaries of ideals, values and policies but to focus on the steps that must be taken, some surely requiring several decades of sustained effort, in order to transform our present limited, partial and patchy education systems into something resembling the vision.

The changes needed may be summarised as the creation of learning communities or educative societies such that the continuing growth and wellbeing of all people is fostered, and supported by all of the relevant agencies and institutions, and is expressed by the values and practices that shape the social order. This means, among others, co-ordinated policies for early childhood care and education (health, social services, employment, pre-schooling), a broad, common core school curriculum with a wide array of choices and options to stimulate and encourage learning throughout childhood and youth, multiple, varied pathways for young adults to enter diverse forms of tertiary education and, in adulthood, the acceptance that professional, civic, social and personal life can provide opportunities and challenges which become the core of continuing learning and development.

For public policy purposes, including funding arrangements, programmes and courses, institutions and agencies will need to be "recognised". Inevitably this will mean a degree of arbitrariness in decision-making and allocations. Partnerships will entail compromises and shared responsibility needs to be based on contractual fairness, for example between employers and employees. These and many other practical issues are beginning to be addressed on a much larger scale. A visionary utopia, say the sceptics; a set of directions to be worked out in depth and detail as the twentieth century of universal schooling merges into the twenty-first century of universal, lifelong learning, say the reformers. There are echoes of the struggle to achieve universal schooling a century ago.

THE UNFINISHED AGENDA: EDUCATION FOR ALL

The implementation of lifelong learning does not mean a turning away from established policies. Rather, it calls for more intensive action on them. We are still grappling with the unfinished agenda of the twentieth century and, globally, we must continue to do so as the next steps in the development of our educational ideas, beliefs and practices are taken.

In the year 2000, the major international organisations with educational roles and responsibilities combined with national governments, voluntary agencies, academic institutions and individual scholars and researchers to review educational progress world-wide in the preceding decade (Skilbeck, 2000). In 1990, an international movement, "Education For All" (EFA), had been launched in Jomtien, Thailand, to address major outstanding gaps and weaknesses in education worldwide. This vast, daunting undertaking comprised analysis of existing provision, declaration of goals and directions and a commitment to carry out a decade of work to reach globally agreed, specific targets. The Jomtien *Framework for All — Meeting Basic Learning Needs* (Education For All International Consultative Forum, 1990) invited countries to set targets with reference to six dimensions (Table 2.1); it was not assumed that all the numerical targets could be met within a decade but they were to provide direction and spur effort. Although focused on quite basic requirements and unmet needs and slanted toward developing countries, it should not be assumed that Education For All is relevant only to poorer and less economically developed countries, a common misconception especially about the education remit of UNESCO and UNICEF. The EFA targets embraced all countries in a common endeavour to expose deficiencies in provision, access, attainment and opportunity world-wide. For example, in only a handful of countries today is there anything approximating a comprehensive, affordable, professionally advanced and fully inclusive system of early childhood care and education. In all countries, there are problems of adult literacy, and school resistance, failure and attrition.

Table 2.1: The Six Dimensions of the Education for All Targets

1. Expansion of early childhood care and developmental activities, including family and community interventions, especially for poor, disadvantaged and disabled children;

2. Universal access to, and completion of, primary (or whatever higher level of education is considered as "basic") by the year 2000;

3. Improvement of learning achievement such that an agreed percentage of an age cohort (e.g. 80 per cent of 14-year-olds) attains or surpasses a defined level of necessary learning achievement;

4. Reduction of the adult illiteracy rate (the appropriate age-group to be determined in each country) to, say, one half its 1990 level by the year 2000, with sufficient emphasis on female literacy to significantly reduce the current disparity between male and female illiteracy rates;

5. Expansion of provision of basic education and training in other essential skills required by youth and adults, with programme effectiveness assessed in terms of behavioural change and impact on health, employment and productivity;

6. Increased acquisition by individuals and families of the knowledge, skills and values required for better living and sound and sustainable development, made available through all education channels including the mass media, other forms of modern and traditional communication, and social action, with effectiveness assessed in terms of behavioural change.

Source: Education For All International Consultative Forum, 1990.

In April 2000, in Dakar, Senegal, the world education community came together to review achievements. From a global perspective, and despite notable achievements and great gains in some regions and many countries, the stark reality is that we have yet to achieve the foundations, let alone the superstructure, of lifelong learning. Instead, there are great disparities, in some instances growing, between countries which have achieved universal schooling to ages 16–18 and beyond and high overall standards of educational attainment, and others where the majority remain illiterate and only a minority attend basic schools and then often for only a few years. The impact of poverty, civil unrest, warfare, disease, famine, inept or corrupt government, insufficient and inadequately focused international development efforts, ensures that education is quite decidedly not "for all". It is not simply a matter of low rates of enrolment and attendance, but of *exclusion* of the most vulnerable, the most impoverished, the most remotely located: girls and women; children with disabilities; working children; children suffering the impact of HIV/AIDS; people in war zones; and refugees. By contrast, an inclusive policy, internationally, nationally, regionally and locally, would, by all deliberate means, reach out to the excluded.

It is necessary to keep this global condition in mind, not as a signal of an international environment that may seem remote from many individual national policy and institutional concerns but, in a rapidly globalising world, as a reminder that the problem of the "have-nots" is no less a problem of the "haves", even if they do not realise it. "Globalisation" refers not only to economic trends and policies such as liberalisation of trade and investment, free capital flows, moves toward a global marketplace, and the commercial practices of multinational corporations. Equally, it connotes the movement of people across national boundaries, the diffusion and intermingling of cultures and efforts to create and maintain some semblance of world order and justice. The market is of ideas and knowledge, not just of goods and services. The reach of the new technologies is global, enabling people regardless of location to become part of global networks of communication, exchange, knowledge and ideas. There are ethical and environmental issues at stake, exceedingly complex and difficult legal, political and diplomatic challenges and the dynamics of rapidly changing, worldwide cultures of technology, communications and media. The inadequacy of present global governance and regulatory arrangements in the face of changes of this scope and scale is all too evident. As yet, the part education can play in humanising global society and processes, liberating and empowering people and producing a more just and capable global community has received all too little attention in the debate over globalisation.

LEARNING FOR ALL IN A GLOBALISED AGE

Of course, the efforts needed to civilise and reap social benefits of globalisation — to make its many dimensions seem like gains to humanity and not just to the favoured few — go far beyond the scope of education policies and agencies. Nevertheless, a curriculum for lifelong learning in the dawning era of global awareness, citizenship and internationally responsible conduct needs to incorporate knowledge and understanding of the world society and the world economy, of law, rules and codes of conduct, of cultures and communities around the globe. It should aim to develop personal and society-wide understandings and values directed at international as well as national, local and personal issues. A curriculum is needed that enhances global capability and insights, building on but transcending the local and national boundaries of present-day education. How to live a worthwhile life through knowledge, understanding and competence defined globally is one aspect. A corollary is that, in global scenarios, the unequal and inequitable distribution of wealth, extremes of poverty and prosperity, violence, hardship and deprivation in particular regions and communities can no longer be drawn together as a category of "the other", sharply demarcated from the interests and concerns of the well-to-do, whether individuals, communities or countries. A curriculum for lifelong learning in the global society will treat the problems, setbacks and failures of parts of the world as concerns for the whole world and will develop readiness and ability to address them. The "all" in "lifelong learning for all" is a global, not simply a national and a local issue.

There is thus no reason for complacency at the national level in those countries which, according to international indicators, are prosperous, stable, enjoy high living standards and levels of education resourcing, funding, institutional provision, participation and measured attainment, have constructed lifelong learning frameworks for themselves and are experiencing a good quality of life. Their educational achievements are impressive — reflecting economic prosperity and a readiness to invest in education, sharing the bounties of production more equitably across the nation and laying the foundations of future growth for all are noble ideals, but from a global perspective three problems stand out in the realm of practical education politics. First, the prevalence of education policies and practices that have yet to capture the social, cultural, ethical, political as well as the economic dimensions of globalisation. Schooling is still heavily nationalistic, and curricula are generally weak on the global interconnectedness of contemporary life. Second, disturbing levels of non-completion of schooling, low standards of attainment, failure and dropout feature to varying degrees even in the most advanced countries. Third, there are quite inequitable patterns of resource distribution which threaten to increase dramatically the gap between rich and poor — those who gain access to the fruits of education and those who don't or can't.

The schooling model of education is a great achievement of nation states. It has been enormously successful in many countries but, as a model of successful, effective learning for all, in a rapidly changing, new world order, it is flawed. The nearer we get to achieving the goals and targets of universalism in participation and desirable standards of attainment (however defined), the more difficult is the road, the more uncertain the direction to take. Without further fundamental changes, notably in the setting of learning targets, in the design of the curriculum, in the methods and procedures of teaching and in the learning environment and material and psychological conditions affecting them, we will not have a satisfactory foundation of universal, lifelong learning for a global age. True in both the most and least educationally advanced countries, this realisation is a daunting reminder that, far from being a panacea or a mere extension into adulthood of established patterns of teaching and learning, effective policies and programmes of lifelong learning creativity and innovation of the highest order are called for.

How can creativity and innovation best be fostered in education systems and in individuals of all ages? Can we build on the best that schooling has to offer, identifying growth points that can be further developed to increase the chances of all young people learning successfully and continuing to do so throughout life? It is worth recalling some earlier attempts to reshape education systems; for example, a reassessment of established teaching and learning processes was important in the renaissance of curriculum thought and development which started in the 1950s, extending into the 1960s and early 1970s (Skilbeck, 1990). There were of course antecedents, and curriculum analysis and debate has been a fundamental and continuing part, not to say a foundation, of the development of modern systems of schooling since the eighteenth century. Throughout the twentieth century, reform efforts have been a feature of many systems. The record is far from being one of consistent success, but reforms that are evolutionary, well planned, build on what already exists, extend and enlarge working models and practices, are comprehensible to practitioners and are appropriately resourced, have been effective (Tyack and Cuban, 1995; Miles, 1998, pp. 37–69).

There were important changes of direction and in the concept of curriculum itself which gathered momentum in the second half of the twentieth century. The initial stages of what was to become an international movement were limited to particular subject areas, notably mathematics and the natural sciences. The motives, too, were at first mainly rather narrow since the early work was carried out in the United States, spurred on in a Cold War climate by reports of Russian advances in science and technology and a wave of internal criticism of standards of student attainment in American schools. There is no question but that funds were made available — from both private and public sources — and initiatives undertaken in a spirit of international competitiveness rather than cooperation. National advancement, not global awareness and citizenship, was the key preoccupation. For governments, the global competitiveness of their economies was and has since remained an over-riding priority.

The enlisting of education to advance national interests is longstanding and has become an integral part of strategies for competitive national development. The engagement of education with the generation of wealth has never been far beyond the reach of education policy. The sale of education services on the international market is not new but during the past decade has become a major instrument of national policy in several countries, notably in relation to higher education. Current interest by national systems in lifelong learning, in the uses of communication and information technology and the popularity of slogans like "knowledge society", express a preoccupation with national prosperity and ways to sustain or enhance it in an internationally competitive environment. Important as this is in motivating public and political interest in education generally and in lifelong learning, there is a serious risk of narrowness in policy and distortion of values if other perspectives are not also brought to the fore. Creativity and innovation can indeed be stimulated but we should be asking for what purpose, in which contexts and with what effects?

The advancement of prosperity has been and remains one major strand in policies and programmes of curriculum renewal and development. This is perhaps most evident in the argument that a successful modern economy requires a highly skilled, broadly competent workforce, with high levels of employment and improved productivity reflecting in part a high overall standard of education (OECD, 1994). In terms of schooling, this means economically and socially relevant curricula, low dropout, ever rising rates of participation in some form of tertiary education and improvements in the quality of teaching and learning.

The effects of these ways of thinking over several decades since the 1960s are numerous and varied. They may be summarised as a continuing drive both to market education internationally and, within nation states, to strengthen studies in science and technology, languages useful for commercial international positioning, broadly defined vocational competencies and values and attitudes which favour competitiveness and an achievement orientation and predispose students to favour economic engagement and productivity. Although there may be no negative view espoused about other forms of knowledge and experience — the humanities, the arts, leisure activities and social sciences other

than those with an economic hue — resources and policy initiatives have tended to be concentrated on what is deemed to be
economically and socially useful skills and knowledge, in a global
environment perceived to be harsh and increasingly competitive.

This kind of economic argument is strong and persuasive and
has been responsible for substantial investments in educational
development. It is in no way to diminish its impact on educational
policy to state that it is not a sufficient basis and has at times
proved unsatisfactory.

Concern continues to be expressed about students turning
away from science and from some branches of technological education. Resources are being steered toward information technology and national innovation policies commonly target information sciences, bio-technology and other "cutting edge" fields that
hold promise of economic returns and enhanced competitiveness
in the belief that highly focused R&D will have numerous spin-
offs and advance a country's economic interests. In education,
however, attempts in several countries to ground curricula more
comprehensively in science and technology and in vocational
preparation have not worked, or only partially so (Skilbeck, Connell, Lowe and Tait, 1994). There is an uncertain link between student interests and motivation, and declared needs and priorities
for national development. Education policy has aimed to achieve
a different balance by demonstrating the importance of science
and technology in contemporary society and preparation for
working life as a central function of schooling, to overcome poor
standards of attainment, and to develop vocational competence in
the large number of young people who are not succeeding at
school or who discontinue study at an early age. While for many
students, a strong vocational orientation in the curriculum and
specific programmes of preparation for working life have undoubtedly been successful, for a very significant minority they are
not working. Very low enrolments in science in upper secondary
and tertiary education demonstrate a low yield from decades of
policy initiatives and investment in improved curricula, pedagogy
and teacher education. Undue emphasis on national goals and

priorities, competitiveness and adult views about what countries "require" is likely to lead to the failure, not the success, of inclusive policies for lifelong learning for all.

This brings us to other perspectives that need to be considered in formulating curriculum strategies and opportunities at all levels and stages of schooling: namely, the cultivation of personal values and interests and the development of a civic culture and social cohesion conceived in international as well as national terms. Again, sketching the lines of descent of present policies over the past half century, it appears that the socio-civic rationale with a strong nationalistic bias has been more to the fore than the international and personal ones. Combined with the prominence of the economic rationale, it presents students with a distinctive challenge: to prepare for adult life by meeting goals and attaining standards which while they may be of great personal interest to many students (but by no means all), are nevertheless extrinsic and usually remote in their beneficial outcomes. They are framed as expectations and requirements of life in the nation state — to study particular subjects and combinations of subject matter by (compulsorily) attending school, performing in tests and examinations whose norms are grounded in characteristics of large populations, not the distinctive concerns of each individual, and as values and ways of behaving which conform to a model of the good citizen and worthy adult member of society. As with the vocational orientation, the socio-civic perspective, while fundamental in the objectives, purposes and structures of formal schooling, does not succeed in sufficiently engaging the interests and commitment of all students. It needs to be broadened on the one hand and, on the other, connected more directly with personal values and interests. Significant numbers of students feel alienated, fall into delinquent patterns of behaviour and either reject the values enshrined in formal schooling or are indifferent to them.

The inescapable conclusion is that, despite the enormous investment and the succession of policy initiatives and developments aimed at "capturing" youth for education through programmes grounded in economic, social and civic values and processes, schooling everywhere is only partially successful in laying the foundations for continuing learning. The explanation lies in the relative neglect of the personal interests, circumstances and values of individual learners — not on the part of those teachers and schools working very hard at times and with outstanding success in this regard, but in the wider policies, frameworks and formal requirements of schooling, and in the life conditions of many students and their families.

The issue is structural and cultural. A curriculum that does not engage, build on and systematically develop and sustain the interests of individual learners is an inadequate basis and platform for present, let alone lifelong learning. While some students will recover from the perceived irrelevance, the disappointments and the frustrations of schooling and overcome their early negative and hostile attitudes to learning, many will not. The school curriculum needs to be refocused to ensure, as far as humanly possible, successful, effective learning by all students in a setting which draws them into global awareness and values and cultivates a wide range of competencies. Success must be an attainable target, enjoyable if demanding engagement must become a reality for all students at school with no exceptions. The structural disablements that are a function of curriculum, pedagogy, standard-setting through examinations, school organisation and other signals that in practice serve as barriers to learning must be eliminated if lifelong learning for all is to become a practical programme and not merely a catchy slogan. The school alone cannot overcome problems of the home and the wider community of which children and young people are part but it can identify itself with all the positive forces in society which are working toward improvement and amelioration of all the adverse circumstances affecting children's learning.

Two basic conditions need to be satisfied in devising curricula at the level of schooling — from pre-school programmes to tertiary studies. First, the learning activities and experiences must be such as to equip students with tools, techniques, competencies, knowledge and understanding that will be demonstrably of value and use to them. The students themselves need to be in no doubt about the social, economic and personal value of their studies, even if their longer term horizons are overlaid by immediate pre-occupations. Such curricula cannot be devised by educators alone but must draw in a broad array of community interests and expertise through education design and development partnerships. Second, and as a corollary, the learning activities and experiences must capture the personal interests and motivations of all individual students, enabling them to continue their personal development through successful encounters with whatever requirements are set. Again, this means treating the workplace, the home, the neighbourhood and the wider community as resources and sites for learning, as much as the specialised institutions of schooling.

What needs to be overcome is the view that in order for systems and institutions to achieve and maintain "standards", goals must be set in an unduly restrictive pedagogical environment, thereby and as an artefact ensuring that many students will fail at the first opportunity or close the book on continuing learning. Moreover, we must get beyond that point of understanding whereby curriculum is defined as a catalogue of required subjects leavened with a few options and so-called "co-" or "extra-curricular" activities. Subjects are a source and a resource and mastery of specified subject matter is or can be made a reasonable requirement of all students — provided it is organised into manageable learning tasks for each individual learner. But mastery of timetabled, syllabus-defined subject matter is only part of the curriculum. A larger, more sophisticated mapping exercise is required, to ensure that the overall experience of life at school, its "outreaches" in the form of home assignments, sporting and cultural events, social interaction and values and norms of school life, are all embraced. Depth of knowledge and understanding are essential and must become universal in a "knowledge society" that is also democratic and functions beyond the level of a technology of information processing. Good educational institutions provide for all of this, but while the provision and opportunity may be there, the engagement of every individual student in a worthwhile set of continuing learning experiences is not. The foundations of a curriculum for lifelong learning depend not just on good policies, plans, designs and provision, but on the learning experiences as *lived* and *valued* in formative ways by all students.

A CURRICULUM FOR LIFELONG LEARNING?

Clearly, the narrower, institution-bound concept of "curriculum" needs to be recast for policies and strategies of lifelong learning. Relevant to many elements of the process, it is nevertheless restrictive and even misleading in considering others. This may explain, at least partly, the relative neglect of curriculum issues in the literature of lifelong learning. But there is an older concept and at the same time there are broader usages which provide a starting point for a curriculum analysis. Literally, "a course to be run", curriculum is best thought of as the totality of learning experiences which are provided for and undergone in the pursuit of educational goals and values. These experiences, while often directed according to institutional purposes and requirements, are not limited to or restricted by them. The goals and values may be society-wide — for example, those which provide a basis for system-wide policies of schooling — they may be institutional or they may be personal or communitarian.

For a meaningful discussion of lifelong learning, it is necessary to take all these dimensions into account. Ultimately, lifelong learning for all is a society-wide, personal and communal quest for knowledge, understanding, competence, values and a worthwhile, fulfilling life. This cannot be reduced to the specific curricular activities of formal education institutions, on-the-job training certification requirements and so forth, although all have something to contribute. A curriculum map or chart for lifelong learning would need to embrace them and to pinpoint changes needed to achieve the purposes of lifelong learning.

While it is scarcely possible to produce such a map in the sense of a comprehensive, inclusive overview of society-wide learning opportunities, action on curriculum is needed at all levels and stages and with reference to the needs and expectations of different categories of learners whose learning expectations and needs are well understood and provide targets for action. There is need for better monitoring and more systematic evaluations of what is available. The first and overriding priority for policy-makers and practitioners alike is to ensure that curriculum design and development at whatever stage and in whatever setting should consistently have lifelong learning as an explicit target and criterion in resource allocation. As noted above, the discourse of the formal education system has begun to move in this direction: "laying good foundations through universal pre-school education", "laying the foundations for continuing learning", and "learning how to learn" as targets in primary and secondary schools; "lifelong learning as a principle in the design of undergraduate curricula" are examples of a change in the language. But it is doubtful whether this change is as yet resulting in practical new curriculum designs and strategies. Policy-makers, administrators, teachers, support staff, researchers and those responsible for assessing learning and for examinations have a responsibility to demonstrate that this shift does in fact take place. It is important that adults who have had poor or inadequate learning opportunities at school have access to appropriate study opportunities, for example in improving literacy skills. Acquiring a basic capability in computing, developing competence and self-confidence for employment and community participation are increasingly recognised as targets for courses and study programmes for adults.

Ultimately, the curriculum principles, designs, standards, criteria, resources and so on that are in place or are clear goals for the elements of formal education systems and to some extent for the informal sector as well, will develop and be modified to incorporate the vision of lifelong learning for all. There are major challenges, some familiar and of long standing, others of more recent origin.

At the policy level, there needs to be a sound balance of provision and opportunity among the economic, socio-civic and personal purposes and aspirations identified earlier in this chapter. This balance raises significant resource and equity issues since while there may appear to be ample provision and opportunity relating to all three categories overall, it is frequently restricted in practice due to people's financial circumstances and geographical location. Choice is thereby distorted.

A major weakness in education systems everywhere is the lack of coherence among the different elements: courses and programmes which do not lead on in a sequential way; lack of recognition of prior learning for purposes of entry to particular programmes; inadequate arrangements for credit transfer and so on. While there has been considerable progress for example in formal recognition of competence, regardless of how and where attained, and in the establishment of system-wide qualification agencies which incorporate national standards and levels that facilitate comparisons of qualifications and attainments, large parts of the informal sector of adult education are still not touched by these developments. As a result of this and of major deficiencies in public funding policies, continuing education over the lifecycle is still by and large a policy morass.

Coherence, moreover, is not just a matter of structural linkages, articulated pathways, formal recognition and intelligent policies of resourcing and incentives. It is very much an outcome of personal learning decisions and strategies: "Learning how to learn" means learning how to orchestrate learning and produce patterns of meaning and understanding, as much as it means developing specific skills and habits. These are sophisticated cognitive strategies, calling for high levels of self-confidence and awareness. Adults, no less than children, commonly need encouragement and support in developing them. The multiplicity of pathways and the great variety of learner interests and preferences and their life circumstances, mean that there will be diversity of curricula and pedagogy rather than homogeneity. Varied maps and multiple routes of learning are the keynotes. Nevertheless, there are tools, techniques, strategies of learning, embedded in and only accessible through systematic study in a range of domains (core curricula) which all learners must acquire in order to proceed and develop capability throughout life.

Numerous pathways, diversity of provision, the individual choices of learners and divided responsibility raise difficult problems of coherence which can only be addressed through enlarged partnership and greatly improved working relationships among the different sectors and responsible bodies both public and private.

Ensuring that there is equitable opportunity, encouragement and incentives for all people to learn throughout life is a global challenge for which there is society-wide responsibility. It is to the educators, however, that society will look for practical capability in making the dream a reality.

References

Aspin, D., Chapman, J., Hatton, M. and Sawano, Y. (eds.) (2001), *International Handbook of Lifelong Learning*, Parts 1 and 2, Kluwer International Handbooks of Education, Vol. 6, Dordrecht/Boston/London: Kluwer Academic Publishers.

Aspin, D. and Chapman, J. (2001), "Towards a Philosophy of Lifelong Learning", in Aspin, D., Chapman, J., Hatton, M. and Sawano, Y. (eds.) *International Handbook of Lifelong Learning*, Part 1, Dordrecht/Boston/ London: Kluwer Academic Publishers, pp. 3–33.

Atchoarena and Hite (2001), "Lifelong Learning Policies in Low Development Contexts: An African Perspective", in Aspin, D., Chapman, J., Hatton, M. and Sawano, Y. (eds.) *International Handbook of Lifelong Learning*, Part 1, Dordrecht/Boston/London: Kluwer Academic Publishers, pp. 201–28.

Australian National Training Authority (ANTA) (1998), *A Bridge to the Future: Australia's National Strategy for Vocational Education and Training 1998–2003*, Brisbane: ANTA.

Candy, P.C., Crebert, G. and O'Leary, J. (1994), *Developing Lifelong Learners through Undergraduate Education*, Commissioned Report No. 28, National Board of Employment, Education and Training, Canberra: Australian Government Publishing Service.

Coffield, F. (ed.) (1996), *Higher Education and Lifelong Learning*, papers presented at School for Policy Studies, Bristol University, Newcastle, Department of Education, University of Newcastle-upon-Tyne on behalf of DfEE, ESRC and HEFCE.

Connell, W.F. (1980), *A History of Education in the Twentieth Century World*, Canberra Curriculum Development Centre, New York: Teachers' College Press.

Delors, J. (1996), *Learning: The Treasure Within*, Report of the International Commission on Education for the Twenty-first Century, Paris: UNESCO.

Duke, C. (2001), "Lifelong Learning and Tertiary Education: The Learning University Revisited", in Aspin, D., Chapman, J., Hatton, M., and Sawano, Y. (eds.) *International Handbook of Lifelong Learning*, Part 2, Dordrecht/Boston/London: Kluwer Academic Publishers, pp. 501–28.

Education For All International Consultative Forum (1990), *Framework for Action — Meeting Basic Learning Needs. Guidelines for Implementing the World Declaration on Education For All*, Jomtien, Thailand, 5–9 March, Paris: UNESCO.

Hasan, A. (2001), "Lifelong Learning: A Monitoring Framework and Trends in Participation", in Aspin, D., Chapman, J., Hatton, M. and Sawano, Y. (eds.) *International Handbook of Lifelong Learning*, Part 1, Dordrecht/Boston/London: Kluwer Academic publishers, pp. 379–402.

Miles, M. (1998), "Finding Keys to School Change: A 40-year Odyssey", in Hargreaves, A. Lieberman, A., Fullan, M. and Hopkins, D. (eds.), *International Handbook of Educational Change*, Part 1, Dordrecht/Boston/London: Kluwer Academic Publishers, pp. 37–69.

Ministerial Council on Education, Employment, Training and Youth Affairs (MCEETYA), Australia (1997), *National Policy: Adult Community Education*, Melbourne: MCEETYA.

Ministerial Council on Education, Employment, Training and Youth Affairs (MCEETYA), Australia (1999), *The Adelaide Declaration on National Goals for Schooling in the Twenty-first Century*, Melbourne: MCEETYA.

Ministry of Education, Finland (1995), *Education, Training and Research in the Information Society — A National Strategy*, Helsinki: The Ministry.

OECD (1994), *The Jobs Study: Facts, Analysis, Strategies*, Paris: OECD.

OECD (1996), *Lifelong Learning for All*, Paris: OECD.

OECD (1997), *Towards a New Global Age: Challenges and Opportunities*, Paris: OECD.

OECD (1998), *Education Policy Analysis 1998*, Centre for Educational Research and Innovation, Paris: OECD.

OECD (2000), *Education at a Glance, OECD Indicators*, Paris: OECD.

Skilbeck, M. (1990), *Curriculum Reform: An Overview of Trends*, Paris: OECD.

Skilbeck, M. (2000), *Education For All 2000 Assessment — Global Synthesis*, Education for All International Consultative Forum, Paris: UNESCO.

Skilbeck, M., Connell, H.M. Lowe, N. and Tait, K. (1994), *The Vocational Quest: New Directions in Education and Training*, London: Routledge.

Swedish Ministry of Education and Science (1994), *Agenda 2000 — Knowledge and Competence for Next Century*, Stockholm: The Ministry.

Tyack, D. and Cuban, L. (1995), *Tinkering Toward Utopia: A Century of Public School Reform*, Cambridge, MA: Harvard University Press.

SECTION TWO

SECONDARY CURRICULUM REFORMS:
IRISH PERSPECTIVES

Chapter 3

POLITICS AND PARTNERSHIP IN CURRICULUM PLANNING IN IRELAND

Gary Granville

INTRODUCTION

The reflections that follow are those of a former "insider" participant in the process of national curriculum planning, now working
in the allegedly dispassionate and cerebral groves of academe.
Former participants are dangerous commentators. Too often they
are concerned with presenting apologias, with settling old scores
or with rewriting history. The observations that follow attempt
neither "to bury" nor "to praise" former colleagues, in the sense
that Shakespeare's Mark Antony used those terms. Instead, this
chapter presents a model within which the process of Irish curriculum planning can be addressed and to offer some personal
commentary on some features of that model.

> Who are the members of NCCA? Do they know how things
> are done in Ireland? Do they read the daily papers? . . . They
> are like First World War generals . . . not knowing anything
> about front line conditions.

Thus wrote a teacher in a letter to *The Irish Times* on 2 February
1999, expressing indignation with policy issues emanating from
the National Council for Curriculum and Assessment (NCCA).

The letter was concerned with assessment for public examinations, one of the few curriculum issues to appear regularly in the media and to generate public debate in Ireland. However, its significance in the present context is its treatment of the membership of the NCCA. One of the hallmarks of the NCCA is its representative composition, designed specifically to remove divisions between "generals" and the "frontline troops".

The practice of curriculum design in Ireland has undergone significant changes during the period 1985 to 2000. From being a highly centralised and sometimes mysterious process within the state Department of Education (Mulcahy, 1981; Coolahan, 1981), curriculum planning at national level has taken on more open and participative procedures. The establishment of the Interim Curriculum and Examinations Board (CEB) in 1984, and subsequently, the NCCA in 1987, marked a very significant transfer of authority. The Education Act (1998) established a statutory role for the NCCA, a role that became effective from 12 July 2001. The main brief of this body is "to advise the Minister on matters relating to:

a.   the curriculum for early childhood education, primary and post-primary schools, and

b.   the assessment procedures employed in schools and examinations on subjects which are part of the curriculum. (Ireland, Government of, 1998, p. 38)

The establishment of the NCCA as a statutory body has its antecedents in the specific history of curriculum development in Ireland (Crooks and McKernan, 1984, Mulcahy, 1981), in the international pattern of educational restructuring (Hargreaves, 1994) and in the evolution of Irish national economic and social planning (Hardiman, 2000). In the international experience of educational politics, the emergence of the NCCA can be seen as an example of ostensible devolution, with an underpinning element of increased central control. This apparently paradoxical conjunction of democratic structures masking autocratic powers has been most graphically demonstrated in the influential New Zealand experience of educational restructuring (Gordon, 1992). The process of extending participation while tightening central control has been described as "free-market Stalinism . . . the contradictory drive to extend the market while simultaneously increasing the powers of the . . . state" (Barber, 1996, p. 55). The NCCA experience is worth examining insofar as it reflects some, but by no means all, of these features. More importantly, however, it should be examined in the context of social partnership, the model of planning that has been at the heart of the growth of the Irish economy in the latter years of the twentieth century.

This chapter examines the operational experience of the CEB/ NCCA since the inception of the former in 1984. The focus is on the structures and processes of national curriculum design rather than on the substantive issues of the school curriculum itself. The chapter is in two parts. The first part applies a specific model of organisational analysis to the NCCA to identify its defining features and functions. Using that analysis as a base, the second part reflects on the NCCA experience in terms of its historical evolution, its underlying operational premises and its particular manifestation of partnership as an instrument of professional and public policy formulation. Prior to undertaking this analysis, it is necessary and appropriate to indicate the theoretical lens through which the study is conducted.

FRAMES FOR ORGANISATIONAL ANALYSIS

It is impossible to develop one theory of organisation that can be simultaneously general, accurate and simple enough to provide for all the different contexts of both public and private management. Weick coined the expression "The Law of Commensurate Complexity" to describe the inadequacy of organisational theory to make sense of complex operations and experiences. He went on to say that:

> . . . much organisational research is uninformative and pedestrian partly because people have tried to make it general and accurate and simple. In trying to accommodate all three of

> these aims, none has been realised vigorously; the result has
> been bland assertions. (1985, p. 41)

Analysis of the operations of the NCCA and its committee system
is hampered by the lack of immediately appropriate tools. The
experience of the NCCA committee system, at one level, may be
analysed in terms of conventional management literature. However, the NCCA operates as more than a collection of committees
under the banner of a national Council. It is a cultural and political phenomenon in its own right. Consequently, its analysis requires a more sophisticated conceptual framework than provided
by conventional organisation theories.

Bolman and Deal's (1990) four-frame model of organisational
analysis is both liberating and revealing. In an attempt to address
the sort of analytical weaknesses described by Weick, this model
provides for a variety of perspectives, not necessarily mutually
exclusive. Rather, they can be layered one upon the other like
lenses through which to view the organisation in question, without recourse to the "bland assertions" typical of much organisation theory. The four frames for evaluation are set out as follows:

- *The structural frame*: a sociological perspective, this concentrates on the roles and relationships within the organisation;

- *The human resources frame*: a social psychology perspective, this
  is concerned with the individual needs and talents within the
  organisation;

- *The political frame*: a political science perspective, this is concerned with the processes of conflict resolution, of coalition-
  making and of negotiation;

- *The symbolic frame*: an anthropological perspective, addressing
  those elements of ritual, ceremony and theatre which give
  meaning to the experience of those involved.

Through the cumulative perspectives generated through the multiple lens of these four frames, a more rounded and three-
dimensional image of what goes on in any organisation may be

produced. It is particularly useful in a study of a public sector institution, where many interests and bodies are involved, and where objectives and outcomes are less easily defined than in the private sector.

The first two frames — the structural and the human resource frames — are located in mainstream management literature. They are concerned with the management of organisations and they relate broadly to the concepts of linearity, certainty and rationality, which are the hallmarks of most theories of organisation. These frames can help to illuminate the internal operations of the NCCA committee system in terms of operational efficiency and effectiveness.

NCCA in the Structural Frame

A defining feature of the NCCA, on its establishment in 1987, was its representative nature. Unlike the earlier CEB (1984–87), the NCCA comprised members nominated by the designated partners in education,[1] under the chairmanship of a Ministerial appointee. Equally significant in the establishment of the NCCA was the compositional specification of the critical secondary tier of curriculum and course committees.

The compositional formula of the NCCA was to be replicated in many other educational bodies and committees over the subsequent decade. For example, the National Council for Vocational Awards (NCVA), established in 1993, operated with a similar Council and series of subcommittees, slightly different in actual membership but designed on the same partnership principles.

Two issues in relation to the representative committee system of the NCCA are of particular interest in the context of the wider concept of partnership:

- The operation of the committees as *representative* as distinct from *participative* democratic structures, and

- The actual experience of the committees in terms of their brief as public policy entities, in terms of quality, equity and long-term outcomes.

Conventional management literature treats committees as necessary features of the landscape, but not generally the most attractive one. Some positive features of committees have been
identified (Weihrich and Koontz, 1993, p. 242) such as: facilitating
group deliberation; avoidance of a single location of power; en-
gendering group loyalty through representation; facilitating
co-ordination of activities; facilitating the transmission or sharing
of information; consolidating authority; motivating members
through participation; and avoiding precipitative action. However, some commentators in the context of public policy formulation have challenged the adequacy of such largely lukewarm and
begrudging recognition of the worth of committees. Considine's
(1992) research in Australia portrays a positive image of committees operating as "lateral structures", bringing together expertise
and specialist experiences in a manner that traditional public sector chains of command could not facilitate. The purpose of these
structures was to enhance the quality of policy decisions and to
do so in an effective and efficient manner.

Boyle (1991) sets out a model (see Figure 3.1) for the evaluation of efficiency and effectiveness within the public sector. He
stresses in particular the importance of long-term *outcomes* (as distinct from the more short-term *outputs*) in terms of quality evaluation. Managerial and political preoccupation tends to be with the
outputs of policy, given the political accountability time-scale.
Economy, equity and quality of service are particular features of
the public service that must be incorporated into any evaluation.

Figure 3.1: Public Sector Comparative Performance Indicators

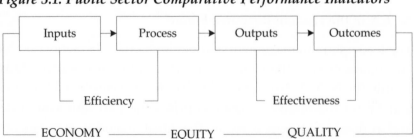

The NCCA, as a public sector agency charged with advising the Minister for Education and Science on matters relating to curriculum and assessment, has operated since its inception through a system of committees that can be subjected to evaluation on similar terms to those proposed by Boyle. Using his model, NCCA course committees may be evaluated using the criteria set out in Table 3.1.

Table 3.1: NCCA Committee Performance Indicators

Inputs	Expertise, participant costs, resources, etc.
Process	Meetings, drafts, consultations, etc.
Outputs	Syllabus, guidelines, sample material, etc.
Outcomes	Implementation, student response, etc.

A definitive evaluation of the impact of curriculum reform must await the long-term outcomes of syllabus and curriculum as implemented by teachers and ultimately as experienced and assimilated by students. The work of the NCCA committees is only one element of that reform process. However, in the shorter term, it is possible to venture some interim commentary on selected aspects of the work of the NCCA committee system. The matrix of sequenced indicators suggested by Boyle offers a useful general frame for the evaluation of the system as a model of public sector performance. However, these indicators are unlikely to be entirely satisfactory in an evaluation of the educational quality of the curriculum in professional terms.

NCCA in the Human Resource Frame

The leadership, management and deployment of personnel within an organisation is the central concern of human resource study. Within the NCCA, two types of personnel are employed. The first and by far the largest group comprises the part-time committee and council members who, in the great majority of cases, are nominated to represent their parent bodies among the partners in education — teacher organisations, management organisations, parents and others. The second group comprises the professional executive staff, either full-time employees or officers seconded for a specific period from their professional positions, usually as classroom teachers. In examining the NCCA within this frame, a key source is the experience of practitioners within the system.

A survey of 80 members of NCCA senior cycle course committees was undertaken in 1994, approximately 65 per cent of the senior cycle committee membership at that time (Granville, 1994),[2] to ascertain views and perceptions of their experience. The research was carried out at a time when the committees in question were coming to the end of their immediate tasks of drafting a revised syllabus in the Leaving Certificate subjects in question.

The survey was concerned with a number of issues, some of a generic nature, derived from an earlier public sector analysis of lateral structures in Australia (Considine, 1992), and some more specific to the process of curriculum design in Ireland. For the purposes of this chapter, three specific issues dealing with aspects of the representational nature of the committees are isolated from the survey:

- Professional-political role conflict

- Individual contributions to committee work

- Willingness to serve again.

Professional-Political Role Conflict

Respondents were asked to comment on the frequency and nature of professional conflict that they experienced between their own personal views on matters of curriculum design and those of their parent body, whom they were representing on the committees. Some forty-six per cent of respondents declared that they *never* experienced conflict between their own personal views and those of the body they represented. A further forty-nine per cent indicated that they *rarely* experienced such conflict, while only five per cent stated that they *often* felt such conflict (see Figure 3.2).

Figure 3.2: Role Conflict

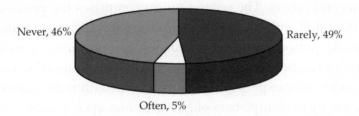

Never, 46%   Rarely, 49%

Often, 5%

The nature of representation is such that nominated delegates of an organisation can reasonably be expected to agree with and adhere to their parent body's overall policy on particular issues. Representatives on course committees are usually either elected by the membership or selected by the executive committee of their parent body. Such nomination procedures are unlikely to result in many "maverick" delegates appearing on committees.

There may be negative implications in this for imaginative, innovative thinking on curriculum planning. If participants do not experience some tension between the developmental work with which they engage and the policy positions previously adopted by their parent bodies, there may be cause to question the essence of that developmental process.

Two observations may be made here:

- Firstly, given that course committee composition gives a majority of places to teachers, there may be a certain validity in Burke's (1992) view that teachers exercise a "virtual veto" over curriculum development. Perhaps more significantly, such a veto will tend to be based on pre-ordained policy parameters set by political forces prior to the professional operation of the course committees.

- Secondly, it may be significant that the Leaving Certificate Applied, arguably the NCCA's most innovative and imaginative reform, was devised and developed outside the formal course committee structure. (Gleeson and Granville, 1996)

Individual Contributions to Committee Work

Respondents were asked to identify the particular strengths that they themselves brought to the work of their committee. A range of attributes was proposed to members, some derived from the Australian public sector research, others more specific to operations of the NCCA. Committee members were asked to rate themselves on a five-point scale from very strong to very weak.

The personal quality given the highest rating by most respondents (58 per cent) was "consensus forming", followed by "subject expertise" (55 per cent). The capacity to represent the views of their nominating organisation was rated highest by some 43 per cent of respondents, while the capacity to oppose the views or positions of others was rated highest by 25 per cent.

Of particular interest is the rate of response to the query on expertise in curriculum development (see Figure 3.3). One-third of respondents indicated that curriculum development was their weakest or next-to-weakest contribution to committee work. As the national body responsible for the development of curriculum policy, such a high proportion of committee members citing this area as their area of greatest weakness is a matter of some concern.

Figure 3.3: Expertise in Curriculum Development

As noted earlier, many committee members rated subject expertise (or "expertise in teaching the subject" as one respondent noted) as among their strongest qualities at the committee table. The distinction between subject expertise and curriculum development is very significant however: subject expertise tends to presuppose an existing format of knowledge content with its own integrity and conventions. Curriculum development is not necessarily based on such suppositions. Instead, traditional subject definitions and syllabuses are perceived as only one of a range of possible formulations of knowledge, skills and attitudes.

A committee lacking in collective self-confidence in relation to curriculum development will be unlikely to embark on major innovations in relation to its subject area, unless key office holders exercise very strong leadership. In this respect, the survey highlighted the particular importance accruing to the role of Education Officer and to that of the Chairperson of a committee.

The position of Education Officer is held by a person appointed by the NCCA to support and lead the professional work of course committees and to liaise with the permanent executive staff in terms of overall policy directions. While the Education Officer is not a member of the committee, and has no formal vote in committee decisions, the position remains a very significant one. The Education Officer is almost invariably an experienced classroom teacher of the subject in question, seconded usually on a part-time basis, for a period of months or years. Most of the research and documentation attendant to the work of committees is carried out by the Education Officer.

The Chairperson of a committee is elected from within the membership of that committee. As well as the usual procedural responsibilities of chairing meetings and suchlike duties, the chairperson is expected to liaise with the NCCA executive and especially the Education Officer. From time to time, the Chairperson will advise the executive on matters relating to the committee's work, meet with personnel from other committees in a cognate area and brief the NCCA council members at key stages in the work of a committee.

In terms of the exercise of key roles, respondents recognised their importance, especially that of the Education Officer. Some fifty-two per cent indicated that the role of Education Officer was the "most significant", with thirty-seven per cent citing the Chairperson as exercising the key role.

In matters of overall curriculum policy, these two key roles are crucial for effective curriculum decision-making. In particular, the role of Education Officer is of vital importance for curriculum development as distinct from syllabus revision. If the committee membership lacks self-confidence in its own capacity for curriculum development, the onus for leadership in this area falls upon the NCCA executive staff including the Education Officer.

Willingness to Serve Again

A good test of any experience is the willingness of participants to undergo that experience once more. Members of the course committees were asked to indicate their willingness to serve once more on an NCCA course committee — some 79 per cent indicated their willingness to do so (see Figure 3.4). This can be seen as quite a positive response and an encouraging one from the perspective of the NCCA. It indicates a general satisfaction with the process and procedures involved in this aspect of national curriculum policy formulation.

Figure 3.4: Willingness to Serve Again

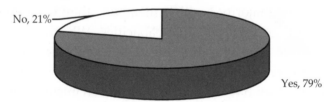

Conversely, three-quarters of university representatives said they would not serve again on an NCCA course committee. Some of the comments made by these members are indicative of the scale of alienation from the process. One member described the work of the committee as "unimaginative, uncreative, conservative"; another referred to the perceived overload of "political appointees, including trade union appointees"; while a third respondent wrote that "too many of those present have a poor grasp of their own subject".

This appears to be an indictment of the NCCA committee system. However, the views of university representatives must be tempered by a number of other considerations. A long-held view of Irish education has been that first and second levels are dominated too much by the needs and perceptions of third-level education, in particular the university sector. The NCCA operations have been the most open and formally inclusive model of curriculum design, whereby the role and interest of university representation is recognised but not to the extent of dominance or veto. The somewhat jaundiced view of many university representatives might reflect a latent resentment of this perceived diminution of status. Interestingly, in this regard, the views of NCEA[3] representatives on committees were much more benign, and in line with those of other members.

Additionally, university representatives tend to be subject specialists. Deliberations of committees tend to be more concerned about classroom transactions than subject matter *per se*; the teacher's comment cited above ("expertise in teaching the subject") is apposite in this context. This too could be a contributory factor to the sense of alienation expressed by university respondents.

Finally, it is noteworthy that the university representatives were the most individualistic in their membership of the committees. Unlike the majority of other members, they were effectively operating in their own personal capacities. When asked to indicate the form of reporting they engaged in with their nominating bodies, the university representatives had the least structured system, in some cases having no reporting mechanism or procedure whatsoever. This lack of a mandate on the one hand, or of a forum for discussion and advice on the other, may have served to inhibit the representatives when it came to participating in the inherently political exercise of shared decision-making. This reverts to the political issue at the core of the NCCA operation. Accordingly, it may be that, in the application of the political and symbolic frames, the four-frame model will be most revealing.

NCCA in the Political Frame

Bolman and Deal (1990, p. 190) state that "the political frame insists that organisational goals are set through negotiation among the members of coalitions". This is further echoed in the concept of "negotiated governance" which has been the dominant ethos of

Irish public policy in the 1990s (O'Donnell, 1995). The political
frame has particular resonance in the work of the NCCA committees where a constant process of negotiation can be observed.

The work of the committees typically is concerned with the
production of a syllabus by a certain date: parameters of time in
school are given and a general outline of assessment possibilities
is provided. The substance of what is to be decided is then negotiated through a committee, with varying degrees of conflict or di-
vergence of views, depending on the specific context. The matrix
provided in Figure 3.5 — the conflict resolution grid (Griffin,
1991, p. 207) — shows the field of possibilities within which a
process of conflict resolution may be carried out.

Figure 3.5: Conflict Resolution Styles

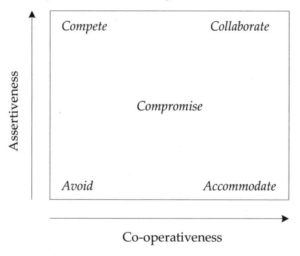

The vertical axis represents the degree of assertiveness applied by
a party to the committee. For instance, it could be the NCCA itself
in setting the brief and demanding adherence to certain principles, or any of the bodies represented on a committee in addressing an issue on which it holds a strong position. In its purest form,
the assertive approach is manifest in a commitment to compete at
all levels and at all stages in a process to ensure that pre-set objectives are achieved or maintained.

The horizontal axis represents the degree of co-operativeness a party might wish to employ on any issues. At its most extreme, the co-operative approach accommodates any suggestion in order to minimise conflict, often without regard to the implications of such compromises.

On this basis, ineffective committees tend to operate around the bottom-left quadrant, avoiding contentious issues without making any attempt to resolve them. Typically, however, committees tend to move towards the centre, the zone of compromise. In this zone, satisfactory resolution of issues is possible and substantial progress can be made on issues that might initially have been problematic. However, the pursuit of compromise can often be quite unsatisfactory, leaving all parties dissatisfied and some essential issues unresolved.

The most successful committee is most likely to operate in the upper-right quadrant, the collaboration zone. This area involves the various parties in joint enterprises and in new territory. It may sometimes involve all parties in entering new territories, developing new models of practice and in many cases, jettisoning some practices or principles hitherto deemed sacrosanct. A defining example of parties engaging in the collaboration zone would be the peace process in Northern Ireland leading up to the 1998 Good Friday Agreement; a retreat to operations in the assertive/competitive zone can also be discerned in this example. The series of national agreements on social and economic policy in Ireland involving government and social partners can also be seen as examples of parties engaging in the collaboration zone.

Anecdotal Evidence

In applying this managerial grid to the NCCA experience, a number of anecdotal incidents may be helpful. Successful committees develop a sense of shared commitment and loyalty, a sense of ownership of the process as well as the product of their work. For instance, the English course committee at junior cycle produced a radically innovative syllabus for the Junior Certificate, in terms of conceptual analysis and structure. Two features of the new sylla-

bus that created considerable controversy were the lack of prescription of literary texts and the inclusion of media studies. This
syllabus emerged after an intensive process of sometimes heated
but always informed debate and discussion within the committee.
At the outset, most members of the committee would have been
reluctant to recommend a syllabus containing no prescribed literature. However, sustained debate and deliberation resulted in the
agreed syllabus being recommended. When the syllabus was issued, it generated significant public debate and dissension. Criticism of the syllabus was voiced from within the membership and
leadership of one organisation in particular.

One of the representatives of that organisation on the committee had initially been very dubious about some of the ideas being
proposed. After a number of public criticisms of the syllabus, the
present author approached that representative and asked whether
he might be considering revising his position on the document.
His reassuring reply was expressed in the language of classic
gangster movies: "When I'm bought, I stay bought!". The response was jocular, but indicated a personal and professional
commitment to a position consciously arrived at, despite the political difficulties it might cause.

Another incident also illustrates the seriousness of purpose of
"negotiated governance" as interpreted within the NCCA. The
revised syllabus for one modern language contained some relatively small changes to the weighting of marks in the examination,
in line with a policy of harmonisation of assessment schemes
across all languages. The parties to the committee agreed all the
details, but the subject association in question felt that the final
decision was taken too precipitously. A campaign of opposition
was initiated, which included fairly intensive political lobbying.
This created certain anxieties, not least for the Minister for Education at the time, as the Council prepared to consider the final syllabus recommendation. The chairperson of the committee was
invited to address the Council, as is the norm for the final presentation of a committee's recommendation.

In any dispute involving teacher dissatisfaction, the easy route for a teachers' union is to play for more time, "to kick for touch" at least. In this case, the chairperson of the committee was a representative of a teachers' union. He had been, and would be again, a trenchant critic of the Department of Education and of the NCCA. In this case, however, he challenged and dismissed the reported opposition and assured the Council that the proposals for the subject were not only the consensus view of the committee but would be overwhelmingly accepted by teachers. All anxieties were banished and the issue was clinically dead by the end of the presentation. This was a case of a committee, through its chairperson, accepting responsibility for its work and not avoiding the problem or even accommodating dissenting views when they had been aired and addressed already.

Not all course committees operate so well. On some critical issues, the work of committees in reaching collaborative consensus has failed to convince the various memberships outside the committees. For example, assessment policy, so often the stumbling block in curriculum matters, proved to be a constant problem in shaping the new Leaving Certificate Applied programme. The Steering Committee of the programme agreed a formula for assessment that included an element of teacher involvement in the process. Support for this position was obtained at an executive council meeting of the Association of Secondary Teachers of Ireland (ASTI). However, at the subsequent annual conference of that union, delegates directed that their representatives withdraw support for the proposals and that teachers be instructed not to co-operate with the system should it be imposed (ASTI, 1994). The result was that the model had to be readjusted to eliminate even the modest proposal that had been made in respect of teachers' input to student assessment.

Another example of a committee reaching a consensus not strong enough to resist external pressure was in the vexed area of technology education. A committee produced a report outlining a developmental model for technology education, incorporating the new subject Technology as well as the established subjects of

Materials Technology (Wood), Metalwork and Technical Graphics. However, the Teachers' Union of Ireland (TUI) annual conference was presented with a number of motions of opposition to the model. One union leader, positively disposed to the proposed approach, explained to the author his dilemma in these terms: "The second last thing I want is to block developments in technology; but the last thing I want is to be hanged, drawn and quartered at the Easter congress." The union conference strongly rejected the proposed strategy for technology education, with barely a voice heard in defence (TUI, 1993).

Zones of Conflict

These examples illustrate in their various ways the strengths and weaknesses of the committee system, the difficulties it encounters and the complexity of relationships that exist, not just within committees but between those committees and various other agencies. These faultlines of relationships can be related to some further characteristics of the political frame of organisational analysis described by Bolman and Deal — the zones of conflict. These zones of conflict can be outlined as follows (see Table 3.2).

Table 3.2: Zones of Conflict in Committees

Conflict Zone	Characteristics	NCCA examples
Horizontal Zone	Between two or more interest groups	Inter-union rivalry; union–management issues
Vertical Zone	Between two or more levels in a power structure	Committee versus NCCA, or Dept. of Education
Cultural Zone	Between two or more systems or modes of operation	Integrated, interdisciplinary study versus subjects

The NCCA is engaged in a constant process of group activity where conflict is often a factor. This activity involves a variety of interest (the horizontal edge), tiers of influence (the vertical edge) and philosophical traditions, practices and approaches (the cultural edge). Goals, clearly articulated at the level of rhetoric, may be unstable, ambiguous and contested at the level of implementation. Bargaining and negotiation are therefore regular features of NCCA business. Power is central to the process and the intensity of the conflict is a function of the authority of the NCCA itself.

The NCCA committees work in a more or less permanent state of conflict at the horizontal and vertical zones: this conflict is rarely of serious dimensions and is usually resolved within the committees themselves. In curriculum terms, however, potentially the most innovative and dynamic zone of conflict is that of the cultural zone, as described above. The structures of the NCCA committee system are such that cultural conflicts occur quite infrequently. Course committees are established on the basis of traditional, formal subjects and implicit in the establishment of the various committees is an acceptance of the cultural parameters of the status quo. The phenomenon of a committee deciding that its own subject area is no longer valid, or that it should be subsumed into or linked with another subject area is rarely encountered.

The structural strangulation of the zone of cultural conflict is reinforced by the findings of the survey, referred to earlier, in which members of committees gave themselves a low rating in the area of curriculum development. In fact, cultural conflicts on curriculum issues have tended to occur on faultlines between the committees as constituted and the views of others outside the committee system, sometimes supported by the professional executive staff of the NCCA. Thus, for instance, the curriculum approach that emerged through the development of the Junior Certificate School Programme — school-centred, teacher-driven, cross-curricular teaching and learning — was received with some suspicion by established junior cycle committees. Advocacy of this programme came from the CDVEC Curriculum Development Unit (CDU), until then a marginal, almost subversive agency in curriculum development (Granville and Malone, 2001) and from within the NCCA executive staff. Similarly, the integrated, cross-curricular approach of the Humanities and SESP (Social, Environmental and Science Project) projects, developed by the CDU in

Dublin and by its sister agency, the Curriculum Development Centre (CDC) in Shannon, was treated with some suspicion by the English, History and Geography committees. The later emergence of the new subject Environmental and Social Studies (ESS),[4] a paler version of the Humanities and SESP programmes, was a pyrrhic victory for the advocates of an integrated curriculum.

The most radical and divergent curriculum innovations, however, have emerged through structures established under the NCCA but outside the mainstream committees. In addition to the Leaving Certificate Applied, already mentioned, the Link Modules of the Leaving Certificate Vocational Programme and the Junior Certificate School Programme are other examples that have been adopted by self-defining communities of practice in schools.

There may be significant deficits, therefore, in the NCCA mode of curriculum development, as compared to the developmental process employed by the regional curriculum development agencies in Dublin and Shannon. In particular, the sense of ownership by teachers of the emerging curriculum, and the degree of innovation involved, may be considerably less in the NCCA model of curriculum development.

Yet for a national curriculum agency, the firm political base provided through the resolution of the vertical and horizontal zones of conflict in the committee system may be more important than issues of ownership and innovation. The role of the NCCA, as a national curriculum agency, is concerned with curriculum and assessment specification for all schools within the state. It has the power to establish the structural parameters and the educational rhetoric within which the curriculum is interpreted and mediated at school level. This does not guarantee the realisation of the espoused ambitions. Neither does it guarantee the quality of those ambitions. However, the changes in the very language of curriculum and the rhetoric of curriculum discourse that has occurred over the past fifteen years is testament to the power of the NCCA as a national partnership body. While local curriculum initiatives at school or district level will tend to have more impact in terms of ownership and of innovation (the zone of cultural conflict), the vertical and horizontal zones define the context within which these may occur.[5]

NCCA in the Symbolic Frame

The political frame is closely related to the symbolic frame in the account of Bolman and Deal. Within the symbolic frame, an organisation is seen as a forum where various interests and individuals can come together for a shared purpose even, or especially, when they are dealing with "questions that cannot be answered, problems that cannot be solved" (1990, p. 253). The essence of curriculum development is captured in this formulation. Curriculum questions have no single correct answer, curriculum problems no single correct solution. The curriculum will never be "developed" in the sense of being completed and closed. The process of development is itself the heart of the mission. In this context, "events and processes are more important for what they express than for what they produce" (p. 244) and the work of the NCCA can be seen as the enactment of "secular myths, rituals, ceremonies and sagas" as much as the technical operation of educational planning.

The NCCA committees achieve their greatest potency in the realm of symbolism. Viewed from this perspective, the NCCA and its committees are not simply pragmatic tools of management. They become not simply official instruments of national education policy formulation, but also theatres of action, negotiation and diplomacy wherein the education partners act out dramas of conflict and conciliation — "drama as politics as drama" (Cruise O'Brien, 1969).

This symbolism resides in the representative nature and relatively broad base of the NCCA and its committees. It provides a basis for the "ownership" of the curriculum by these partners. It is manifest in the rhetoric of the NCCA: at its most graphic, a video and a newsletter produced by the NCCA on the introduction of the Junior Certificate programme in 1989 consisted essentially of talking heads and quotations from representatives of the partners. The messengers were the message.

This symbolism of partnership and participation has been used also in a negative manner. On at least two occasions, the ASTI has withdrawn from the NCCA and its committees. On one occasion, this was precipitated by the NCCA's implementation in 1990 of Ministerial plans to introduce continuous assessment of pupils within the Junior Certificate programme. Similarly, in the school year 2000–01, the ASTI withdrew its participation in all committees during the course of the pay dispute with the government. These withdrawals symbolised the alienation felt by the ASTI vis-à-vis the thrust of educational policy. It also indicated a more profound sense of disengagement from a process that claims to enhance the professional role and status of teachers.

NCCA AS A COMMUNITY OF PRACTICE

The experience of the NCCA can be seen as the development of a community of practice in national curriculum design. The concept of a community of practice refers to shared and implicit understandings and operations developed by participants, adhering to common guidelines but, more importantly, defining and shaping those practices themselves (Lave and Wenger, 1991; Wenger, 1998). The NCCA experience should be understood in terms of its historical evolution, its operating premises and its operational practices.

The history of the NCCA can be viewed in terms of three distinct stages of development. A loose historical analogy can be drawn with revolutionary France at the end of the eighteenth century, the prototype for most subsequent revolutions. The initial years of audacious ambition were epitomised by the Jacobin revolutionaries daring to invent their own calendar, as they redefined their social and political terrain. This was followed by the pragmatic search for survival, stability and respectability under the Directorate. This in turn reverted to traditional autocracy, imperial strength and confidence under the Napoleonic regime.

The revolution in Irish curriculum planning, I suggest, followed a similar pattern. In the early years of the CEB (1984–87) the *sans culottes* of curriculum advocacy breached the walls of the educational Bastille and new ideas proliferated (Crooks, 1988; Hyland, 1990). The ambition and audacity of the new order extended to the exploration of new forms of curriculum organisation — a wheel of curriculum levels, primary and post-primary curriculum re-alignment (CEB, 1984), areas of experience (CEB, 1986). This was followed by a period (1989–95) of pragmatism and consolidation, during which the NCCA tried to establish credibility in the power game of education (Granville, 1995). Subsequently, the NCCA became a centrally established and secure national agency. The rivalries and suspicions of the past no longer defined relations between the Department of Education and Science and the NCCA. The two bodies now operate, if not as equals, at least as mutually recognised and supportive agencies and as national power centres in education. The joint series of consultation meetings and complementary publications (DES, 1999; NCCA, 1999) on the Junior Certificate programme and its assessment arrangements, held around the country by the DES and the NCCA in the winter of 1999–2000 symbolised this *entente*. The establishment of the NCCA as a statutory body in 2001 confirmed this in legislation. The change in role from outsider in 1984 to establishment power broker in 2001 has been a steep learning curve for the NCCA. Its participant members have forged a distinct operational culture and community of practice in that short period.

The three-stage historical evolution of the NCCA can be related to three types of control that have been used to describe the professional cultures of organisations (Perrow 1999; Hannan, 1987; Weick, 1995). Within this typography, an organisational culture, like that of the NCCA, can be analysed in terms of the following types or "orders" of control being exercised at any time:

- *First order control*: this involves direct supervision of all activities, total engagement of the supervisor in the operation. The early days of the CEB/NCCA were typified by this approach: a committed and zealous council membership, appointed to break new ground, aided by a small professional staff similarly driven. The scale of task in those early days was vast, in the sense of addressing the entire set of curriculum possibilities, unbounded yet by operational implications. The first engagements with curriculum specifics — the introduction of courses for the new Junior Certificate — was imbued with a spirit of radicalism (Granville, 1995) and engaged the direct and concerted attention of the entire professional staff.

- *Second order control:* this describes the institutionalisation of routines and procedures within the organisation. Direct engagement is replaced by a more distant control system, at one or more removes from the centre. As the NCCA committee system grew, from the initial seven committees in 1989 to an ever-increasing range of committees operating at primary, junior cycle and senior cycle levels, inevitably the emphasis of executive staff shifted to administration more than leadership or even management. Similarly the role of the Council members, now nominated by designated bodies rather than as personal appointees, moved from intensive personal engagement to a more supervisory and distant role. Committees operated to a common brief and a format and procedure for syllabus definition was established for all committees.

- *Third order control:* this level of operation is dominated by premise controls, by assumptions taken as given or implicitly understood. An organisation that has achieved a measure of self-confidence and generalised recognition tends to operate at the level of third-order controls. New entrants to the organisation are likely to have prior knowledge of its culture and operational practice. Its code of operations will have generated a sense of self-evident validity, with its operating premises rarely questioned or indeed stated. This very confidence and security is potentially a source of major risk. It is in this category of premise control that what Perrow (1999) refers to as "normal accidents" or "professional blindspots" can occur. These are the oversights that are so enormous that they are inconceivable to the participants. They don't make sense (Weick, 1995, p. 143). Yet established organisations, systems and cultures regularly produce such "third order failures".[6]

Irish schools have been operating in a culture of premise controls for many generations. Education achieved a certain status in Irish society. Uncontested assumptions were commonplace: so, schooling is a good thing, teachers know what they are doing and assessment schemes are almost godlike in their integrity. In recent years these premises have begun to be challenged. In a society where more than eighty per cent of the population completes second-level education, the mystique of education is less dominant than heretofore.

In national curriculum terms, it may be that the NCCA is operating in a phase of third order or premise control, where curriculum assumptions are made unconsciously and amendments and developments are circumscribed by past experience and present practice. As such, it runs the risk of equivalent failures. Indeed, already there may be a case for such accusations.

Specific and targeted criticism has been made of certain curriculum-related aspects of Irish schools. This criticism has tended not to come from within the institutional structures of education but from outside the pale. Thus the Conference of Religious in Ireland (CORI) has been the most trenchant critic of the role of assessment in the Irish education system (Archer and McCormack, 1998). Irish schools have been criticised also in terms of premise failures in relation to systems of "streaming" pupils (Hannan, 1993). Schools operating rigid streaming were seen to be implementing policies of operative goals (as distinct from stated or rhetorical goals) designed to alienate certain pupils and to encourage early school leaving. The culpability of educational leaders was seen to be no less significant by virtue of their lack of intent.

The unaltered status of Gaeilge (Irish language) as the only compulsory subject for young people from age 6 to 18 years may also be a case of a professional blind spot. Despite recurring evidence of failure to achieve stated and implied educational, linguistic and cultural objectives, the subject has retained its form and status amidst a flurry of curriculum changes, a glaring anomaly apparently incapable of resolution. Likewise, the inability of the education system to address the issue of sexuality and relationships until direct Ministerial intervention in the mid-1990s, might be seen to have been such a failure. While both these issues were, and continue to be, highly charged politically, the education community in general tended to avoid engagement with them, to the extent that they became almost invisible on the educational agenda.

These and other examples of cognitive dissonance in educational planning are not unique to NCCA. Indeed, it is fair to concede that the NCCA has been and is better placed to identify such potential weaknesses than other educational bodies, including the Department of Education and Science. One of the premise controls at work within the NCCA culture is the concept of representation and consultation which, if nothing else, ensures that the decision-making process is open to as many voices of comment as possible. This reduces, but does not eliminate, the risk of "normal accidents" or premise failures.

The rationale of representation emerged in education policy-making some years before the concept of partnership became a defining characteristic of public policy through the 1990s. Social partnership as set out in the National Economic and Social Council report, *Strategy into the 21st Century* (1996), became the platform upon which national economic and social planning was based. The notion of partnership formalised in policy-making has been variously described as "negotiated governance" (O'Donnell, 1995), "competitive corporatism" and "organised decentralisation" (Hardiman, 2000).

However, the mere presence of partners on a shared committee does not betoken success: shallow compromise or endless confrontation is as likely to occur as achieved ambitions, unless certain criteria or dimensions of partnership are present. It has been suggested that the creative dynamic of such partnerships depends on three criteria:

1. Functional interdependence, bargaining and deal-making;

2. Solidarity, inclusiveness and participation; and

3. Deliberation, interaction, problem-solving and shared understanding. (O'Donnell and Thomas, 1999, p. 123)

The concept of partnership in policy-making has become a relatively uncontested area, in political terms. However, in curriculum terms, reservations have been expressed about the limitations of partnership. In particular, the tendency for a partnership approach to curtail the range of options and experience available to the policy-makers and to institutionalise a virtual veto on developments has been cited (Burke, 1992; Gleeson, 1998). Any formal system of representative partnerships can only accommodate a certain number of identified partners, invariably the largest and most powerful. Thus the "usual suspects" syndrome emerges, with largely the same labels, and frequently the same faces appearing at the various representative forums of educational partnership. One glaring weakness in the current structures, for instance, is the lack of voice for the learners themselves — school pupils and adult learners returning to education.

The national programme of partnership has been under more or less constant review by the partners, and by partnership bodies. The National Economic and Social Forum review of the partnership system identified seven problems associated with the process (O'Donnell and Thomas, 1999):

1. The limits of consensus

2. The limited terms of inclusion

3. The difficulty of linking national representation and/or policy formation to local action

4. Effectiveness in achieving real change

5. The proliferation of partnership bodies

6. Problems of monitoring

7. The relationship between social partnership and representative democracy.

Similar commentaries on partnership as an approach to public policy formulation emphasise the dynamic and organic nature of the process. It is inherently participative with its own sometimes problematic relationship to representative or more particularly, to parliamentary democracy. It requires constant monitoring and adjustment. No such system of review has operated in the education domain in general, or within the NCCA model of representation in particular.

CONCLUSION: ROMANS, GO HOME?

Without an operational practice of review and monitoring, the symbolism of partnership can lose its potency. The NCCA has moved from being a new and radical form of policy formulation to being an establishment body, a fixture in the educational landscape. In doing so, it has perhaps lost some of the cutting edge it claimed in its early days. Around and within the NCCA, a culture of operations and a community of practice has developed. This culture is dominated by subject-centred syllabus revision at curriculum level, and by institutional power-plays at policy level. The opportunities if not the inclination to address the broader or more fundamental issues of policy or the possibilities of alternative approaches are restricted by the conventions of practice. Compromise and pragmatism tend to dominate over time.

The partnership principles embodied in the NCCA are a mark of the opening up of educational decision-making over the past few decades. From being an enclosed and centralised process, national curriculum design is now a more open, inclusive if not entirely transparent process. Potential conflicts are minimised through the participation of all major parties, particularly teachers. The revised primary curriculum introduced in 1999 is a clear example of the product of such participation. A major initiative, incorporating some significant developments and changes in practice, affecting approximately 3,200 primary schools and almost every family in the country, was introduced with a minimum of rancour. All such issues had been dealt with in the process of partnership.

The value of the NCCA committee system is most clearly manifested in terms of accountability, transparency and representation. It provides a clear model of partnership at a time when such models are demanded in all spheres of public policy. Perhaps the greatest triumph of the system is that despite its limitations it has produced professional output of the highest quality and it has facilitated the emergence of other initiatives through parallel and related systems.

Questions about the quality and substance of changes and developments in the curriculum remain, but they must be addressed in the context of the remarkable achievements that the NCCA system has produced. Participation and partnership have replaced the autocracy of the state in curriculum design. The essential thrust of this chapter has been to suggest that the achievement of such a process should be recognised and acknowledged but that it is not a sufficient end in itself. There is a need to reassess and to review the form of partnership involved and to explore new models of participation.

The model of social partnership, so important in Irish public policy, is equally important in Irish education. Like the national social and economic partnerships, there is a need for monitoring, reviewing and developing the models of partnership in curriculum planning. The Education Act leaves the door slightly ajar when it refers to the composition of the NCCA, allowing for a membership that might extend beyond the strictly representational. Such flexibility might allow for the development of the NCCA to include other voices, to develop more sophisticated in-house training for committee members, to pilot and foster innovative practices and, crucially, to increase the professional capacities of its extended executive staff.

This chapter has examined the NCCA experience as a unique combination of professionalism and partnership in public policy formulation. The process of curriculum development is likely to cause dissent, frequently of a creative nature. Some real or potential weaknesses have been identified in relation to its organisational effectiveness and the quality of its professional engagement in curriculum development. However, significant strengths have been identified in the political and symbolic dimensions of the NCCA. In particular, the provision of a forum for public debate and professional engagement in curriculum development has been a major achievement. This field is replete with "questions that can't be answered, problems that can't be solved" (Bolman and Deal, 1990, p. 253), and thus the symbolism of partnership becomes at least as important as its outcomes.

This chapter opened with an oblique reference to classical Roman history through the prism of Shakespeare's writing. It may be appropriate to close with another reference to Roman civilisation, through another eminent prism. The classic scene in the Monty Python film *The Life of Brian* comes to mind, where a tiny Judean political group is trying to foment rebellion against the Romans. The agitator asks the rhetorical question "what have the Romans ever done for us?" After numerous literal responses, in exasperation he enquires one last time:

> Alright then, apart from sanitation, medicine, education, wine, public order, irrigation, roads, fresh water systems and public health, what have the Romans ever done for us?
>
> *Brought peace?*
>
> Peace! Oh, shut up!

Any criticism of the NCCA contained in this chapter is presented with an awareness of what these Romans have done for us.

References

Archer, P. and McCormack, T. (eds.) (1998), *Inequality in Education: The Role of Assessment and Certification*, Dublin: CORI.

Association of Secondary Teachers, Ireland (1994), Annual Conference Report, Dublin: ASTI.

Barber, M. (1996), *The Learning Game*, London: Gollancz.

Bolman, L.G. and Deal, T.E. (1990), *Reframing Organisations: Artistry, Choice and Leadership*, San Francisco: Jossey-Bass.

Boyle, R. (1991), *Inter-unit Comparative Performance Indicators: An Underused Resource*, Dublin: IPA.

Burke, A. (1992), *Teaching: Retrospect and Prospect*, Oideas 39, Dublin: Stationery Office.

Considine, M. (1992), "Alternatives to Hierarchy: The Role and Performance of Lateral Structures inside Bureaucracy", *Australian Journal of Public Administration*, Vol. 51, No. 3, pp. 309–20.

Coolahan, J. (1981), *Irish Education: History and Structure*, Dublin: IPA.

Crooks, T. (1988), "The Interim Curriculum and Examinations Board", *Compass*, Vol. 16, No. 2, pp. 7–26.

Crooks, T. and McKernan, J. (1984), *The Challenge of Change*, Dublin: IPA.

Cruise O'Brien, C. (1969), "Drama as Politics as Drama", in Cruise O'Brien, C. and Wallach, W. (eds.), *Power and Consciousness*, London: University of London Press, pp. 215–28.

Curriculum and Examinations Board (1984), *Issues and Structures in Education*, Dublin: CEB.

Curriculum and Examinations Board (1986), *In Our Schools*, Dublin: CEB.

Department of Education and Science (1999), *Assessment in the Junior Certificate*, Dublin: DES.

Gleeson, J. (1998), "Curriculum and Assessment: Some Political and Cultural Considerations", in Archer, P. and McCormack, T. (eds.), *Inequality in Education: The Role of Assessment and Certification*, Dublin: CORI, pp. 47–81.

Gleeson J. and Granville, G. (1996), "The Case of the Leaving Certificate Applied", *Irish Educational Studies*, Vol. 15, pp. 113–32.

Gordon, L. (1992), "The State, Devolution and Educational Reform in New Zealand", *Journal of Education Policy*, Vol. 7, No. 2, pp. 187–203.

Granville, G. (1994), "Professionalism and Partnership: The NCCA Committee System as a Mechanism for National Policy Formulation", MSc Dissertation, Trinity College, Dublin (unpublished).

Granville, G. (1995), "Dissemination of Innovation: The Experience of the NCCA", *Irish Educational Studies*, Vol. 14, pp. 143–58.

Granville, G. (1999), "Politics and Curriculum Policy", a paper presented at the annual conference of the Educational Studies Association of Ireland in University College Dublin, March.

Granville, G. and Malone, R. (2001), *Poverty Awareness in the Classroom*, Dublin: CDU/CPA.

Griffin, R. (1991), *Management*, Boston: Houghton Mifflin.

Hannan, D. (1987), "Goals and Objectives of Educational Interventions" in Crooks, T. and Stokes, D. (eds.), *Disadvantage, Learning and Young People*, Dublin: Curriculum Development Unit, pp. 37–53.

Hannan, D. (1993), "School Organisation Issues at Senior Cycle", a paper presented at an NCCA Senior Cycle seminar in University College Dublin, March.

Hardiman, N. (2000), "Social Partnership, Wage Bargaining and Growth", in Nolan, B., O'Connell, P.J. and Whelan, C.T. (eds.), *Bust to Boom: The Irish Experience of Growth and Inequality*, Dublin: IPA, pp. 286–309.

Hargreaves, A. (1994), *Changing Teachers, Changing Times*, London: Cassell.

Hyland, Á. (1990), "The Curriculum and Examinations Board 1984–87: A Retrospective View", in McNamara, G., Williams, K. and Herron, D. (eds.), *Achievement and Aspiration*, Dublin: Drumcondra Teachers' Centre.

Ireland, Government of (1998), Education Act, Dublin: Stationery Office.

Lave, J. and Wenger, E. (1991), *Situated Learning: Legitimate Peripheral Participation*, Cambridge: Cambridge University Press.

Mulcahy, D. (1981), *Curriculum and Policy in Post-primary Education*, Dublin: IPA.

National Council for Curriculum and Assessment (1999), *Junior Cycle Review: Progress Report*, Dublin: NCCA.

National Economic and Social Council (1996), *Strategy into the 21st Century*, Dublin: Government Publications.

O'Donnell, R. (1995), "Decision-making in the 21st Century: Implications for National Policy Making and Political Institutions", *Political Agenda*, Vol. 1, No. 1, pp. 29–36.

O'Donnell, R. and Thomas, D. (1999), "Partnership and Policy Making", in Healy, S. and Reynolds, B. (eds.), *Social Policy in Ireland*, Dublin: Oak Tree Press, pp. 117–46.

Perrow, C. (1999), *Normal Accidents*, Princeton: Princeton University Press.

Teachers' Union of Ireland (1993), Annual Conference Report, Dublin: TUI.

Weick, K. (1985), *Social Psychology of Organising*, Philippines: Addison-Wesley.

Weick, K. (1995), *Sensemaking in Organisations*, London/New Delhi: Sage.

Weihrich, H. and Koontz, H. (1993), *Management: A Global Perspective*, London: McGraw-Hill.

Wenger, E. (1998), *Communities of Practice*, Cambridge: Cambridge University Press.

Endnotes

[1] The composition of the NCCA was drawn from teacher unions, school management bodies (including religious interests), parents, IBEC (the employers' representative body), ICTU (congress of trade unions) and the Department of Education. Designated sub-committees comprise teacher union, school management, subject association and, if appropriate, higher education representatives.

[2] Most of the survey data referred to in the rest of this paper is drawn from Granville, G. (1994), "Professionalism and Partnership: The NCCA Committee System as a Mechanism for Curriculum Policy Formulation", MSc. (Ed. Mgmt) TCD.

[3] National Council for Educational Awards (incorporated within the newly created Higher Education and Training Awards Council in 2001) has been the awards body for non-university third-level education institutions in Ireland.

[4] ESS is a recognised subject for the Junior Certificate and can be offered by schools as a single alternative to the individual subjects History and Geography. It was introduced in 1993, restricted to those schools, mainly vocational schools, which in the past had not provided both History and Geography to junior cycle pupils.

[5] A crude and frivolous analogy may be drawn with the early technology of television sets. Irish television owners in the 1960s engaged in much groping and twiddling of buttons, as they sought to improve the quality of reception on their screens — vertical and horizontal hold buttons were adjusted when images began to slide. The actual content of the television programmes was beyond the control of the button turner. Perhaps a similar relationship exists between the NCCA and local curriculum development in agencies such as the CDU and CDC and in school-based initiatives!

[6] An example of a third order failure in Irish society is the incidence of child sex abuse. For generations, this was unspoken and unacknowledged until, through the latter years of the twentieth century, the horrific truth began to emerge, at first in drips, then in torrents.

Chapter 4

CULTURAL AND POLITICAL CONTEXTS OF IRISH POST-PRIMARY CURRICULUM: INFLUENCES, INTERESTS AND ISSUES

Jim Gleeson

INTRODUCTION

Educational innovation is best understood from the three perspectives identified by House (1981, p. 18ff), each focusing on different concerns — technological, political and cultural. The technological perspective is dominated by inputs and outputs, the political concerns centre on power and authority relationships, negotiation between the main players and the legitimacy of the authority system, while "shared meanings resting on shared values" are central to the cultural perspective. Curriculum innovation is seen very differently depending on the dominant perspective. From the technological perspective, innovation is "conceived as a relatively mechanistic process [where] the concern is economic and the primary value that of efficiency" (House, 1981, p. 26), directed at a passive teaching force, often through the Research, Development and Diffusion model. From the political perspective, innovation is a matter of negotiating compromises between various interest groups (teacher unions, management, churches, Department of Education and Science). The cultural perspective is concerned with the study of the innovation process itself, the effects of the innovation and its

perceived meanings. While the technological perspective is by far
the most dominant, House's contention that the political perspective has become a major competitor with the technological is becoming more accurate according as the modern state becomes more
involved in education and curriculum (Kennedy, 1995).

This chapter considers Irish post-primary curriculum from both
the cultural and political perspectives and identifies some relevant
issues arising from this analysis. It is based on twenty years' involvement in curriculum development, relevant literature and on
in-depth interviews with some thirty key curriculum decision-
makers (Gleeson, 2000b). Key socio-cultural contextual factors considered include the prevalence of the rhetoric/reality dichotomy,
the neglect of social studies and educational research, the associated anti-intellectual bias and the dominance of economic and
technical interests. The political perspective involves treatment of
key power relations, the prevalence of fragmentation and the representational nature of the current partnership approach to curriculum policy-making. This analysis raises many issues including the
nature of Irish curriculum reform and contestation, the marginal
status of curriculum issues in education discourse and alternative
models of partnership for curriculum decision-making.

The Cultural Perspective

Situating the Analysis: Some General Background

The importance of socio-cultural context has been identified by
Cornbleth (1990), Grundy (1987), Goodson (2001): "to analyse sustainability of change we must understand the conditions of
change, and to do this we have to develop our historical and eth-
nographical studies" (Goodson, 2001, p. 52).

Ireland's participation in the OECD's Washington Conference
of 1961 led to the *Investment in Education Report* of 1966 and the
resulting expansions supported by World Bank funding. As Hannan (1987) points out, adherence to the dogma of "human capital
formation" theory has been an extremely important factor in the
legitimation of Irish education policy since then. But the national

economic difficulties of the 1980s meant that pragmatic considerations became paramount in Irish education policy-making. During this period, Ireland was "characterised by its youthfulness" (OECD, 1991, p. 13) with half the population under 25, thirty per cent under 15 while school enrolments were continuing to rise. Irish post-primary education participation rates expanded almost threefold between 1965 and 1998 and school completion rates rose from twenty per cent in 1960 to approximately eighty per cent at present. While state involvement in education expanded dramatically during the 1990s, educational expenditure, as a percentage of GDP, decreased between 1988 and 1998.

Irish education has been influenced by many other factors (Gleeson, 2000a) including insularity, colonial past, Catholic Church control, Classical Humanist ideology and state examinations (OECD, 1991) and the considerable influence of external agencies such as OECD and the EU[1] (O'Connor, 1998). The exercise of power is a key concern in this chapter and the conservative nature of the Irish party political framework as outlined by Bew et al. (1989) provides a crucially important contextual factor for Irish education. As O'Sullivan (1989, p. 265) remarks, "the absence of ideological cleavages in educational thinking among political parties in Ireland provides a breeding ground for slogans". But the rhetoric of slogans can be far removed from reality!

Rhetoric, Reality and the Discourse of Curriculum Reform

Lee concludes that (1989, p. 652) traditional Ireland is characterised "by a capacity for self-deception on a heroic scale". In the course of a personal interview, Lee referred to this in terms of the Irish "say/do dichotomy", citing Anthony Clare's conclusion that "there is certainly a terrific gulf between what people say and what they do in Ireland" and Eamon De Valera's reported observation that "while one could say what one liked in England as long as one did the right thing, one could do what one liked in Ireland as long as one said the right thing".

In the course of personal interviews, several well-placed observers remarked on the prevalence of the rhetoric/reality dichotomy in Irish education (Gleeson, 2000b, p. 298). Ó hUalla-cháin, a former Inspector and Principal Officer was very aware of this dichotomy: "not much development took place after the initial launch of Vocational Preparation and Training (VPT), which involved a fair amount of fanfare. Every new initiative that's introduced is the same". Duffy (General Secretary of the Joint Managerial Body from 1977 to 1996) feels that

> there has been a great deal of rhetoric in relation to curriculum change in Ireland — some people think that talk about change is change. [For example] the Minister thinks that wonderful things are happening in schools.

McKay, the long-standing representative of the Irish Vocational Education Association (IVEA) on the National Council for Curriculum and Assessment (NCCA) commented that "phrases like equality of educational opportunity have been bandied about but I don't think any serious effort was made to actually do anything". Donohoe, the Irish Congress of Trade Unions (ICTU) member of the NCCA, commented that "the White Paper contained a lot of rhetoric about the Arts in Education but I have great difficulty finding it in the curriculum" and "despite the rhetoric of learning how to learn, [in reality] there's a great finality about the system".

Sugrue (1997, p. 25) has highlighted the strength of the rhetoric/reality dicotomy at primary level:

> in a number of survey studies conducted in the Irish context during the past twenty-five years, teachers overwhelmingly endorse progressive ideology. However when data on actual practice are isolated from these studies teachers seem to endorse a child-centred rhetoric while practising a more formal pedagogical style.

The rhetoric (or is it a slogan?) that proclaims that the 1990s has been a decade of unprecedented change in Irish post-primary education is widely accepted. This sits somewhat uneasily alongside the reality that recent mainstream educational reforms have primarily involved a change in subject content rather than classroom practice. Notwithstanding complaints of "innovation fatigue", often associated with legitimate pay demands, the experience of the author (Gleeson et al., 2001) as well as the findings of Callan (1997), Mackey (1998) and Marino Institute of Education (1992) suggest that little has changed in the culture of our schools or in classroom practice. It is the author's contention that part of the explanation for this paradox lies in the uncritical adoption of "loose curriculum discourse". Certain distinct though related concepts are used as if they were interchangeable:

- Curriculum *reform*, characterised by the phenomenon of "the launch". This comes from the top, is not necessarily concerned with "deep change" and tends to get snowed under by the realities of the "classroom press". Where evaluation is included it tends to be of a "bureaucratic" rather than "democratic" nature as defined by McDonald (1976).

- Curriculum *innovation*, often used to mean "experimentation". The adoption of innovation without the realisation of change is a common occurrence (Fullan, 1991, p.42).

- Curriculum *development*, though suggesting change for the better, as in human development, often means syllabus and content change only.

- Curriculum *change*, which at the objective level (Fullan, 1991, p. 32–46) involves "deep change" at three levels: materials, practice and practitioners' beliefs/values.

Neglect of Social Studies and Educational Research

Lee (1989, p. 609) concludes that the smaller Northern European countries devoted significantly more resources than Ireland to the study of society: "there was therefore no gut craving to learn more about the nature of Irish society". Because of what he calls this "relative indifference to thought", Lee (1989, p. 578) argues that makers of social policy in insular, postcolonial Ireland "had little contact with the supply of ideas in Ireland, much less in the wider world". Notwithstanding the influence of the Catholic Church during most of the twentieth century, Lee (1989, p. 610) cites the former Professor of Sociology at Maynooth, subsequently a member of the Catholic Hierarchy, to the effect that "the Catholic Church had failed to provide a richly Christian body of thought on any social topic".

Nor did the education system promote inquiry. Lee (1989, p. 573) sets out the historical legacy as context:

> the Irish secondary school system in the early decades of independence inculcated many worthy qualities. Neither intellectual independence nor intellectual originality were normally among them.

Sugrue (1997, p. 45) concludes that Irish primary teachers are characterised by a "widespread anti-intellectualism (which) has a particularly Foucauldian ring to it where 'docile minds' and 'docile bodies' appear to be the object of the system". This inattention to intellectual analysis is clearly linked with the dominance of a consensualist ideology in Ireland (Lynch, 1987).

Insofar as social science developed in Ireland, the positivist paradigm predominated while critical theory and phenomenology were neglected (as discussed by Kane, 1996, p. 132). The dominance of positivism inevitably promoted a technicist approach and a preoccupation with "facts" while the questioning of meanings was left to literary figures, newspaper columnists and the small community of philosophers. O'Donoghue (1999, p. 149) notes the "almost complete absence of social scientific education through the non-representation of sociology, social administration, anthropology, political science and media studies in the curriculum". The OECD (1991, p. 42) examiners commented on the "dearth of policy-related research" in Ireland. This is hardly surprising in view of the lack of support for social research in general and education-related research and development, especially of an applied nature, in particular as shown by Lee, 1989; Sugrue and Uí Thuama, 1994; Coolahan, 1984; O'Reilly, 1998.

This anti-intellectualist and positivist mindset is well illustrated by the attitudes of several Ministers for Education and in official papers. Minister Mulcahy stated in 1957 that he did not have "a duty to philosophise on educational matters" while Ministers Colley and Hillery adopted the attitude in the 1960s that comprehensive schooling was an organisational rather than an *ideological* matter[2] (O'Sullivan, 1989, p. 243). Discussing the importance attributed to technology in the Education White Paper of 1980, Browne concluded (1985, p. 334): "the context of education is considered primarily as the economy, the arts being associated with leisure". The introduction to the 1983 *Programme for Action in Education* stated expressly that "it would be inappropriate to formulate any philosophy of education in the context of the programme".

In this context, it is hardly surprising that educational research has not been a priority in Ireland. Whatever research exists tends to be empirical and quantitative in nature. For example, of the one hundred pieces of research identified by the CEB in relation to the primary curriculum, not one is qualitative (CEB, 1985). O'Reilly concludes his study of the Vocational Education Committees (VECs) with the observation that the politics of education "is still very much an untilled field" while education policy research in Ireland has been "organised on a chronological basis with little or no explicit theoretical of interpretative analysis" (1998, p. 47ff).

The Dominance of Economic and Technical Interests in Irish Education

Against the background of this socio-cultural context, it is hardly surprising that House's technical and political perspectives dominate Irish education. As O'Sullivan (1992, p. 464) notes, the Irish frame of education and social discourse has become increasingly "coterminous with the theme of education and the economy", with the result that "cultural identity, language, civic competence and moral development were excluded as themes". Ever since the publication of *Investment in Education* (1967), tension has existed between the uneasy bedfellows of human capital production and equality of educational opportunity. Despite its citation as an ideal by successive Ministers for Education and Department officials, equal opportunity "was never confronted as a concept demanding analysis and elaboration" (O'Sullivan, 1989, p. 243). It took some twenty years before there was a curriculum response in the form of Junior Certificate to the raising of the school-leaving age in 1967 and the introduction of universal post-primary education.

Strong economic interest groups such as the Confederation of Irish Industry (CII) began to influence schooling and curricula during the 1980s. The State and economic interests coalesced, according to Fuller (1990, p. 172), to "redefine cultural capital as legitimated in schools, in accordance with the perceived need to link education and economic planning even more closely and to shape school curricula accordingly [preparing] for the higher visibility, status and take up of applied subjects and for the gradual erosion of the Humanities". Worthwhile knowledge was redefined by the introduction of new technological subjects at Junior and Leaving Certificate levels (Lynch, 1989). The education system transmits the dominant cultural emphasis of the present time as if it were unproblematic, with the education system playing an instrumental role in "motivating the small number of high achievers who will be capable of creating jobs for themselves and others" (p. 185).

From the perspective of the Department of Education and Science (DES), maintaining the confidence of the international community has always been an overriding interest in relation to curriculum reform. Margaret Walsh (interview), Ministerial Adviser to Mary O'Rourke (1987–1991), recalled that "the bottom line always was, what's wrong that they want to change it?" She sees education as "a very valuable national asset" that "the government should have control over" and cites the satisfaction of the Industrial Development Authority with the standard of education achieved through the present system: "Irish education is perceived — correctly or not — to be a system that seems to work reasonably well." In her experience that perspective "coloured decision-making on everything including curriculum reform because, as Minister, you have to stand up in the Dáil and defend your mistakes before introducing changes in education; one has to ask, is this going to rock the boat?"

The dominance of the technical mentality is closely related to this emphasis on economic development. Habermas has identified three knowledge-constitutive interests or paradigms — technical, practical and emancipatory (critical).[3] Within the technical paradigm, which closely resembles House's technical perspective, abstract knowledge is packaged as subjects that contain unquestioned truths. The emphasis is on instrumental knowledge in the form of scientific explanations, presented in terms of outcomes or product and with little attention to process. This corresponds closely to the Irish post-primary curriculum as characterised by the OECD (1991). Callan (1995, p. 100ff) argues that the main concern of various Irish political forces[4] has been "with fitting people into a society that is allowed to remain unproblematic".

Within the practical interest paradigm, the emphasis is on meaning-making and interpretation. School-based action research work undertaken by the Marino Institute of Education during the early 1990s offers a rare enough example of an Irish post-primary initiative based on practical interest. It emerges from related publications (McNiff and Collins, 1994; McNiff *et al.*, 2000) that such research activity is found during the early years of post-primary schooling and in the context of out-of-school, alternative education initiatives rather than Leaving Certificate teaching where the academic stakes are higher.

Within the emancipatory interest, the dominant concern is with the distribution of power and with the emancipation of the student through the process of learning. The Conference of Religious in Ireland (CORI) has been the main proponent of this paradigm; for example, their response to the Green Paper on Adult Education of 1999 is called *Education for Transformation*. As McCormack, then head of CORI's Education Secretariat, explained:

> we fight our corner as one of many partners out there. The institutional church does it on the basis of their authority. We have to bring the light of the gospel to bear on the system,

> whereas the school managers have a vested interest to main-
> tain the system. (interview)

The Irish system displays all the characteristics of a system where technical rather than practical or emancipatory interests are dominant (Grundy, 1987):

- The sub-culture of subjects is dominant, as exemplified in the rejection of the Interim CEB's proposal to move to "Areas of Experience" (see Granville, Chapter Three in this book)

- The curriculum and the learning environments are controlled from the centre, with teachers implementing designs handed down from above

- The technical bias of post-primary curriculum

- Insofar as teachers value "theory", they are concerned with its practicality (Kiely, 2003)

- A strong emphasis on the external measurement of the product.

This latter emphasis is reflected in the enormous attention devoted to technical aspects of curriculum and assessment at post-primary: e.g. the introduction of additional levels and a wider range of grades; the priority afforded the publication of Examiners' reports; the inclusion in the Education Act (1998) of legislation to do with grade appeals; the inclusion of assessment objectives in syllabus documents. It is ironic that the only available definition of Leaving Certificate grades is in terms of points for third-level entry.

The dominance of the technical mentality is also reflected in various other ways: the growing involvement of the Irish Business and Employers Confederation (IBEC) in education policy-making; the name change from Department of Education to Department of Education and Science (DES) in 1997; the appointment at that time of a Minister of State with special responsibility for science and technology. Irish educational discourse reveals this technical men-tality through the frequent use of technical language such as: "de-livery" mechanisms, used in relation to INSET and curriculum; frequent references to the "products of our system", "targets", "strategies", "overhaul"; "teacher *training*" rather than teacher education; the overriding concern with "covering the course". Looney (2001, p. 151), Chief Executive of the NCCA writing about the drift of curriculum discourse "towards the technical", comments that "the curriculum has become something for teachers, students and schools to overcome, to manage, to conquer. There is little empowerment associated with it."

THE POLITICAL PERSPECTIVE

Within this socio-cultural environment, Irish education has been heavily influenced by a curious combination of political and pragmatic interests.[5] Crooks, Deputy Director of the Curriculum Unit of City of Dublin VEC from 1972 to 1988, believes that political aspects of education overshadowed curriculum policy-making, which is seen by key decision-makers as "playing around at the margins". In his experience, what "really matters" is "control, structures, buildings, interests, pension rights, the actual things that happen in schools" rather than curriculum:

> they worry about exams because there will be Dáil questions if things go wrong. . . . Curriculum is reduced to a technical art where exam papers have to be proofread and marked. . . . Very few people outside of History teachers think of how important it is to teach people about our culture and our past. (interview)

While curriculum is generally regarded as apolitical in Ireland, in the way that Cornbleth suggests, the influence of political parties and personalities on Irish education and curriculum matters has been significant (see Johnson, 1992). The prevailing clientelist system of government (Bew *et al.*, 1989), allied with a rather unstable party political system that provided eight different Ministers for Education during the 1980s, makes for a volatile, fragmented approach to education policy (see OECD, 1991, p. 38ff). The Minister of the day can be enormously influential and a trend has developed whereby individual Ministers adopt "pet projects" with relevance to curriculum e.g. O'Rourke emphasised European languages, Bhreathnach championed CSPE while Martin chose ICT as his initiative (Gleeson, 2000b).

Prevalence of Fragmentation and Discontinuity

Cornbleth (1990, p. 17) believes that the dominance of the techno-cratic model results in the elevation of curriculum documents to a status above that of classroom practice and to the decontextualisation of curriculum in two related ways:

> curriculum as product and its construction are arbitrarily separated from curriculum policy-making and use [and] curriculum and its construction are seen as apolitical or neutral, apart from or above competing values and interests.

Both outcomes are evident in Ireland where fragmentation and discontinuity in the relationships between various official agencies is clearly in evidence. The pathology of the DES unearths a history of clear lines of demarcation between the administrative side and the Inspectorate, between the secondary and vocational inspectors and between the primary and post-primary inspectors (Gleeson, 2000b). Within Irish schools there is ample evidence of fragmentation and differentiation by gender (the exceptionally high proportion of single-sex schools), academic ability (Hannan, 1987; Smyth, 1999) and social class (Lynch, 1989). O'Reilly (1998, p. 238ff) concludes from his study of the Vocational Education Committee (VEC) system that "the segmented post-primary system generated a form of competitive conflict for key educational resources". Hyland (2000) reports evidence of fragmentation within the non-formal education and training "support services for disadvantaged young people" who drop out of school.

Much of this prevailing fragmentation is promoted by considerations of power, control and protection of sectoral interest. From the perspective of curriculum, relationships between the Interim CEB and the NCCA on the one hand and the DES on the other have been fraught with difficulties. When the Interim Curriculum and Examinations Board (CEB) was established it was proposed that it should have responsibility for both curriculum and assessment.

While this would have freed up inspectors to engage in quality control in schools it was strongly resisted by the majority of the DES who did not want to lose control of the examinations at any cost.[6]

The 1983 Department of Education Working Party on the establishment of a national board for curriculum and examinations wisely adopted integrity as between curriculum design, implementation and assessment as a core value. But today, centralised examinations dominate rather than serve pupil learning and the curriculum–assessment relationship is far removed from the "seamless robe" envisaged at that time, much more so than in many other jurisdictions (O'Donnell et al., 1998). Once the NCCA's Course Committee has produced the Syllabus documentation, the Department assumes primary responsibility for the implementation and assessment of the new programmes. Ó Ceallaigh (former CEO of the NCCA), in conversation with the author, referred to this dichotomy as the "bamboo curtain" between his organisation and the DES. The DES position is captured in the classic request made by a senior member of the Inspectorate to a member of the NCCA Executive: "send over the document and we'll take it from there".

While the NCCA was, in theory, given responsibility for both curriculum and assessment, its role in relation to examinations has been somewhat peripheral in practice. According to her adviser, Minister O'Rourke, like most other Ministers for Education, believed that she should keep control over the examinations so as to maintain national standards and maintain the confidence of foreign multinationals in the Irish education system. The decision to establish an independent Examinations Unit as recommended by Cromien (2000) would appear to have been taken for pragmatic and administrative rather than educational reasons. It will be interesting to see how the relationship develops between this Unit and the NCCA.

There has been slippage also between the Interim CEB and the NCCA. Ó Ceallaigh (1985, p. 9) (then CEO of the Interim CEB), reported that the Board had identified three areas of need in relation to the junior cycle curriculum:

- A broader and more balanced curriculum with an increased emphasis on skills and processes;

- A curricular structure that is sufficiently flexible to recognise and accommodate curriculum initiatives at school and regional level;

- Assessment procedures that are determined by the aims and objectives of the curriculum.

None of the above goals has been successfully achieved to date. While the NCCA has adopted the CEB's principle of curriculum breadth and balance and the curriculum framework based on Lawton's (1983) eight areas of experience, it then defines this framework in terms of subjects as Course Requirements (NCCA, 1993, p. 26). While the NCCA has come up with some creative suggestions for the achievement of breadth and balance through the establishment of "full" and "short" courses, no progress has been made in relation to the definition of a national common core curriculum, despite the best efforts of NCCA. The concept of core curriculum is not even mentioned in the 1998 Education Act and the Junior Cycle review group has not made any proposals in this regard. "Subject politics" provides the most obvious explanation for this neglect (Goodson, 1994; Hargreaves, 1994).

The CEB proposal that schools or consortia of schools be allowed to develop their own courses and submit them to the Board for validation with a view to national certification is nothing more than a memory.[7] This excellent idea had the potential to promote action research and achieve some balance between the centre and the periphery. Unfortunately, it has been caught up in the worldwide trend towards the centralisation of education and curriculum policy-making: "the 1980s made it clear that central government were not prepared to preside over the fragmentation and disintegration of national education effort" (Kennedy, 1995, p. 73). Insofar as localised curriculum development and a centralised examinations system are extremely difficult to reconcile, the original NCCA proposal is incompatible with centralised assessment systems such as the Irish one. The failure to act on the CEB's third principle has been discussed earlier.

The influence of party political factors on Irish curriculum policy-making is nowhere reflected as clearly as in the changing fortunes of the NCCA. Granville (interview) believes that the NCCA's influence went in a "series of peaks and troughs", depending very much on who was Minister at the time. One peak occurred during O'Rourke's ministry when the Junior Cert was ready to roll: "It seemed at the time that the NCCA was more or less an alternative Department of Education." Then that wave passed and the NCCA had hardly any input at all in the preparation of the 1992 Green Paper during Brennan's ministry. Granville identified the 1993 publication of *Towards a New Century*, "the blueprint for the White Paper curriculum thinking", as the next peak, though this was internally driven. He believes that "the influence of the NCCA has been increasingly peripheral" since that time, though it remains to be seen what influence its statutory status will enable it to exert.

Partnership and Sectoral Interest

The economic difficulties of the 1980s gave rise to the adoption in Ireland of a rather unique model of government by social partnership (Gleeson, 1998). Logan and O'Reilly (1985, p. 475) identify the assumptions underpinning the 1983 decision to introduce the CEB in terms of the need *"to broaden the social base of decision-making* so that the process of selecting knowledge, skill or experience for inclusion on the national curriculum will address the *common good"* (my italics). However, Minister Hussey's desire to have a representative rather than a representational Board[8] encountered very strong opposition from the main sectoral interests, particularly the teacher unions (Gleeson, 2000b). Minister O'Rourke subsequently established the NCCA and its Course Committees on a representational basis and this arrangement is now enshrined in the 1998 Education Act. The CEB structures for consultation with "designated bodies" ceased with the establishment of the NCCA but have been reinstated in the Act.

The representational nature of the NCCA provides an excellent example of how partnership "Irish style" is predicated on a sectoral agenda — DES, teacher unions, school management bodies, representatives of the parent associations and industry/business — giving the lie to the argument that curriculum is apolitical. The Irish teacher unions are particularly strong by international standards, as noted by Skilbeck in a personal interview. Along with school management bodies, they effectively control the NCCA and its Committees (Gleeson, 2000b). Union representatives inevitably prioritise teachers' working conditions, while the school management representatives concern themselves with the implications of change for staffing and resources. According to David Barry, former president of the union, the ASTI,

> in its participation in policy-making will seek to ensure the welfare of its members rather than work objectively to create a good education system, where these objectives are in conflict. (1989, p. 160)

When the NCCA was omitted from the first Education Act (1998), the teacher unions were the first to object because of the control that the Unions could exercise on curriculum through the NCCA. Walsh, Chair of the Interim CEB and NCCA (1984–1991), recalled that:

> while the union members of the Council represented the views of their members very admirably, they failed to cast them aside and deal with what I thought we were about, the well-being of the Irish community and the development of a curriculum for the next millennium. (interview)

The representational basis of the NCCA has ensured that curriculum reforms, once agreed at Course Committees and Council, have not encountered opposition from the teaching force — with some exceptions, as outlined by Granville in Chapter 3 (see, for example, the ASTI objections to the Leaving Cert Applied).

Granville's (1994, p. 83) sample of Course Committee members considered their competence in curriculum development to be low. He also found that ninety-five per cent of his respondents "never or rarely experienced conflict between their personal views and those of their nominating body", prompting the observation that such a high level of conformity "might inhibit the introduction of innovative ideas and initiatives" (see Chapter 3 for a more detailed analysis).

In the context of our small island, many of the same people meet very frequently in their capacity as sectoral representatives. The prevailing anti-intellectual, technicist and consensualist (Lynch, 1989) ethos provides a most hospitable environment for "cosy consensus" and compromise born out of familiarity. The control and management of schools were the dominant concerns at the 1993 National Education Convention (NEC) (Gleeson, 1998) whereas little attention was given to curriculum, seen as safely in the hands of the representational NCCA.

The constitution of the NCCA on a representational basis (Gleeson, 2000b) raises important power and control issues. Who takes responsibility for the whole curriculum? Who speaks for the ordinary citizen? Whose voices are heard within this representational framework? Bruton (1998) believes that:

> the voices which dominate the debate are those of the providers. No one expects a union, whose job it is to win better conditions for its members, to be able to tell the whole story.

As Lynch (1989, p. 124) argues, education:

> matters most to those who gain most from it presently, namely the middle classes. They have learned the educational formula by rote, it is in their interests that it does not change. As a power group the middle classes are well positioned to have their interests defined as the public interest in education.

McCormack of CORI, the most likely representative of the voiceless, recalled in a personal interview that her experience of policy-related education discussions was one of isolation:

change is very difficult when you're working with vested interests. Sitting around the table, it's notoriously difficult to look at issues from a systemic perspective. On a number of occasions we have found ourselves as a sole voice. There's an enormous amount of brokerage going on.

Post-primary students depend ultimately for their say on their parents at election time (see Lynch, 1999). What about the silent majority of teachers who do not become actively involved in union activity? Do they experience a sense of ownership of the decisions reached through partnership? Roche and Geary (1998) found that the close partnership relationship between employers and unions at national level is not being replicated in the workplace, where most change is management driven. White, Assistant General Secretary of ASTI (interview) acknowledges that partnership doesn't transfer down to the grassroots level and that, no matter how hard his Union tries:

> the problem is teachers are very practical people and they concentrate on doing their job, getting good exam results, they only become aware of changes when someone tells them.

The vacuum resulting from the absence of critical debate has enabled the continuation of a hegemony whereby the increased participation rates in post-primary education during the 1980s and 1990s have resulted in the redistribution rather than the redefinition of cultural capital in Ireland. Hannan (1987) argues that the effects of social and educational exclusion are more serious in Ireland than elsewhere — the very high degrees of cultural homogeneity, the weakness of social democratic parties and policies, the private ownership of schools and the absence of regional education agencies with responsibility for ensuring equality of opportunity — with the result that:

> we have effectively built up a potential underclass, most of whose members are excluded from actively participating in the economy and who disproportionately constitute those with serious drug addiction problems or who end up in the equivalent of Mountjoy. (p. 8)

Lee (1989, p. 610) concludes that the self-interest of the dominant power groups rather than clerical hostility to independent thought offers the best explanation of "Irish intellectual retardation". As Hannan (1987, p. 162) argues, this hegemony goes unchallenged because any dissatisfaction with the system is publicly voiceless and unorganised:

> the ideological climate and class forces within Ireland are such that the pursuit of egalitarian citizenship rights has no active political priority or urgency. Partly, as a result, the educational process over the past twenty years has clearly worked to the benefit of the majority of the middle class.[9]

Evidence of attention to these fundamental social justice issues is sparse in Irish curriculum debate, which has been dominated by various technical and political issues such as: modes and techniques of assessment; "turf wars" in relation to subjects e.g. technology education, or the perceived dropping of History and Geography from the secondary core curriculum in 1995; "national" issues to do with the Irish language; "economic" issues such as the declinining numbers taking the physical sciences at Leaving Certificate level; "religious/moral" matters such as the introduction of Relationships and Sexuality Education (RSE).

Partnership and the Legitimation of State Policy

House (1981, p. 19) argues that, from the political perspective, the "legitimacy of the authority system" is a primary value. Jansen (1990) and others have developed the notion of compensatory legitimation: "according as the range and scope of the state's activities increase, there is a corresponding, or indeed, disproportionate increase in the need for legitimation" (Weiler, 1990, p. 16). According to Weiler, the partnership model provides an ideal support system for those who are primarily concerned with the legitimacy of the decision-making process and the symbolism of change and innovation. Werner (1991) describes the use of partnership in the preparation of the *Year 2000* document in British Columbia as an exercise in "defining curriculum policy through slogans". As O'Sullivan (1989, p. 265) argues, the use of slogans is a prominent feature of Irish educational thought, instanced in examples such as "equality of educational opportunity, cherishing all the children of the nation equally, community schools and discovery learning".

Adherence to the dogma of "human capital formation" theory has been an extremely important factor in the legitimation of Irish education policy since the 1960s (see Hannan, 1987). In the context of increasing secularisation and rapidly declining vocations to the religious life, and consistent with international trends (Kennedy, 1995), the Irish State is increasingly assuming the powerful place previously occupied by the Churches. From the perspective of education we have seen the publication of three White Papers, the Education Act (1998) and many other pieces of legislation over the past ten years. Because of the need for legitimation of policy, particularly in a sensitive area such as education, consensus-seeking through partnership has played an increasingly important role in education policy-making. For example, the Minister for Education was the most frequent user of the discourse of partnership at the innovative National Education Convention (1993), followed by the relative newcomers, the parents, while the traditional stakeholders, the Teachers' Unions and School Management bodies, hardly used the language of partnership at all (Gleeson, 1998, pp. 53–4). The 1995 Education White Paper quotes extensively from the Convention Report. Keating, Ministerial Adviser at the time of the preparation of the Education White Paper, recalled that the Convention Report "was the major reference document that we kept referring back to". McCormack (CORI) was of the view that:

> most of what was being done was with a view to setting up the legislation rather than addressing educational issues *per se*, with the result that curriculum wasn't adequately dealt with there at all. (interview)

The effectiveness of this legitimation process is evident in various ways. Students and teachers have become increasingly utilitarian in their attitudes to knowledge, with the former becoming adept at calculating the points-scoring capabilities of particular subjects and their utility in the labour market. The Points Commission (Ireland, Government of: 1998, p. 108) noted a "narrowing of the curriculum arising from the tendency to teach to the examination and an undue focus on the attainment of results".

SOME ISSUES ARISING

Beginning from the critical perspective of curriculum as social process, adopted by Cornbleth (1990, pp. 12–41), some of the relevant issues arising from the above analysis of the Irish sociocultural and political context are now considered. These include the nature of curriculum reform, the marginal status of curriculum, the nature of curriculum contestation and the future of partnership.

The Nature of Curriculum Reform

Hord (1995, p. 87ff), in her analysis of the American experience, identified four cycles of reform since the early 1980s. She calls the first cycle "fix the parts", the "quick fix" approach involving incremental, superficial, change. This was followed by "fix the schools", focusing on the organisational setting for change. Teacher development became the goal during the third cycle of change, while the final stage has involved the attempted restructuring of the fundamental structure of schooling across social systems.

Irish curriculum reform has been characterised by successive "launches" of "quick fix" approaches and by increased state involvement, culminating in an unprecedented amount of legislation and the proliferation of centralised "implementation groups". This increased state involvement is reflected in the DES decision to use the former Teachers' Centres (re-designated Education Centres and enshrined in the 1998 Education Act) as a delivery mechanism for reform (Gleeson, 2001). Arguably the two most critical components of "deep change" — those focusing on schools and teachers — have been, up to the late 1990s, seriously neglected in the Irish context of a rising school-going population and difficult economic circumstances. Resource provision for teacher professional development was totally inadequate prior to the establishment in 1995 of the In-Career Development Unit (ICDU) with European Social Fund money under the general umbrella of human resource development. Expenditure on teacher in-service education rose from 0.04 per cent of total expenditure during the period 1986–88 (Gleeson, 1992, p. 111) to 5.85 per cent in 2002 (Department of Finance, 2002, p. 121). Some 85 per cent of this increase has been spent on start-up programmes for new syllabuses/programmes (Gleeson and Leonard, 1999). Apart from the pilot project on Whole School Evaluation and the recent introduction[10] of the School Development Planning Initiative (Breathnach, 2001), the importance of school context for the effective implementation of curriculum change has been overlooked in Ireland.

Teachers inevitably experience curriculum reform from the immediate perspective of the "classroom press", where they are overawed by what Hord (1987) refers to as "management concerns". From this perspective there is little opportunity or motivation for teachers to revisit and question previously taken-for-granted beliefs about practice, a necessary precondition for change (Fullan, 1991, p. 43). The Irish history of teacher professional development accentuates the difficulties.

From the perspective of curriculum change, the state's newfound interest in promoting curriculum reform has caused a crisis of identity for the two main curriculum development centres at Dublin and Shannon (Trant, 1998). These centres pioneered many innovative programmes in the context of an inhospitable climate during the 1970s and 1980s. They now depend for their survival on becoming the agents of the DES in what Schon (1971) calls the "proliferation of centres" model of dissemination (Gleeson, 2001). Trant (interview), Director of the Curriculum Development Unit (CDU) of the City of Dublin VEC, recalled that "in the early days, [we] had the stage to ourselves and we could afford to challenge". He believes that their current involvement as support agencies helps the Department to legitimate the new programmes:

> the Department is now driving these big new programmes . . . the new deal [is] an act of genius on their part, they recognise

> that it would not be quite wise for them to call all the shots . . .
> so they [allow us to] facilitate the implementation [with the re-
> sult that] we are not challenging anybody anymore.

Ó Donnabháin, Director of Shannon Curriculum Development
Centre, voiced similar concerns:

> We have absolutely no power, no authority. There is no inno-
> vation as such. I just implement the policy as it is given to me
> from above.

Marginal Status of Curriculum-Related Issues

The low status of Curriculum Studies within Teacher Education
provision (post-primary) comes as no great surprise, given the
strong positivist orientation of Irish educational research. Goodson
and Hargreaves (1996, pp. 7–8) see the emphasis on the Foundation Disciplines (Psychology, Sociology, Philosophy and History of
Education) in the university-based teacher education departments
in terms of the "devil's bargain" whereby teacher educators sought
"to maximise status and esteem within the university milieu". In
the Irish context, the regulations of the Teacher Registration Council identify "Studies in the Foundations of Education" as an essential component of initial teacher education. There is an associated
requirement that Professional Studies *must* include general methodology and specific methodology and should *normally* include
studies in other areas including curriculum studies, understood in
subject rather than "whole curriculum" terms. When these regulations were revised during the late 1980s (Ireland, Government of,
1987, p. 8), the relative status of the foundation disciplines and curriculum studies remained exactly the same as had been set out in
1928! There is no requirement that student teachers be introduced
to curriculum development and school-based action research, the
central planks of teacher professional development (Stenhouse,
1975; Trant, 1998).

The treatment of the respective Directors of the Shannon and
Dublin curriculum development agencies epitomises the failure of
the Irish educational community to appreciate the demands of

"deep change" as against superficial "reform". If these two men worked in the UK, they would both have been appointed Professors of Education in prestigious universities long ago. As McDonald (1991, pp. 6ff) argues, "the totally unintended but most significant and lasting impact" of the curriculum development movement in the UK was that it "implanted in higher education the seeds of its reconstruction" under the title "curriculum studies". The "veterans" of the curriculum development projects:

> poured into the departments of education at the universities and the polytechnics, the local education advisory services, even the national inspectorate and senior school positions [bringing] a hands-on knowledge of the practice of schooling that would transform those atrophied institutions by challenging their traditions and offering them a new role.

Trant has been a research fellow at Dublin University since 1972 while Ó Donnabháin enjoyed a short-lived appointment as Adjunct Professor at the University of Limerick.

From the DES perspective, as O'Brien, former Assistant Secretary, recalled, "when it comes to the crunch, it is not curriculum that's the big issue . . . it's structure and management and power and control". Due to work pressures on Department officials, there was a lapse in the *Rules and Programmes for Secondary Schools* for several years during the 1990s, yet examinations remained subject to minute attention at all times.[11] From his time as Ministerial adviser, Keating recalled that:

> curriculum wasn't one of the pressure points in the system. Curriculum was pretty marginal during the last two governments. The school managers were worried about areas like in-service and implementation groups but the teacher unions or churches weren't strong on the actual development of the curriculum. The pressure points in the system were issues of control and regionalisation.

From the perspective of the NCCA, Gary Granville recalled that, when it became known that he was leaving the NCCA in a career move in 1996, many commented on the timeliness of his move, on the basis that "the NCCA is finished now . . . the work is done . . . you have really done it all". As they saw it, the syllabus revision process was complete, the new programmes were now in place and there was nothing left to do. The very limited resources and staff at the disposal of the NCCA since its establishment until its recent designation as a statutory body provides further evidence for the marginal status of curriculum. McKay, the longest-serving member of the Council, remarked to the author that "the fact that they have produced so much quality stuff is a tremendous tribute to them". Gary Granville spoke of his embarrassment when meeting international colleagues working in parallel agencies:

> Other agencies would talk about their information and publications unit. I was the information and publications unit for two hours every month maybe at best, whereas the others would have a full-time staff, not to speak of a printing press.

There are indications that the recently acquired statutory status of the NCCA is beginning to result in better funding for research.

The Nature of Curriculum Contestation in Ireland

Apple, in a public lecture at Mary Immaculate College, Limerick in May 2001, argued that the only worthwhile reason for a national curriculum is that it gives rise to significant public debate in relation to what should be included in the core. While Ireland does have a national curriculum, Irish educational debate has largely eschewed ideological issues within the context of the dominance of positivism. For example, the controversial 1992 Education Green Paper had virtually no impact on that year's General Election debate. Even more surprisingly, the control exercised by schools in determining students' life chances features very little in public debate (Hannan with Boyle, 1987, p. 164). As Bruton (1998) commented as Opposition spokesperson on Education:

> debate in Ireland about education almost invariably centred on inputs not on outcomes — on pupil–teacher ratios, on capi-

> tation, on ex-quota staffing, rather than on literacy and nu-
> meracy, on pupil progress, on course drop-out.[12]

It is hardly surprising in this context that debate about curriculum, the "story that we tell our children about the good life", has
been limited.

Olson (1989, p. 106) ponders the general persistence of technical rationality, notwithstanding the maturation of states. He concludes that, within the technical rationality model, there is "tacit
agreement" to assume consensus, emphasise techniques and
avoid public debate about the fundamental values of schooling.
Curriculum issues are seen in terms of "problems" to which solutions can be found without any critical analysis. Questioning of
previously taken-for-granted assumptions would delay much
needed "reform" where the dominant attitude says, "if it ain't
broke, why fix it?"

In this environment, the dominant focus has been on:

> updating curriculum content. The concern has been to "get
> into" the curriculum subject knowledge relevant to changing
> demands in the labour force and to addressing economic and
> technological needs. (Callan, 1995, p. 97)

Fundamental curriculum issues have been neglected in the pursuit of what Callan (p. 100) calls "piecemeal adjustments or align-
ments to a host of social and cultural issues . . . leading to an
enlargement of curriculum contents with resultant pressures on
schools to respond" — what Hord calls the "quick fix" approach.
Given the dominance of the "transmission model" of teaching and
terminal assessment (see OECD, 1991), it is not surprising that
overload is one of the most recurring problems in the Irish post-
primary curriculum. The learning outcomes are seldom debated.
For example, the 1999 report from the Chief Examiner for Higher
Leaving Certificate History noted that "some candidates depend
almost entirely on class notes and potted/printed synopses"
(Flynn, 2000). O'Toole (2000) comments on the Chief Examiner's
Report for Higher Level English (for 1997) that:

> it is hard to avoid the impression that the system is producing students who are very good at learning and repeating but not so good at analysing and responding. The system passes on skills very effectively but does not, on the whole, encourage students to use them creatively.

Irish curriculum debates (Gleeson, 2000a) are best characterised as technical-rational (Carr and Kemmis, 1986) in nature, with relatively little contestation in relation to substantive issues. While the CEB adopted a modified version of Lawton's Areas of Experience in 1984, there has been little debate around the relationship between curriculum and culture or around the issue of core curriculum. Whereas curriculum content, pedagogy and assessment have all been subject to contestation in the UK (Ball, 1990, p. 21), assessment is the only one of these areas that is seriously contested in Ireland. The author painfully recalls how assessment absolutely dominated the deliberations of the Leaving Certificate Applied (LCA) Steering Committee, with the result that substantive issues, such as parity of esteem, school management implications, school–community liaison and pedagogy were neglected.[13]

Debates about the meaning of the "good life", the "good of education" (Dunne, 1995), curriculum and working life (Ó Donnabháin, 1998) rarely occur in Ireland. When they do, the focus tends to be on Gross National Product rather than on indices of the quality of people's lives, such as that proposed by Douthwaite (1992) or the Social Progress Index proposed by the Conference of Religious in Ireland (CORI, 1999, p. 77). Whereas one might expect the Catholic Church to promote such debates, as Davis (1999, p. 224) notes:

> the near abandonment by Catholic curriculum theorists of "integral humanism" is reflected in many otherwise laudable defences of the merits of Catholic education. These pass over the curriculum for the most part in silence or else make reassuring statements about the normative content of what is taught in Catholic schools outside the RE department.

The Irish situation is no exception. It was clear from the author's interview with Bishop McKiernan, Education spokesperson for the Irish Catholic Hierarchy from 1976–1991, that the Hierarchy takes a reactive stance in relation to curriculum matters, being interested in Religious Education rather than whole curriculum: "the bishops weren't unhappy with what was there, to be taught within the atmosphere of Catholic schools".[14]

Ideological differences have seldom featured in Irish education debate. O'Sullivan (1989, p. 261) concludes that, with the exception of the North Mayo/Sligo project, developed and managed by the Irish Foundation for Human Development from 1978–1982:

> liberal functionalism persists as the only salient paradigm for linking school and society. . . and this remains so despite the raising of many critical issues about Irish social structure by social researchers and religious and church groups in recent years.

Skilbeck believes that curriculum in Ireland:

> is still a protected territory . . . still the secret garden being controlled by the NCCA . . . the Inspectorate, the teachers, Subject Associations. You cannot expect radical changes when people think that curriculum is non-problematic. (interview)

While it must be acknowledged that the Interim CEB initiated a serious curriculum debate from 1984 to 1986 (Crooks, 1987), the momentum was lost when the Board was disbanded. On the establishment of the NCCA, the focus quickly shifted to syllabus development, with Course Committees replacing the Department of Education's Syllabus Committees. The dominant perception of curriculum remains one of syllabus document as defined in the 1980 Education White Paper and *Rules and Programmes for Secondary Schools*. In the context of the prevailing consensualist ideology (Lynch, 1987), it is hardly surprising that few contentious curriculum issues have surfaced between the NCCA and the DES and that the differences that have emerged have been in relation to particular subjects or structures rather than underlying curriculum principles. Insofar as curriculum and assessment focused debate does occur, it is short-term in nature and takes place *within* the relevant teacher unions and management bodies rather than in the public arena.

Time to Rethink Partnership in Education?

McDonald and Norris (1978, p. 7) advised the education community in the UK to "look up for a change!" and focus on the evaluation of the processes of policy formulation. Broadfoot (2002, p. 62) notes that work is ongoing "to develop hypotheses of the relationships in Norway[15] between politics, public administration and agents within the educational system". She highlights the need for policy-makers to engage with practitioners because of their "inherent responsibility to understand the uniqueness that emerges from historical and current influences on the genesis of new policies". In the Irish context, it is encouraging to find Looney, newly appointed Chief Executive Officer of the NCCA, calling for an analysis of curriculum policy from a *policy* perspective (2001, p. 150).

My argument is that the politics of partnership, Irish-style, buttresses the technical perspective, legitimates official policy and maintains the interests of the dominant sectors in society. Schwab identifies two models of partnership: *democracy* where "power comes to be exercised through mechanical numerical majorities" and *polity*, where "power is collaboratively shared among groups or categories of citizen" (quoted in Reid, 1984, p. 109). Partnership in Ireland clearly falls into the first category, with a resultant failure to see curriculum decisions in terms of what Reid (1978, p. 112) calls "justifiable acts *with public significance*". The polity model would enable all members of the community to engage in deliberative discussion where:

> curriculum development becomes the process by which the citizenry in partnership with teachers create and recreate an educational culture to support their deliberations about what it means to induct children into the culture of the society. (Elliott, 1998, p. 35)

For polity to become a reality, decision-makers must move beyond representing their sectoral interests and the value of critical
discussion and research findings in decision-making must be acknowledged. In such an environment, curriculum problems are
seen as "uncertain practical problems" (Schwab, 1978). This contrasts with the "narrowness of view" that prevails in the technical
perspective where "the questions that should be asked and how
they should be answered" are defined in a manner that is "inimical to good deliberation" (Reid, 1984, p. 61). Within this paradigm,
"problems get treated not because they are problems that matter,
but because they are problems for which some procedural tech-
nique exists" (Reid, 1978, p. 60). From this perspective, "failure
must lie in the schools" whereas "the practical reasoning model
suggests that if the problem is not being solved in action, then the
process through which the action was decided on was perhaps at
fault" (Reid, 1999, p. 67). The antidote is for curriculum to be seen
in terms of "institutionalised practice . . . and the curriculum itself
as a social and cultural institution" (p. 112).

CONCLUSION

The OECD (1991, p. 76) concluded that the basic goals and values
of the Irish education system have:

> tended to be *tacit* rather than *explicit* [my italics] during a pe-
> riod when major transformations in the society, economy and
> culture have been occurring; curriculum, assessment and ex-
> amination changes have been continual but piecemeal.

Curriculum, seen as document, has been of marginal importance.
The symbiotic relationship between curriculum development and
teacher development identified by Stenhouse, long accepted at the
margins by the curriculum development community (Trant, 1998),
is beginning to be acknowledged more widely e.g. in the deliberations of the new support services at primary and post-primary
levels. The essentially political role of schooling in the distribution
of wealth and privilege, in the transmission of culture and the

development of citizenship remains largely unacknowledged. Insofar as education is about preparation for democratic and egalitarian citizenship, the prevailing model of partnership has to be reviewed. Leithwood et al. (2002) identify vision and goals as key policy levers for large-scale reform, the dominant change strategy of the current time. The original vision of the CEB in terms of broadening the social base of decision-making in relation to the story we tell our children must be rekindled. This demands the intervention of critical friends from outside the present circle of power brokers. While the teacher education community has a potentially powerful role to play in this enterprise, there is a real need for the leaders in Irish society to become involved.

Whereas successive American Presidents and British Prime Ministers have continuously prioritised education — often for political ends — in their public pronouncements, the lack of party political attention to educational issues in Ireland, even at election time, is remarkable. It is, however, encouraging to hear the President of Ireland (McAleese, 2000) identify the transformative power of knowledge and learning in a way that can:

> reach well beyond the world of economics . . . [and] emancipate or develop tastes, sensibilities, interests, talents, passions, enriching the life of the person and of society . . . [and] cannot be measured only in enhanced earning power.

Within such a paradigm it becomes possible to develop a "form of cultural criticism that sets the stage for transformative action [and to] help educators make sense of the tacit ways power operates to shape education" (Kincheloe, 1999, p. 81). Without such a critical perspective the technicist and political factors identified above will continue to dominate Irish curriculum policy, discourse and practice.

References

Ball, S.J. (1990), *Politics and Policy Making in Education*, London: Routledge.

Barry, D. (1989), "Impact of an Interest Group", in Mulcahy D.G. and O'Sullivan. D. (eds.), *Irish Educational Policy*, IPA: Dublin, pp. 133–62.

Bew, P., Hazelkorn, E. and Patterson, H. (1989), *The Dynamics of Irish Politics*, London: Lawrence and Wishart.

Breathnach, S. (2001), "School Development Planning: An Opportunity for Teacher Professionalism", in O'Flaherty, L. (ed.), *Issues in Education, Volume 5, Teaching as a Profession*, ASTI: Dublin, pp. 67–74.

Breen, R., Hannan, D.F., Rottman, D.B. and Whelan, C.T. (1990), *Understanding Contemporary Ireland, State, Class and Development in the Republic of Ireland*, Dublin: Gill and Macmillan.

Broadfoot, P. (2002), "The Making of a Curriculum", *Scandinavian Journal of Educational Research*, Vol. 46, No. 1, pp. 47–64.

Browne, T. (1985), *Ireland: A Social and Cultural History 1922–1985*, London: Fontana.

Bruton, R. (1998), "Bold Strides Needed to Tackle Disadvantage", *Irish Times*, 10 November.

Callan, J. (1995), "Equality of Learning in Quality Schooling: A Challenge for Curriculum Implementation", in Coolahan, J. (ed.), *Issues and Strategies in the Implementation of Educational Policy*, Maynooth: Education Department.

Callan, J. (1997), "Active Learning in the Classroom: A Challenge to Existing Values and Practices", in Hyland, A. (ed.), *Issues in Education*, Vol. 2, Dublin: ASTI, pp. 21–8.

Carr, W. and Kemmis, S. (1986), *Becoming Critical, Education, Knowledge and Action Research*, London: Falmer.

CEB (1985), *The Primary Curriculum*, Dublin: CEB.

Coolahan, J. (1984), "The Fortunes of Education as a Subject of Study and Research in Ireland", *Irish Educational Studies*, Vol. 4, pp. 1–28.

Coolahan, J. (ed.) (1994), *Report on the National Education Convention*, Dublin: National Education Convention Secretariat.

CORI (1999), *Social Transformation for Lifelong Learning, Towards a Policy on Adult and Community Education*, Dublin: CORI.

Cornbleth, C. (1990), *Curriculum in Context*, London: Falmer.

Cromien, S. (2000), *Review of Department's Operations, Systems and Staffing Needs*, Unpublished Report, Dublin: DES.

Crooks, T. (1987), "The Interim Curriculum and Examinations Board 1984–87", *Compass*, Vol. 16, No 2, pp. 7–26.

Davis, R.A. (1999), "Can there be a Catholic Curriculum?" in Conroy, J.C. (ed.), *Catholic Education, Inside out, Inside in*, Dublin: Veritas.

Department of Finance (2002), *Revised Estimates for Public Services*, Dublin: Stationery Office.

Douthwaite, R. (1992), *The Growth Illusion*, Dublin: Lilliput.

Dunne, J. (1995), "What's the Good of Education?" in Hogan, P. (ed.), *Partnership and the Benefits of Learning*, Dublin: ESAI.

Elliot, J. (1998), *The Curriculum Experiment: Meeting the Challenge of Social Change*, Buckingham: Open University Press.

Flynn, S. (2000), "Report Defends 1999 History Exam", *Irish Times*, 19 May.

Fullan, M. (1991), *The New Meaning of Educational Change*, London: Cassell.

Fuller, L. (1990), "An Ideological Critique of the Irish Post-Primary School Curriculum", unpublished MEd thesis, NUI, Maynooth.

Gleeson, J. (1992), *Gender Equality in Education in the Republic of Ireland (1984–1991)*, Dublin: Stationery Office.

Gleeson, J. (1996), "Senior Cycle Curriculum Policy", in Hogan, P. (ed.), *Issues in Education*, Vol. 1, Dublin: ASTI, pp. 57–67.

Gleeson, J. (1998), "A Consensus Approach to Policy-making: the Case of the Republic of Ireland", in Finlay, I., Nevin, S. and Young, S. (ed.) *Changing Vocational Education and Training*, London: RKP, pp. 41–64.

Gleeson, J. (2000a), "Sectoral Interest versus the Common Good? Legitimation, Fragmentation and Contestation in Irish Post-primary Curriculum Policy and Practice", *Irish Education Studies*, Vol. 19, pp. 16–34.

Gleeson, J. (2000b), "Post-primary Curriculum Policy and Practice in the Republic of Ireland: Fragmentation, Contestation and Partnership", unpublished PhD thesis, University of East Anglia.

Gleeson, J. (2001), "The Law or the Prophets? Post-primary Curriculum Reform in the Context of Recent Structural and Policy Developments", unpublished paper read at ESAI Annual Conference, Mary Immaculate College, Limerick.

Gleeson, J. and Leonard, D. (1999), "Rhetoric and reality in the implementation of education policy: teacher professionalism development", unpublished paper read at ISATT Bi-annual Conference, Dublin.

Gleeson J, O'Grady, D., McGarr, O. and Johnston, K. (2001), *Case Studies on ICT and School Improvement,* report submitted to OECD, published at http://www.oecd.org.

Goodson, I. (1983), *School Subjects and Curriculum Change,* London: Croom Helm.

Goodson, I. (1989), "Curriculum Reform and Curriculum Theory: A Case of Historical Amnesia", *Cambridge Journal of Education,* Vol. 19, No. 2, pp. 131–41.

Goodson, I. (1994), *Studying Curriculum,* London: Falmer.

Goodson, I. (2001), "Social Histories of Educational Change", *The Journal of Educational Change,* Vol. 2, No. 1, pp. 45–63.

Goodson, I. and Hargreaves, A. (1996), "Teachers' Professional Lives: Aspirations and Actualities", in Goodson, I. and Hargreaves, A. (ed.), *Teachers' Professional Lives,* London: Falmer, pp. 1–27.

Granville, G. (1994), *Professionalism and Partnership: The NCCA Committee System as a Mechanism for Curriculum Policy Formulation,* unpublished MSc thesis, University of Dublin.

Grundy, S. (1987), *Curriculum: Product or Praxis,* London: Falmer.

Hannan, D. (1989), "Irish Poverty, Inequality and State Policy", *The New Nation,* No. 4, pp. 8–10.

Hannan, D. with Boyle, M. (1987), *Schooling Decisions: the Origins and Consequences of Selection and Streaming in Irish Post-Primary Schools,* Dublin: ESRI, Paper No. 136.

Hargreaves, A. (1994), "Introduction", in Goodson, I. (1994) *Studying Curriculum.* London: Falmer.

Harris, J. (1989), "The Policy-making Role of the Department of Education", in Mulcahy, D. and O'Sullivan, D. (eds.) *Irish Educational Policy*, Dublin: IPA, pp. 7–26.

Hord, S. (1987), *Evaluating Educational Evaluations*, London: Croom Helm.

Hord, S. (1995), "From Policy to Classroom Practice: Beyond the Mandates", in Carter, D. and O'Neill, M. (eds.) (1995), *International Perspectives on Educational Reform and Policy Implementation*, London: Falmer.

House, E. (1981), "Three Perspectives on Innovation: Technological, Political and Cultural", in Lehming, R. and Kane, M. (ed.), *Improving Schools, Using What we Know*, London: Sage Publications, pp. 17–41.

Hyland, A. (2000), public lecture, Limerick Inn Hotel, 27 January.

Ireland, Government of (1987), *Registration Council Regulation*, Dublin: Stationery Office.

Ireland, Government of (1992), *Education for a Changing World, Education Green Paper*, Dublin: Stationery Office.

Ireland, Government of (1995), *Charting our Education Future, Education White Paper*, Dublin: Stationery Office.

Ireland, Government of (1998), *Commission on the Points System: Consultative Process — Background Document*, Dublin: Stationery Office.

Jansen, J. (1990), "Curriculum Policy as Compensatory Legitimation? A View from the Periphery", *Oxford Review of Education*, Vol. 16, No 1.

Johnson, M. (1992), "Education as an Issue in Irish Politics, 1957–1981", unpublished MEd Thesis, Trinity College, Dublin.

Kane, E. (1996), "The Power of Paradigms: Social Science and Intellectual Contributions to Public Discourse in Ireland", in O'Dowd, L. (ed.), *On Intellectuals and Intellectual Life in Ireland*, Dublin: RIAC.

Kennedy, K.J. (1995), "An Analysis of the Policy Contexts of Recent Curriculum Reforms in Australia, Great Britain and the United States", in Carter, D. and O'Neill, M. (eds.) *International Perspectives on Educational Reform and Policy Implementation*, London: Falmer.

Kiely, L. (2003), "Teacher's Perceptions of Teaching as a Profession", unpublished Master's thesis, University of Limerick

Kincheloe J. (1999), "Critical Democracy and Education", in Henderson, J.G. and Kesson, K.R. (eds.) *Understanding Democratic Curriculum Leadership*, Columbia: Teachers College Press.

Lawton, D. (1983), *Curriculum Studies and Educational Planning*, London: Hodder and Stoughton.

Lee, J.J. (1989), *Ireland 1912–1985: Politics and Society*, Cambridge University Press.

Leithwood, K, Jantzi, D. and Mascall, B. (2002), "A Framework for Research on Large-Scale Reform", *Journal of Educational Change*, Vol. 3, No. 1, pp. 7–33.

Logan, J. and O'Reilly, B. (1985), "Educational Decision Making: The Case of the Curriculum and Examinations Board", *Administration*, Vol. 33, No. 4, IPA.

Looney, A. (2001), "Curriculum as Policy: Some implications of contemporary policy studies for the analysis of curriculum policy, with particular reference to post-primary curriculum in the Republic of Ireland", *The Curriculum Journal*, Vol. 12, No. 2, pp. 149–62.

Lynch K. (1999), *Equality in Education*, Dublin: Gill and Macmillan.

Lynch, K. (1987), "Dominant Ideologies in Irish Educational Thought: Consensualism, Essentialism and Meritocratic Individualism", *The Irish Economic and Social Review*, Dublin, Vol. 18, No 2, pp. 110–22.

Lynch, K. (1989), *The Hidden Curriculum: Reproduction in Education, An Appraisal*, London: Falmer.

Mackey, J. (1998), "Teaching Methodology in the Junior Certificate", *Irish Educational Studies*, Vol. 17, pp. 284–91.

Marino Institute of Education (1992), *School Communities and Change: The Junior Certificate*, Dublin: Marino Institute of Education.

McAleese, M. (2000), "The Power of Knowledge", unpublished lecture delivered at Newman House, University College, Dublin, 21 February.

McDonald, B. (1976), "Evaluation and the Control of Education", in Tawney, D. (ed.), *Curriculum Evaluation Today: Trends and Implications*, London: Macmillan

McDonald, B. (1991), "Introduction", in Rudduck, J., *Innovation and Change*, London: Falmer.

McDonald, B. and Norris, N. (1978), *Looking up for a Change: Political Horizons in Policy Evaluation*, Norwich: CARE.

McNiff, J. and Collins, U. (1994), *A New Approach to In-Career Development for Teachers in Ireland*, Bournemouth: Hyde.

McNiff, J., McNamara, G., Leonard, D. (2000), *Action Research in Ireland*, Poole: September Books.

NCCA (1993), *A Programme for Reform, Curriculum and Assessment Policy Towards the New Century*, Dublin: NCCA.

NESC (1993), *Education and Training Policies for Economic and Social Development*, Dublin.

NESF (1997), *Early School Leavers and Youth Unemployment*, Forum Paper No. 11, Dublin: National Economic and Social Forum.

Ó Buachalla, S. (1988), *Education Policy in Twentieth Century Ireland*, Dublin: Wolfhound Press.

Ó Ceallaigh, A. (1985), "The Work of the Curriculum and Examinations Board", *Compass*, Vol. 14, No. 2, pp. 7–18.

O'Connor, T. (1998), "The Impact of the European Social Fund on the Development of Initial Vocational and Training in Ireland", in Trant, A., Ó Donnabháin, D. et al., *The Future of the Curriculum*, Dublin: CDU.

O'Donnell, S., Le Matais, J., Boyd, S. and Tabberer, R. (1998), *INCA: The International Review of Curriculum and Assessment Frameworks Archive* (CD ROM), London: QCA.

Ó Donnabháin, D. (1998), "The Work-Related Curriculum", in Trant, A., Ó Donnabháin, D. et al. (eds.), *The Future of the Curriculum*, Dublin: CDU.

O'Donoghue, T. (1999), *The Catholic Church and the Secondary School Curriculum in Ireland*, New York: Laing.

OECD (1991), *Reviews of National Policies for Education: Ireland*. Paris.

Olson, J. (1989), "The Persistence of Technical Rationality", in Milburn, G, Goodson, I, and Clark, R.J. (eds.), *Re-Interpreting Curriculum Research: Images and Arguments*, London: Falmer, pp. 102–9.

O'Reilly, B. (1998), "Vocational Education and Society in Ireland, 1930–1990. A Case Study in the Politics of Education", unpublished PhD thesis, University of Edinburgh.

O'Sullivan, D. (1989), "Ideational Base of Policy", in Mulcahy, D.G. and O'Sullivan, D. (eds.), *Irish Educational Policy*, Dublin: IPA.

O'Sullivan, D. (1992), "Cultural Strangers and Educational Change: The OECD Report Investment in Education and Irish Educational Policy", *Journal of Education Policy*, Vol. 7, No. 5, pp. 445–69.

O'Toole, F. (2000), "Skills Training Leaves Students Unengaged", *Irish Times*, 7 June.

Payne, J. (2002), "A Tale of Two Curriculums: Putting the English and Norwegian Curriculum Models to the Test of 'High Skills' Vision", *Journal of Education and Work*, Vol. 15, No. 2, pp. 117–43.

Reid, W. (1978), *Thinking about the Curriculum: The Nature and Treatment of Curriculum Problems*, London: Routledge.

Reid, W. (1984), "Curriculum, Community and Liberal Education: A Response to the Practical 4", *Curriculum Inquiry*, Vol. 14, No.1, pp. 103–11.

Reid, W. (1999), *Curriculum as Institution and Practice*, London: Erlbaum.

Roche, W.K. and Geary, J.F. (1998), *"Collaborative Production": and the Irish Boom: Work Organisation, Partnership and Direct Involvement in Irish Workplaces*, University College Dublin: Centre for Employment Relations and Organisational Performance.

Schon, D. (1971), *Beyond the Stable State*, London: Temple Smith.

Schwab, J. (1978), *Science, Curriculum and Liberal Education*, Chicago: University Press.

Schwab, J.J. (1983), "The Practical 4: Something for Curriculum Professors to do", *Curriculum Inquiry*, Vol. 13, No. 3, pp. 239–65.

Smyth, E. (1999), *Do Schools Differ?* Dublin: Oak Tree Press.

Stenhouse, L. (1975), *An Introduction to Curriculum Research and Development*, London: Heinemann.

Sugrue, C. (1995), "Critical Reflections on the Process of Charting our Education Future", unpublished paper read at ECER Conference, University of Bath.

Sugrue, C. (1997), *Complexities of Teaching: Child-centred Perspectives*, London: Falmer.

Sugrue, C. and Uí Thúama, C. (1994), "Perspectives on Substance and Method in Post-graduate Educational Research in Ireland", *Irish Educational Studies*, Vol. 13, pp. 102–29.

Trant, A. (1998), "Giving the Curriculum Back to Teachers", in Trant, A., Ó Donnabháin, D. et al. (eds.), *The Future of the Curriculum*, Dublin: CDU.

Tussing, D. (1978), *Irish Educational Expenditures — Past, Present and Future*, Dublin: ESRI.

Weiler, H. (1990), "Curriculum Reform and the Legitimation of Educational Objectives: The Case of the Federal Republic of Germany", *Oxford Review of Education*, Vol. 16, No. 1, pp. 15–27.

Werner, W. (1991), "Defining Curriculum Policy through Slogans", *Journal of Education Policy*, Vol. 6, No. 2, pp. 225–38.

Endnotes

---

[1] For example, with the exception of the Transition Year Programme, the senior cycle developments, Post-Leaving Certificate Courses, Initial Vocational Education and Training and In-Career development programmes could not have happened without European funding.

[2] Hillery stated (Dáil Reports Vol. 203, Col. 684, 11/6/1963) that "to do what is possible is my job and not to have the whole matter upset because of some principle or ideal". Colley said of comprehensive education: "it is not anything ideological or political".

[3] This classification has been applied to curriculum by Carr and Kemmis (1986), Grundy (1987), Cornbleth (1990) and others.

[4] O'Sullivan, 1989, p. 243–5 makes a similar argument.

[5] Lee argues (1989, p. 583) that economists filled the vacuum resulting from the prevailing anti-intellectual bias — "economists can get away with playing the philosopher king because there is so little challenge to the dominant orthodoxy".

[6] As one senior Inspector put it in the course of an interview with the author, "our exam papers received more scrutiny than bank notes in the Central Bank".

[7] The exception to this trend is the activities of the National Council for Vocational Awards, a new body established during the early 1990s, to provide certification for vocational-type courses, often of a Further Education nature.

[8] Membership of the board was determined by proportional affiliation from the various stakeholders. Consequently, members were there more because of their affiliation rather than having particular expertise.

[9] In this context, the EU's commitment to the promotion of equity in social policy may yet be of very great significant for Ireland.

[10] Provided for under the terms of the Education Act (1998).

[11] That has now changed with the recent establishment of the State Examinations Commission (January 2003).

[12] Bruton also observed that "we in Ireland are too quick to congratulate ourselves on the excellence of our education system" and expressed regret that "we have steadfastly refused to shine a light into the darker corners where some nasty surprises lurk".

[13] Nor has this matter been resolved. The OECD noted (1991, p. 55) that "a major reform of assessment, examining and credentialising is long overdue . . . if curriculum reform strategies are to succeed". Similar sentiments were expressed at the National Education Convention (NEC) (Coolahan, 1994, p. 74), incorporated in the White Paper (Government of Ireland, 1995, p. 60) which called for a shift in emphasis away from external examinations to internal assessment and reinforced by the Points Commission (Government of Ireland, 1998, p. 113) when it commented on "the lack of congruence between the aims and goals of the second-level curriculum and the modes and techniques of assessment used for the established Leaving Certificate".

[14] All interviews referred to in this chapter were conducted between 1998 and 1999. For further details see Gleeson, 2000.

[15] According to Skilbeck (personal interview) the Norwegian curriculum documents are widely respected internationally, a point acknowledged by Payne (2002).

Chapter 5

SECONDARY SCHOOL CURRICULUM REFORMS IN NORTHERN IRELAND: A CRITICAL ANALYSIS

Alex McEwen

INTRODUCTION

This chapter provides a critical analysis of recent reforms of Northern Ireland's Secondary School Curriculum. It is in three parts. First, recent reforms in the Province are situated within the wider change agenda pursued by successive British Governments in England and Wales. Second, an outline of current curricular structures and content is provided as a precursor to a more detailed and critical analysis of its shaping influences under a number of emergent headings. Third, the chapter concludes that despite reform efforts, the project of an Enlightenment-inspired curriculum continues to prevail. Consequently, many secondary school pupils will remain poorly equipped to face the challenges and employment opportunities provided in a globalised and increasingly deregulated marketplace.

BACKGROUND AND CONTEXT OF REFORMS

There are a number of political and economic factors that formed the context for the introduction of the National Curriculum in

England and Wales and Northern Ireland. The political right had
been arguing that liberal reforms of the 1960s and 70s, introduced
primarily by Labour governments, had led to lower standards of
attainment by pupils in state schools when compared with the independent sector. This was also true, critics argued, when international comparisons were made. These "orthodoxies" were
challenged chiefly on the basis of resource allocation where, in the
independent sector, the amount spent per pupil is almost double
that for those in the state sector, thus facilitating favourable teaching conditions in the independent schools such as small classes
and up-to-date equipment. International comparisons were challenged also on the basis of how such comparisons were made —
on the disparity between the lower proportion of gross domestic
product spent on education in the United Kingdom in comparison
with other similar countries.

These criticisms of domestic schooling were part of a wider
political project of free market reforms of the economy and public
services. Schools were criticised for being producer-driven — that
they were run for the benefit of the employees and not the cus-
tomer and were not sufficiently focused on facilitating wealth
creation. This criticism was also directed at schools where teaching and learning were seen as having been overly influenced by
liberal educational theory that stressed individual intellectual and
moral growth at the expense of the vocational needs of pupils and
their future contribution to the country's ability to create wealth.
Schools, it was argued, needed the introduction of a consumer
ethos and to be managed and held accountable in a manner similar to well-run businesses. Professions in general also attracted
similar criticisms and, in the case of teachers, their power to frame
curricula had led to significant differences in what pupils were
taught depending on where they lived. The free marketeers saw
this as an impediment to economic mobility and a gross monopoly by teachers, whom they blamed as being at least partially responsible for low expectations and attainment of pupils in state
schools. In addition, teachers, in common with other public sector
professionals, were perceived as being largely unaccountable for

their practice; inspections were criticised as too cosy and non-judgemental with "inspector-speak" widely pilloried for being anodyne and obfuscatory. The creation of the OFSTED (Office For Standards in Education) and the appointment of an adversarial Chief Inspector prepared to "name and shame" failing schools as indicated by inspection reports was evidence of the strength of scepticism that the political right held about schools. Whilst there were undoubtedly under-performing schools which were failing their pupils, current OFSTED policy has been widely criticised due to the absence of valid and reliable criteria for assessing teaching from the viewpoint that such schools need support rather than public humiliation. Not surprisingly, Fitzgibbon (1999) has pointed out that good inspection reports correlate well with schools in affluent areas.

Northern Ireland schools have been spared the excesses of inspection in England; there is no naming and shaming and a professional full-time schools' inspectorate has been retained, unlike the privatisation of inspections in England and Wales. The policy on inspections reflects a wider public confidence in the quality of schooling in Northern Ireland. There is a feeling that, during the period of direct rule, policies were introduced to solve problems that did not exist to the same extent as in England. Another notable aspect of the Reform Order (1989) was the official statutory support to be given to the expansion of religiously integrated schools which up to then had been established and supported from charities and other private funds. This sector began with 28 pupils in a scout hall and has now grown to a school population of 12,000, about three per cent of the school population.

Criticism of schools as largely unaccountable led to the introduction of what are now known as academic "league tables" consisting of pupils' attainment levels at all four Key Stages, with GCSE and A-level grades being expressed as percentages. The thinking behind this crude representation of results is that parents as consumers can "shop around" for the school with the best attainment. The league tables are widely criticised from the point of view that they are only a very crude indicator of the quality of a school's teaching and leadership. No allowance is made for the socio-economic circumstances or ability of the pupils in the school's catchment area, thus leading to quite absurd comparisons between schools in prosperous suburbs with inner-city schools whose pupils are handicapped by multiple economic and social disadvantages. Attempts to ameliorate these comparisons by introducing a value-added component that would take account of schools' circumstances in measuring pupils' attainment in the league tables have been largely unsuccessful in terms of government adoption of proposed schemes at secondary level. At primary level, a very crude attempt has been made through "baselining" that involves testing pupils on entry at year one on literacy, numeracy and social skills in order to measure how much added value the school contributes at the two subsequent Key Stages.

CENTRALISED PLANNING OF CURRICULUM: STRUCTURE AND CONTENT

The subjects of the Northern Ireland Curriculum and the National Curriculum in England and Wales were each planned by a subject panel that created the curricular outline from which teaching syllabuses were to be drawn. In the case of English and History, this led to disputes about the aims and content of English and History teaching which attracted criticism from politicians anxious to promote "traditional literary values", the centrality of British history and "tried and tested" methods of teaching them. In literature, certain areas assumed the status almost of holy writ with an assumption that in some modern representation of Plato's forms of knowledge there were subjects that were sacrosanct and not to be excluded by what was seen as the left-leaning educational establishment thought by the educational right to be largely responsible for the decline in standards.

The Northern Ireland Curriculum was introduced in 1989 through the Education Reform (Northern Ireland) order and is broadly similar to the National Curriculum introduced in England

and Wales by the Education Reform Act (1988). Structurally it is defined in four phases:

- Key Stage One for school years 1–4 and pupils aged 4–8

- Key Stage Two for school years 5–7 and pupils aged 7–11

- Key Stage Three for school years 8–10 and pupils aged 12–14

- Key Stage Four for school years 11–14 and pupils aged 15–16 Culminates in GCSE

Curriculum content is divided into the following subjects:

- Religious Education

- English

- Mathematics

- Science, and Technology and Design

- Environment and Society (History and Geography)

- Creative and Expressive Studies (Art and Design, Music and Physical Education)

- Modern Languages (including French, German, Italian or Irish)

There are six educational themes, each to be taught as an integral aspect of all curricular subjects and throughout compulsory schooling while some themes are confined to secondary curricula as indicated in Table 5.1 below.

Table 5.1: Educational Themes

Primary and Secondary	Secondary
1. Education for Mutual Understanding 2. Cultural Heritage	1. Economic Awareness 2. Health Education 3. Information Technology 4. Careers Education

The curriculum is set out statutorily as prescribed programmes of study according to age, range and ability and these are used by teachers to plan schemes of work. Specified attainment targets are also set out as level descriptors of what should be achieved in a particular subject and are the basis for assessing pupils' progress at Key Stage 3. There are eight levels of achievement covering the four Key Stages and teachers are expected to evaluate pupils' performance over a period of time. It is expected that the majority of pupils will reach level 5 or 6 at Key Stage 3.

A recent change at Key Stage 4 allows pupils, when appropriate, to drop a number of subjects excluding Maths, English and Science in preference to a vocational course such as National Vocational Qualifications that are provided by either the school or a local further education college. This is recognition that for a substantial number of pupils, further study of academic subjects such as History and modern languages is inappropriate in terms of their ability and future career trajectories.

Knowledge, Power and the Curriculum

What principles underpin the organisation of Northern Ireland's statutory curriculum into largely separate subject disciplines? Traditional liberal approaches to this question rely on some underpinning universalistic principles based on the accumulated wisdom of past and contemporary societies. Liberal arguments point to the utility of the traditional subject-based curriculum in sustaining a more or less stable society by introducing successive generations of pupils to this wisdom as it is expressed through literature, history, science, geography. Proponents argue that it is best organised predominantly as single-subject disciplines. The underlying social emphasis in this mostly past-oriented intellectual tradition is on maintaining and justifying the deep structural principles of order in our society. The most cogent arguments for this approach are provided by Peters (1966) and Hirst (1974), who argue that studying curricular subjects is a form of initiation into the knowledge necessary both to function successfully in society, to understand where it came from and how it works. It is essentially an ideational philosophy: that our culture has been shaped and is sustained by the ideas at the core of this liberal tradition and, implicitly at its higher levels, accessible to relatively few. This intellectually elitist viewpoint has had an adverse effect on the popularity of more vocational and applied alternatives. Technical education, for example, despite being one of a triumvirate of curricular routes provided by the 1944 Education Act, was abandoned for pupils of compulsory school age by the early 1960s. Paradoxically, its demise was caused, in part, by some middle-class parents' realisation of the added vocational value of the grammar schools' success in securing attractive employment for their children. Secondary schools that pursued the government's blueprint of preparing pupils for practical work in mostly manual trades or secretarial work experienced diminishing enrolments as parents sought alternatives that were offering a more academic curriculum as a means of upward social and occupational mobility. Consequently, technical education is now taught as a core provision in the further education colleges.

Justification for the curriculum organised as separate subjects stems from the argument that the world can be understood in many different ways. Understanding or appreciation of art and literature as well as other aspects of culture are established through dialogue that is replete with aesthetic judgements that are by definition individual to each person but influenced by wider cultural norms reflecting discussions about "good" art and drama and so on. Such dialogues are open in the sense that opinions are necessarily infinitely variable and, in addition, different generations create their own cultural and aesthetic narratives. Literature, for example, is constantly open to re-interpretation; historians too would be largely redundant if there was one "official" definition of past events although this has not prevented totalitarian societies from attempting such a project and imprisoning those who questioned such histories.

Deconstructing the Curriculum: Its Socio-Political Milieu

The subject-based educational curriculum briefly set out above is structuralist insofar as its proponents argue that it represents the chief intellectual and ethical building blocks of our way of life whilst also providing pupils with the skills and knowledge to participate in society. The curriculum structure is portrayed as unproblematic and its central purpose is the maintenance of a social and political order underpinned by a more general liberal consensus on ideas of justice and equality. Where inequality and injustice occur, the fault is usually attributed to an imbalance or inefficiency of the structures and one of the least painful ways for governments of improving equality is through curricular reforms. Since the rise of free market economics during the 1980s and 1990s, the education system has been in the frontline of those social systems that have borne the brunt of criticisms from the educational and political right of liberal educational policies of the 1960s. The political and educational reflection of more right-wing economics took the form of a virulent criticism of progressive educational policies that had produced, it was argued, declining moral standards, citing a "yob culture" in Britain as a prime example and, in addition, poor economic performance. The response was both structural in the imposition of a standardised national curriculum which remained strongly subject-based and a free competitive market for schooling with the introduction of academic league tables and parental choice of schools. There has been an underlying shift from a social and political narrative focused on equality of opportunity and building a consensual civil society through schooling to a more utilitarian concern with excellence and accountability of schools through a focus on results. This was part of a wider scepticism regarding public bodies in general which were being privatised throughout this period.

Bernstein (1971) describes the curriculum above as a "collected code" consisting of discrete, strongly demarcated subject disciplines. Practitioners see it as a central part of their intellectual purpose to maintain the integrity of their respective subject boundaries and to initiate students into the discipline of the subject: its rules of explanation, what counts as evidence and its key logical pathways. The traditional subject and highly academic curriculum, he argues, reflects a society where social and economic roles and status are relatively fixed. Such a curriculum differentiates strongly between, for example, commonsense and esoteric knowledge; between applied and theoretical, between academic and vocational. These distinctions reflect the sorts of boundaries set by principles of control that are determined by the patterns of social and economic hierarchies in such societies. The uncommonsense, theoretical knowledge of the subject-based academic curriculum reflects a society where the prevailing boundaries of social class, religion, race and gender are matched by knowledge organised within strong epistemological boundaries.

A society where life chances and aspirations are largely bounded by class, religion and gender will be preoccupied with principles of control that justify and perpetuate existing ruling classes. The hierarchical structure of such societies is reflected in a similarly stratified curriculum placing a premium on high-level theoretical and strongly bounded subject knowledge. This, it is argued, is accessible to relatively few who either consolidate their positions of power based on their favourable, in curricular terms, cultural capital, or are sponsored from lower levels of the class structure on the basis of their success in the curriculum. The underlying structural rationale for such a hierarchical ordering of knowledge is social rather than educational, since it is arguable that all pupils could benefit from exposure to the academic curriculum and is indeed the main motivation for much of adult education provision in, for example, the Open University. Its social basis relates to the social structures that such a stratified classification of knowledge supports in so far as it incorporates the "master patterns" of values and knowledge necessary for membership of power elites. This support is double-edged since, at its highest levels, the basis for existing knowledge and power is characterised by uncertainty and permeability, a necessary feature if new ideas and theories are to be discovered. Inherent in this uncertainty principle is the possibility of social and economic change;

existing structures of power are not immutable. Consequently, there is a premium on the processes of selecting those who should study the academic curriculum if current social and economic elites are to be preserved.

New ideas and theories imply change and are therefore potentially subversive of existing structures of power and those in positions of established authority, especially where their positions are revealed as historically or economically transitory. As far as the school curriculum is concerned, most pupils are taught certainty at the expense of a subject's creative uncertainty, often in response to the inexorable demands of an examination system with the added pressure of published "league tables". Such pressures have led to teaching that is largely information-based. The introduction of the new AS-level syllabuses in year 13 in an attempt to broaden the A-level curriculum is currently criticised on this basis. It is claimed that there is little overt opportunity for pupils to see beyond the information and facts to the conceptual frameworks that make informed interpretations and inferences possible. In such a curriculum, boundaries between teacher and pupils are strong, thus signalling a clear pedagogical and intellectual distinction between expert and novice. This decreases as the pupil becomes more expert and is eventually recognised as an equal by other experts, as fully initiated into the discipline.

Bourdieu (1977) argues that the academic curriculum replicates the "master patterns" of social and economic power. It represents ruling class culture as the ideal in terms of family structure, schooling, and social and economic networks. The post-partition educational curriculum in Northern Ireland until recently was an attempt, from the ruling Protestant ascendancy's viewpoint, to consolidate its position of power through the promotion of Britishness as the ideal in the state schools. This policy represented a wider political ideology of cultural Britishness that led to the under-representation of Nationalist culture in official representations of Northern Ireland society. More generally, historically Irish sources that were integral to a northern Protestant identity were consciously omitted. Presentations of Northern Irish culture, as far as curricular choice were concerned, were interpreted by Protestants as synonymous with Britishness and were part of a wider agenda of preserving sectarian patterns of employment, political and cultural identity, all of which supported Protestant hegemony.

From a Nationalist perspective, the curriculum was interpreted in such a way as to preserve an identity in the face of an otherwise hostile political and economic environment. In the past, the different interpretations of the curriculum, in promoting either a British or Irish culture and identity, were most obvious in the schools' differing emphasis in the teaching of History, the Irish language, some aspects of Music and choice of sports. Until recently, for example, nineteenth- and twentieth-century Irish history, especially the development of Irish nationalism, was simply not taught in most Protestant post-primary schools. Protestants were taught British and European history in much the same way as pupils in Leeds or Bristol on the assumption, largely taken for granted in the Protestant community, that the history of Irish nationalism was not only irrelevant for British pupils in Northern Ireland, but potentially subversive. It is still the case that in the statutory history curriculum taught in state and Catholic schools, there is likely to be differences of emphasis according to the particular ethos of the school or the views of individual teachers.

The political, cultural and economic dismantling of the Protestant hegemony through legislation and policies guaranteeing equality of treatment of employment and cultural identities has been reflected in the secondary curriculum. Special cross-curricular themes to be taught through all subjects have been introduced in an attempt to teach Protestant and Catholic pupils about aspects of their respective traditions which they share and respect for those on which they differ. As part of these curriculum reforms, for example, schools are now required to teach the two cross-curricular themes of Education for Mutual Understanding and Cultural Heritage. All pupils must now take these courses with the aim of redressing the balance of sectarian myth concerning "the other side" and the sort of distorted history which accompanies them. However, there is a body of research on schools in the province which suggests that such curricular attempts to promote greater cross-community understanding are compromised by denominational schools. Darby (1987) shows that schools are an important arena for the communication of sectarian ideas and myths for pupils. In building a sense of identity, the research emphasises the significance for both sets of pupils of a hidden curriculum of sectarian attitudes outside the classroom. These are often distorted accounts of a community's history and traditions connected with, for example, the establishment of the Protestant ascendancy after the Williamite Wars of the seventeenth century or, alternatively, the commemoration of the republican uprising of Easter 1916.

Following Bourdieu's argument, the master patterns of Northern Ireland culture were mostly derived from British sources putting Protestant pupils at an advantage, culturally and economically, because of the matching cultural capital they brought to schooling. This was consistent with the curriculum in the state schools but also with important social and economic networks that sustained an inequitable opportunity structure. This was manifest in absolute terms in higher rates of unemployment for Catholic pupils and also relative to employment sectors that required greater skill and commanded higher pay, work dominated by Protestants. In curricular choices, greater numbers of Protestants selected science and maths subjects as a preparation for a career in sectors with higher pay, better career structure and dominated by their co-religionists.

It would be misleading, however, to over-emphasise the sectarian contexts that, in the past, led to particularistic curriculum choices. Most of the former discriminatory employment practices have been dismantled as a consequence of successive legislation outlawing discrimination as part of the normalisation of Northern Ireland and the creation of an agreed civil society. The introduction of the Northern Ireland curriculum on the same lines as the National Curriculum in England and Wales has also provided both state and Catholic schools in curriculum terms with a "level playing field" with respect to curricular choices, their curricula are identical with the exception of the unique position of Irish as a second language taught predominantly in the Catholic-owned schools and the religiously integrated schools. However, because of the strong link between social class and religion in Northern Ireland, Catholics' disadvantages resulting from sectarian discrimination since partition are exacerbated by continuing socio-economic inequalities. In this latter sense, the consequences of economic disadvantage mirrors the wider British context where academic attainment and occupational destinations are equally bound up with the influence of pupils' social class origin.

Cultural Capital and Curriculum Reform

The question arises at this point as to the reasons for the close and continuing relationship between attainment, occupation and pupils' socio-economic origins and their experiences of schooling through the curriculum. This is especially so for many children from manual working backgrounds whose ability is not matched by their attainment and occupational placement. This relationship has been extensively researched ranging from quantitative studies by Goldthorpe (1997) which focus on the unequal outcomes attributed to the effects of social class origins, to studies that examine the educational processes that contribute to lower-than-expected attainment of working-class pupils. Bernstein (1975), for example, argues that classroom language, what he calls "elaborated codes", is continuous with forms of cultural capital synonymous with non-manual patterns of family structure and socialisation. Labov (1972) criticises this work on the basis that the codes are merely linguistic styles or social class markers. The corollary Bernstein calls a "restricted code" which he claims mirrors the close-knit patterns of working-class families and communities and the implicit nature of many patterns of communication. The difference between working-class and middle-class children is that the latter have access to both and learn the socially constructed rules about the appropriateness of their use and the accompanying social roles expected — the classroom being a prime example of formal language use as a learning medium and a dependent learning relationship. Lower-class pupils' socialisation and relationships are framed predominantly in the context of informality of language use and social roles that disadvantage them in the context of more formal modes of transmission determined by the forms of knowledge and pedagogy entailed in subject-based curricula.

Bourdieu objectifies these patterns of socialisation and attitudes to schooling as cultural capital as a means of explaining different educational experiences and attainments of working- and middle-class pupils. The "master patterns" of power and control in capitalist society are embedded in, and transmitted through, the academic medium of subject-based curricula. The traditional academic curriculum, Bernstein argues, reproduces class structures and their class-based differentials by strongly distinguishing between knowledge as control. He argues that this is embodied in the traditional academic curriculum; the concepts that enable the powerful to impose and sustain their meta-narratives of meaning through the media, politics, the economy and schooling. The alternative is knowledge as execution concerned with particular skills and understanding, which render the "master patterns" of power and influence unproblematic.

The principles of control embedded in the subject-based curriculum are supported by the pedagogy and the more general patterns of learning and relationships between teacher and pupil. Collectively, these form "the hidden curriculum" characterised by pupils learning in a predominantly passive way as opposed to an active critical engagement with the concepts underlying the information they receive. The learning process is predominantly competitive with co-operation a residual practice only. This is also reflected in an examination system that assesses individual performance only and places a premium on recall of facts and information in written form as opposed to oral presentations. Learning takes place in a context that assumes acceptance of authority for successful learning. The strong hierarchical distinction between teacher and pupil in a subject-based curriculum means that any serious consideration of individual pupil opinion is delayed until the novice learner is initiated into the subject when, it is assumed, the learner can make an informed judgement based on acceptance into the body of subject experts. This is also the point at which the deep structure of the subjects and their inherent uncertainty is revealed and a comprehensive knowledge of the meta-narratives of power that control the direction of politics, the economy, the culture of ideas and understanding of our human condition become apparent. More radically, such knowledge and the power elites that it supports contains the means of their transformation as former certainties of the school curriculum are exposed to informed critical evaluation and the intellectual basis of power and the structures that support it are revealed as transitory. Bernstein (1971) argues that in its strongest form the subject curriculum is a form of alienation for pupils through its imposition of certainty and through a relationship that discounts pupils' contribution until very late in the learning process. The fact of its continuing strength as the organising principle for the National Curriculum, he argues, is an indication of the extent to which the underlying structure of our society remains "mechanical" in Durkheim's terms. In other words, pupils' access to the type of knowledge that gives insights to power and eventually its exercise is largely "fixed" by socio-economic class, gender, and, in Northern Ireland, religion and ethnicity.

Curriculum Reform as Contestation

It would be wrong, however, to assume that the predominance of the traditional academic curriculum has not been challenged as part of more general social and economic changes whose central ideological core is equity. As educational reform gathered pace in the 1950s and 1960s in terms of the abolition of selection and the introduction of comprehensive schools in response to more general policies of equal opportunity, the predominance of the subject-based curriculum began to be questioned on both philosophical and vocational grounds. Vocationally, it was argued that an education consisting of separate compartmentalised subjects was a poor way of preparing children for the problems they met which usually required a multidisciplinary approach. Philosophically, this was reflected in criticisms of Hirst's (1974) view of a curriculum of discrete forms of knowledge logically separate from commonsense and received wisdom or prejudices used to organise and interpret experience of everyday life. Knowledge in this sense takes us beyond and liberates from the morally and intellectual restricting pressures of the world and gives us the concepts and principles through which we can deal with the multitude of facts and information that daily bombards us. To be educated in this way enables us to distinguish fact from propaganda, to question, in an informed way, the claims made by our political leaders as they seek our approval for policies or our votes at election time.

Criticism of this view of knowledge as a curriculum framework is that for some subjects there is too great an assumption of separateness between everyday life and subject knowledge (Pring, 1995). This is perhaps more so in the case of the humanities and social sciences than in mathematics and the physical and biological sciences. Scientists, however, in response to public awareness and disquiet about the ethical dilemmas of exploiting foetal tissue and cells necessary for the development of future medical advance have begun a "charm offensive" in an attempt to publicise their work through newspapers and magazines in order to allay the public's fears that Huxley's "Brave New World" is not just round the corner. This is especially so in the case of gene therapy, which its advocates argue will eliminate a range of diseases that are currently incurable, due to faulty genes. In order to allay public apprehension about the necessity of foetal research, scientists have responded with high-quality popularisations of their work through television such as the BBC "Horizon" series and in the broadsheet newspapers. Their neglect of the benefits and disadvantages of genetically modified food has produced overwhelmingly negative feedback from environmental protection groups with frightening images of "Frankenstein food", despite its potential for feeding an increasing proportion of the world's population.

For other subjects in the broad area of the humanities, such as English, the technical requirements of teaching the rules of syntax and grammar are mixed in with the more aesthetic and subjective aspects of the appreciation and evaluation of literature and poetry where there are less clear-cut "rules" although, in respect of literary criticism, there is a language and a range of conventions concerning literary judgements. The annual literary competitions such as Booker and Whitbread prizes for best novel and the disputes that arise about winners and losers point to less agreement than might otherwise have been assumed. It seems reasonable to argue that the insight afforded by the study of religion, history, geography and literature complement yet refine and heighten everyday experience of the world and lead to a deeper understanding of more general interpretations of our common human condition.

It is more difficult to argue a similar case with respect to the physical and biological sciences and the various branches of mathematics. In these subjects, knowledge is some distance from common sense. Small particle physics and much of genetic theory is at odds with ordinary experiences of matter and our bodies. However, both subjects have been spectacularly successful in their application, especially in the case of biological science. Perhaps physicists' involvement in the arms industry has led to a less benign view of their discoveries; they omitted to tell us of the risks involved in the development of nuclear power until Chernobyl suddenly brought them home to us. In science the use of mathematics as its "lingua franca" is surely necessary in the context of the highly abstract models used and which are needed if the new knowledge is to be sought and generated. There is a tension, therefore, between more esoteric aspects of a discipline and initiation into subject disciplines where connection with students' life experiences are often ignored in favour of a discipline's integrity.

Knowing That, Knowing How

A central criticism of the subject-based curriculum is the concentration on knowing that something is the case at the expense of the wider range of knowledge embedded in the skills used in everyday life. Much of the criticism arises from the creation of more practical knowledge which has been included in the curriculum. In these newer forms of knowledge, distinction between "knowing that" and "knowing how" is not as clear as in the traditional academic subjects, such as personal and social education, careers education, health education and economic awareness, all of which are intended to give pupils a greater range of social, personal and employment skills. Personal and social education (PSE), for example, is informed by psychology and sociology but it is quite different in form and presentation from A-level psychology or sociology. The difference arises from the different aims of the teachers involved. In PSE the application of psychology and sociology is as important as any reference to theory, whereas in the A-level course, application is a residual aspect of its presentation only. A further criticism of the academic curriculum is that it has been open to one dominant form of assessment — testing by written individual examination — and that much of acquired knowledge remains inert afterwards. The status of knowledge and its assessment has also tended to devalue other applied areas of knowledge and the skills that are used. This has also led to an underestimation of the knowledge base on which practitioners draw for competence in their work.

A more vocational curriculum ethic is evident now also in the reform of A-level syllabuses as a consequence of a series of Dearing reports (1996) that were critical of an overcrowded curriculum. A central element of A-levels will be what are called "key skills". There are six of these: the three core skills of communication, application of number and information technology will be assessed at four levels of competence in addition to a portfolio. Students may take a further three at level five: problem-solving, managing own learning and working with other people. These six elements will be offered as a separate Key Skills qualification. The

Key Skills component is part of a wider reform of the way in which A-levels are to be taught. Instead of the former pattern of linear single-subject courses assessed by final examination at the end of two years, the structure will now be modular with students taking three to five "half" A-level modules examined at the end of the first year. In the second year, students will specialise in three of these for a full A-level award. These reforms, while broadening the base of what counts as "knowledge" as legitimised by the curriculum, may continue to perpetuate and protect existing elites, thus preserving inequalities and injustice.

Education for Competence

The reforms of the A-level curriculum reflect a wider vocational narrative that challenges the dichotomy between liberal and vocational approaches to knowledge. I argued above that these two philosophies are often posited as opposing curricular rationales. The liberal ideal stresses intellectual excellence as a means of liberating people to live a full purposeful life and make the best of their talents in pursuit of their aims in life but also in their contribution to the common good through work and as an educated citizen. For proponents of this view, there is often an assumption that everyone agrees on what exactly the common good is, whereas continuing inequalities in health, wealth and employment opportunities suggest that a more critical approach is necessary when considering how the common good is to be achieved and its rewards distributed. The political right often responds that the common good necessarily involves some element of inequality simply because not everyone has the ability to be a High Court judge, although they, like other power elites in society, seem to be remarkably similar in terms of social class and education. Consequently, it is argued by this group that some means of selection is inevitable if educational resources are to be used efficiently.

Intellectual excellence in subject-specific terms has been the chief means of selecting people for strategically important positions. The evidence, however, suggests that social class remains a more significant determinant than ability for recruitment to the various economic and cultural positions of power. Emphasis on intellectual ability as a route to success has had the effect of diminishing the value of vocational and technical education, which is often perceived merely as a form of training. Pring (1995) argues that this is based on a false distinction between theory and practice. The former is associated with abstract thinking; its strength is that it takes people beyond the immediacy of everyday experience. It is liberating in the sense that such an education enables people to understand the principles that underpin these: to discriminate, for example, between fact and propaganda. In curricular terms this tradition has tended to have a baleful effect on some subject teaching more than others. One of the clearest examples is science teaching where emphasis on abstract models and description seem to be proportional to the fear of being associated with anything vocational or technical: only the able need apply seems to be the message. Consequently, the majority of children are denied an understanding of the physical world in which they live; it becomes a series of abstract models presented through three different subjects and often completely separate from pupils' everyday experiences.

There is some irony in this approach to science, since it is these subjects that are used chiefly in the training of doctors. Competent clinicians will harness science in the diagnosis of illness in the sense that it will be embedded in their observation and treatment of patients. This enables the doctors to have ongoing reflective conversations between accumulated experience of patients and also their scientific knowledge. Given the pace of medical advances, this sort of reflection must now be at a premium for competent practice. The emphasis on combining abstract thinking with competent performance is the rationale behind the courses offered by the National Council for Vocational Qualifications. The General National Vocational Qualification (GNVQ) is currently offered at three levels: foundation (one year full-time and equivalent to four GCSEs at grades D–G); intermediate (one year full-time and equivalent to four GCSEs at grades A–C); and advanced (two years full-time and equivalent to two A-levels). The latter courses can be mixed with AS and other NVQ units. They have proved to be the most popular as far as schools and colleges are concerned and are presented by the Qualifications and Curriculum Authority as a vocational A-level. The most popular courses offered currently are business studies, construction, engineering and health studies. In Northern Ireland these are confined mostly to the further education colleges and non-selective secondary schools.

The GNVQ has not made any significant inroads into the selective grammar schools, which is part of the courses' wider problems of low uptake by able pupils and low completion rates: currently about 42 per cent of those taking the courses. More positively, the GNVQ has been successful in its acceptance by universities as an entrance qualification as an equivalent to A-levels and also in the more general context of the university sector wishing to widen access by attracting more students from non-traditional backgrounds. The most comprehensive survey of GNVQ provision provided by Wolff (1997) concluded that the qualification had suffered from some degree of "mission drift" in so far as it had become more general and had lost a good deal of its specific focus as a preparation for employment. The report concludes:

> At one level they have been a success. Centres have adopted them, and students have enrolled on them; they are a major component of post 16 study for full timers and they offer a route for progression from GCSE to higher education.

More critically the report adds:

> There are, nonetheless, major areas for concern. Dropout rates are high, GNVQs are predominantly educational rather than vocational qualifications, conceptualised in terms of a 21st century economy . . . many students are offered only a very narrow choice of programme. (Wolff, 1997, p. 118)

CONCLUSION

In a post-industrial society, to what extent can the subject-based curriculum meet the needs of future generations of children? The current curriculum reflects a modernist rationale in so far as it is based on meta-narratives of rational social and economic progress and is underpinned by intellectual and moral universals. The violent history of the twentieth century, as the outcome of eighteenth-century Enlightenment-derived narratives, has engendered widespread scepticism about the virtues of rationalism and the usefulness of such an approach in the face of unrestrained global capitalism. Critics now argue that such developments have produced widespread social and economic dislocation in the movement of refugees from the impoverished south to the work-rich north and the growth of fundamentalist religions and ethnic ideologies as a means of preserving a cultural identity in the face of the economic and cultural colonising effects of American and European capitalism. Such developments are also symptomatic of the weakening of national boundaries and identities caused by the globalisation of production and new forms of identity free of the limitations of nation states. Modernist schooling has been criticised by Foucault (see Ball, 1995) as aimed at producing "docile bodies" whose oppression comes from national systems of bureaucratic schooling bearing down on individuals. The disciplinary power of schools, factories, hospitals and offices are, he argues, all designed to bring us under greater control.

Postmodern society demands flexibility and the ability to reinvent ourselves as former certainties disappear and traditional foundations for creating a sense of self alter radically. The current curriculum, focused on certainty derived from meta-narratives of rationality and ideas of ordered progress, appears to be stuck in time. The compression of time and space implicit in information technology means that knowledge is instantly available to pupils and has potential to render redundant the teacher's position as a subject authority. Analysis presented here suggests that the curriculum and the authority structure it engenders are remnants of the requirements of mass education of the nineteenth century with its emphasis on hierarchical power relationships in the management of schools and classrooms and the continuation of paternalism. Post-industrial society is demanding newer more adaptable skills for citizenship and work, which places a premium on our ability to find and use appropriate sources of information rather than the more passive model of a curriculum embodying clear roles for teacher and taught; where pupils are active in knowledge creation. This is also the case with the current predominance of the individualist and competitive pattern of assessment in the current curriculum. Changing patterns of work appear to demand greater group and networking skills as the economy shifts from a mainly manufacturing base to service industries.

References

Ball, S.J. (1995), *Foucault and Education*, London: Routledge.

Bernstein, B. (1971), "On the Framing and Classification of Educational Knowledge", in Young, M., (ed.) *Knowledge and Control*, London: Macmillan, p. 51.

Bernstein, B. (1975), *Class, Codes and Control*, London: Routledge and Kegan Paul.

Bourdieu, P. and Passeron, J. (1977), *Reproduction in Education, Society and Culture*, London: Sage.

Darby, J. (1987), "Segregated Schooling: The Research Evidence", in Osborne, R.D., Cormack, R.J., and Miller, R.L., *Education and Policy in Northern Ireland*, Belfast: Policy Research Institute, pp. 38–54.

Dearing, R. (1996), *Review of Qualifications for 16–19 Year Olds, Summary Report*, Middlesex: SCAA Publications.

Fitzgibbon, C. (1999), "The Work of OFSTED, Fourth report Vol. 1", Report and Proceedings Parliamentary Select Committee on Education and Employment.

Foucault, M. (1967), *Madness and Civilization*, London: Tavistock.

Goldthorpe, J.H. (1997), "Problems of Meritocracy", in Halsey, A., Lauder, H., Brown, P. and Stuart Wells, A., *Education, Culture, Economy, Society,* Oxford: Oxford University Press.

Hirst, P. (1974), *Knowledge and the Curriculum,* London: Routledge and Kegan Paul.

Labov, W. (1972), *Sociolinguistic Patterns,* Philadelphia: University of Philadelphia Press.

Peters, R.S. (1966), *Ethics and Education,* London: Allen and Unwin.

Pring, R. (1995), *Affirming the Comprehensive Ideal,* London: Falmer Press.

Wolff, A. (1997), *GNVQs 1993–1997A National Survey,* London, Further Education Development Unit, Institute of Education University of London and the Nuffield Foundation.

SECTION THREE

PRIMARY CURRICULUM REVISIONS: IRISH PERSPECTIVES

Chapter 6

WHOSE CURRICULUM IS IT ANYWAY? POWER, POLITICS AND POSSIBILITIES IN THE CONSTRUCTION OF THE REVISED PRIMARY CURRICULUM

Ciaran Sugrue

Never before has the success, perhaps even the survival, of nations and people been so tightly tied to their ability to learn. Consequently, our future depends now, as never before, on our ability to learn. (Darling-Hammond, 1997, p. 2)

INTRODUCTION*

Commentators suggest that education is already at the top of the agendas of national governments (Riley, 2000); "the times they are a changing" and schools, teaching and curricula need to be altered, amended, revised or radically changed to reflect these changed and changing circumstances. But, as Tyack and Cuban (1995, p. 8) indicate, "Educational reforms are intrinsically political in origin." The politics and power relations around schooling in Ireland are often

* I am particularly grateful to the following for their helpful comments on earlier versions of this chapter: Mark Morgan and Jimmy Kelly (St Patrick's College), Gary Granville (NCAD, Dublin), Pádraig Ó Donnabháin (DES), Jim Gleeson (UL) and John Owen (Melbourne University and visiting scholar at OISEUT).

invisible, and particularly in the past decade when a consensual, partnership approach to policy formulation and curricular innovation has been privileged, practised and lauded (Government of Ireland, 1995; Coolahan, 1994). In such circumstances it is more difficult to appreciate that "Groups organize and contest with other groups in the politics of education to express their values and to secure their interests in the public school" (Tyack and Cuban, 1995, p. 8). To understand the existing order of things, therefore, it is necessary to undertake an archeology of reform, and recent reforms of the primary curriculum are no different in this respect than any other concerns that signal departures from tradition or established curricular and pedagogical orthodoxies.

The focus of this chapter is the power relations surrounding recent reform of the "revised" primary curriculum that was disseminated to all primary schools in September 1999. There are three major purposes for undertaking this task:

1. To trace the lineage of the revised curriculum by undertaking a critical analysis of its finished documents and supporting reports to identify the manner in which political power relations have shaped the final product; new departures and shifts in emphasis will be identified also in addition to significant omissions.

2. To construct and to model a way of undertaking such a task that may be useful to others who engage in similar exercises; to provide a "set of thinking tools" (Bourdieu, 1989, p. 50) that could be utilised by practitioners and others as a means of self-empowerment.

3. The macro analysis undertaken here can be made more complete and comprehensive by more detailed and fine-grained scrutiny of the process and substance of the reform, something that is necessary throughout the implementation phase.

This chapter, then, may be regarded as an initial map and mapping of the substance and process of primary curriculum reform over the past two decades, but particularly the decade of the

1990s. It is intended to contribute to the field of critical debate in education and to encourage others also to position themselves within the field and to have their voices heard.

This agenda gains in significance for three reasons. One, despite unprecedented change that has been accelerating in scope and intensity, in the number of reports on aspects of the education system and policy documents, there has been relatively little discussion about primary schooling, its goals and pedagogies. In democratic societies, education and schooling are everyone's responsibility, not just policy elites or teachers and their representatives. Consequently, promoting ongoing dialogue about the nature and purpose of primary curricula and schooling is a requirement in a more open, pluralist and (hopefully) more democratic Ireland. Two, due to the postmodern condition of uncertainty, unpredictability and unprecedented possibilities (see Hargreaves, 1994; Giddens, 1991) as well as market forces and globalisation (see Beck, 2000), economic concerns have gained heightened significance in an open economy such as Ireland's. Curricula and the routines of schools and classrooms cannot be inured from such wider socioeconomic forces. As a result, their influences, both positive and negative, need to be articulated and understood as part of the power relations and politics of educational reform. These new conditions of schooling present choices that, in turn, require decision-making. It is necessary to identify the key values, beliefs, knowledge and power positions that shape and influence education policies and practice.

The chapter is in four parts. First, the language of reform, structures, policies and contexts are identified and briefly outlined. Second, theoretical perspectives are discussed as a means of framing subsequent analysis and institutions and players are identified as a means of contextualising and situating this analysis. Third, a detailed and in-depth archeology of the reform process is undertaken. Fourth, the concluding discussion offers an assessment of emergent power relations through the reform process and identifies implications for the substance and process of reform for policy, practice and research in the immediate and mid-term future.

LANGUAGE OF REFORM:
STRUCTURES, POLICIES AND CONTEXTS

The terminology used, and by whom, when referring to re-fashioning the existing child-centred curriculum is very revealing. The official term used to refer to the documentation delivered to schools in September 1999 is "revised". Chambers' (1993) definition of the term "revise" is: "to examine and correct; to make a new, improved version of; to study anew; to look at again." What such definitions do not reveal is whether or not revisions are major or minor, but they do open up the possibility that there are advocates for revision, those who are relatively neutral and those who are opposed. Consequently, it is necessary not only to identify the revisions that are evident in the documentation, but also to trace their lineage by identifying the players in the process, their institutional affiliations and their positioning within the field of primary education. Collectively, those with responsibility for the revised curriculum were to "look again" at what had been espoused policy since 1971. My task is to identify key influences that shaped their thinking and wider socio-economic forces that intruded and became inscribed in the outcomes over the decade of the 1990s.

Reform is deemed more significant than revision in the sense that the former includes "to transform; to restore, rebuild; to amend; to make better; to remove defects from" (Chambers, 1993). The possibility of major revisions notwithstanding, the term "revised" suggests "fine-tuning" rather than radical overhaul, tinkering rather than root-and-branch reform. While the purveyors of the 1999 curriculum have been consistently careful to speak of revisions, is this a covert language for more substantial reforms that remain unarticulated due to power relations within the system?

Distinctions and difference in emphasis are detectable depending on the players who use the terminology. In the Foreword penned by the Minister of the day, it states: "The introduction into schools of the *Primary School Curriculum* is a significant landmark in the history of primary education in Ireland" (1999a, p. *vi*) suggesting that such a "historical landmark" is more than a revision or fine-tuning of its predecessor (Department of Education, 1971). Yet, on the opposite page, there appears to be both agreement and disagreement being voiced by the chairperson, when she states: "The introduction of a revised primary curriculum is . . . a significant educational development." She continues that "this revision" has included taking cognisance of developments in the junior post-primary cycle and that "The revised curriculum also incorporates new content and embraces new approaches and methodologies" (p. *vii*). At the heart of official thinking, therefore, there appears to be ambiguity, if not disagreement, about the amount of continuity and change envisaged in the revised documents. For example, the Minister's piece concludes that this documentation "is an exciting opportunity for change and renewal in primary schools", while the introduction to the 1999 curriculum, written by an NCCA insider, sounds a more ambitious and far-reaching note for the documentation, where it states that the Primary Curriculum Review Body Report (PCRB, 1990) provided the "basis for the *redesign* and *restructuring* that is presented in this curriculum" (p. 2, emphasis mine). Granville's comments in response to an earlier version of this text suggests, I think, that the politics of reform frequently dictate that this ambiguity be retained, even for the same audience on occasion. He says:

> There has always been an ambiguity about the scale and ambition of the NCCA work, depending on the audience. I remember going around the country in the early days of the Junior Certificate, saying two things, often simultaneously: "this is the most significant breakthrough in educational change" and "sure, this is no problem, you'll all be able to handle this just like ye did the old Inter. . . ". (Granville, personal correspondence, November, 2001)

The range and depth of planned change appears ambiguous and alters with an individual's location in two senses: who they are as individuals, the gradient of their career trajectory and where they position themselves in relation to educational matters, as well as their institutional affiliation and location, as union member,

Department of Education and Science inspector, seconded teacher, NCCA employee. This is tacit evidence (at least) that power, position and capital shape policy.

Structures and Context

There are important structural differences between the processes employed to produce the 1971 and the 1999 curricula respectively. The former was the work of a small group of primary inspectors, and criticism was made at the time of the lack of consultation with teachers (McDonagh, 1969). Several subsequent documents reiterate and reinforce a *de facto* situation that the inspectorate had responsibility for "developing curricula" while teachers' responsibility was to implement what they designed. This scenario pertained until the establishment of the Curriculum and Examinations Board, the precursor to the NCCA. The OECD report comments in the following terms in relation to this new body in Irish education:

> The establishment of the National Council for Curriculum and Assessment is the most important innovation in recent years, since it can provide the means whereby a national approach to the curriculum of both primary and secondary levels can be adopted. . . . (1991, p. 66)

The report continues, however, that "There is much to be done" because "the necessary infrastructure for system-wide curriculum development has to be systematically built up, a task requiring both better co-ordination of existing agencies and the installation of new structures (1991, p. 66). These comments are quite explicit: in order to advance the cause of curriculum development nationally, new structures were required.

Curriculum

The term curriculum has been much defined in seminal or classic works by, for example, Stenhouse (1975) and Eisner (1979, 1992). It is rather surprising that, despite its pervasive use through official documentation, even a working definition is not provided.

However, as Granville has made clear, the operational definition used by the NCCA was appropriated from an earlier CEB document (*Issues and Structures*, 1984) and regarded curriculum as "simple and all-embracing" (personal correspondence). Nevertheless, it would be useful to be provided with a "working definition". Increasingly, definitions have become more inclusive, thus embracing the official and unofficial, the formal and informal routines and rituals of schools and schooling, with increasing awareness also that, due to greater permeability of boundaries between school and community, the external climate and more general socio-cultural and economic milieu have considerable shaping influence on what transpires in classrooms. Despite the importance of conceptual boundaries typically supplied by definitions, it may be more productive in the present context to focus on various means of framing curricula and their underlying epistemological assumptions, beliefs and values while locating child-centred curriculum within this framework.

THEORETICAL PERSPECTIVES

This section is in two parts. First, five frameworks, perspectives or orientations towards curriculum design are briefly outlined. Second, a framework for examining power relations within systems is articulated. Both frameworks are a necessary means of surfacing deep structures and power relations in the process of reform, thus indicating the dominant shaping influences, and as a means of signaling possible lines for future directions.

Curriculum Frameworks

Borrowing from Eisner's work in particular, the diagram below provides a brief summary of five dominant orientations or value stances towards curriculum design.

Table 6.1: Five Orientations and Their Priorities

Cognitive Processes	Academic Rationalism	Personal Relevance	Social Adaptation/ Reconstruction	Technology
Learn how to learn: emphasis on process rather than content	Exposure to the "canon" of cultural achievement to develop reason	Learners' interests and needs should be incorporated into curriculum	Meet the needs of society or seek to transform it	Curriculum can be reduced to means-end, measurable; accountable

Source: This figure is an adaptation of Eisner, 1979, pp. 50–73

Since these orientations are already familiar to many, they need not detain us here. Yet, they are significant because each is under-pinned by a basic set of beliefs. Progressive or child-centred teaching is frequently located within the personal relevance perspective but it may also contain elements of cognitive processing and academic rationalism with varying degrees of social adaptation and reconstruction, while in several contexts the technology of testing and performance indicators is becoming increasingly pervasive with negative consequences for teacher and student learning (see McNeil, 2000).

These orientations are unlikely to exist in pure form. Understood as a spectrum or continuum of orientations that have different emphases, they become a useful lens through which reform efforts can be analysed and positioned as a means of identifying influences and emphases. Collectively, they reinforce a view that curriculum "is a social artifact, conceived of and made for deliberate human purposes" and is thus the "most manifest of human constructions" (Goodson, 1994, p. 18). Whatever its underlying assumptions, there are three dimensions to curriculum as it is enacted in schools by teachers and experienced by students: some things are explicitly taught; others are caught incidentally and informally as a consequence of what is explicitly intended — the "hidden curriculum" (Lynch, 1989); and there is what Eisner calls the "NUL" curriculum, what is excluded. As will emerge below, the rhetoric of progressivism has been retained, rehabilitated even, but with some

important shifts in emphasis with significance for future teaching orientations and teacher professional development.

It is neither possible nor appropriate to isolate the social dynamics of educational reform from wider cultural and economic influences or structural relations. Consequently, an additional frame of reference is necessary also that provides a means by which power relations can be brought to the surface and made more transparent as integral to the politics of reform.

Power, Players, Positions

In addition to developing a theoretical lens through which to analyse critically the reforms and the reformers, it is necessary also to map the field of primary education so that the dynamics of the power relations, often invisible, are more apparent and more adequately understood. Bourdieu makes this point when he states: "we cannot grasp the dynamics of a field if not by a synchronic analysis of its structure" while adequate understanding of such a structure needs "a historical, . . . genetic analysis of its constitution and of the tensions that exist between positions in it, as well as between this field and other fields, and especially the field of power" (Bourdieu and Wacquant, 1992, p. 90). For Bourdieu, this entails a "structural history" which documents "each successive state of the structure under examination, both the product of previous struggles to maintain or to transform this structure, and . . . [its] subsequent transformations" (p. 91). His framework is particularly apposite to the analysis undertaken here as it provides a means of documenting over time the manner in which power relations within the field of primary education have evolved, thus shaping the revised curriculum in significant ways. In addition to outlining Bourdieu's framework, the remainder of this section contextualises it within the field of primary education in Ireland, thus illuminating the context by identifying features of its structural history.

Three key terms and concepts are central to Bourdieu's "tools for thinking": *habitus*, *capital* and *field*. Though each element contributes to a "way of seeing" the world (Berger, 1972), they are part of a dynamic interactive whole. He states that "to think in terms of a field is to think *relationally*" (Bourdieu and Wacquant, 1992, p. 96). Consequently, to analyse a field is to describe "the state of relations of force between players [and] . . . the structures of the field, while these set of relations also determine the structure of a particular field" (1992, p. 99). It is particularly difficult to set firm boundaries to a given field, and many fields intersect in a variety of relational ways. For example, primary schooling may be understood as a separate field from curriculum reform, and curriculum as a related sub-set. My preference is to understand the field of curriculum as constitutive of primary education with inadequately defined boundaries in terms of where influence ceases or commences as part of the field of relations.

Within any particular field, there are a number of "agents", each bringing a particular "capital" or expertise to the situation. Bourdieu suggests that there are different kinds of capital in fields such as economic, cultural, social and symbolic. In the field under investigation here each of the players on NCCA (subject) committees and NCCA staff bring a particular capital to the table. However, what they bring to the situation is shaped by the structure of the field and their own positioning within it. Consequently, the players or agents in the politics and power relations of reform cannot be divorced from the organisations or structures in the field to which they have allegiance or affiliation. For this reason, he suggests that one of the functions of the research process necessary for analysing a particular field is to "map out the objective structure of the relations between the positions occupied by the agents or institutions who compete for the legitimate form of specific authority of which this field is the site" (Bourdieu and Wacquant, 1992, p. 105). However, it is the field rather than the agents "which is primary and must be the focus of the research operations" (p. 107).

Not everybody engaged in primary schooling has been an agent in the production of the revised curriculum. Consequently, it may be asked, how does one become an agent? Bourdieu argues that part of the challenge of the research process is to identify the "forms of specific capital" that agents possess to legitimise their entry. His response to this question is to suggest that "People are at once founded and legitimised to enter the field by their possessing a definite configuration of properties" (1992, p. 107). Because the reform process in the Irish context espouses a "partnership" approach (Ireland, Government of, 1995), an important element of agents' "capital" is affiliation to an institution such as a college or university, an organisation such as the Department of Education and Science, National Parents' Council or trade union. A striking illustration of this phenomenon is presented in the revised curriculum documents. Membership of the various subject committees that drafted documents are invariably identified by their respective institutional/organisational affiliation, which suggests that affiliation is a significant element of the "capital" that the various players bring to the curriculum game.

The glue that binds a particular field is power, and relations are shaped by a variety of factors. Bourdieu describes the field of power relations in the following terms:

> The field of power is a field of forces defined by the structure of the existing balance of forces between . . . different species of capital. . . . It is a space of play and competition in which the social agents and institutions which all possess the determinate quantity of special capital (economic and cultural capital in particular) sufficient to occupy the dominant positions within their respective fields. At any one time within a field, what is happening is "a *division of the work of domination*". (1992, p. 76, n. 16)

Only agents with the requisite capital become major players in the power politics of reform. Throughout, these agents are engaged in "struggles to transform or preserve these fields of forces. And the relation, practical or reflective, that agents entertain with the game is part and parcel of the game and may be at the basis of its transformation" (Bourdieu, 1982: 46, in Bourdieu and Wacquant, 1992, p. 101, n. 52).

Players in the reform game do not act in a vacuum. Their "habitus" is a vital element of this dynamic. Habitus is fundamentally about individual posture or stance within a particular field, but this too is relationally determined as "socialised subjectivity" where there is mutual simultaneous shaping between individual and field (1992, pp. 121–2). Consequently, my teaching experience or membership of the inspectorate or teacher union will bear on my habitus to the extent that "when habitus encounters a social world of which it is the product, it is like a 'fish in water': it does not feel the weight of the water and it takes the world about itself for granted" (p. 128). However, it is not simply a matter of identifying an agent's own positioning within the field as a means of unlocking its inner power relations, for not all actors are simply pre-programmed by the field. Rather, he suggests that the reality is messier and the dynamics do "not imply that all small capital holders are necessarily revolutionaries and all big capital holders are automatically conservatives" (1992, p. 109). It may even be the case that at different times and on different occasions agents can defend the status quo or seek to transform it. As Bourdieu suggests, in each field within what he terms "the structure of social space" there is "its dominant and its dominated, its struggles for usurpation and exclusion, its mechanisms of reproduction . . ." (p. 106). Because the actors are "fish in water" and take the milieu largely for granted, it is necessary to expose its contours so that shaping influences of product, milieu, actors, their habitus and capital become more visible, thus constructing a social history of the reform endeavour that captures its dynamic relational nature.

Actors' behaviour is shaped also by career trajectories which add to the dynamics of the reform process. For example, members of NCCA committees who subsequently found employment in the inspectorate or in Colleges of Education may have acted differently to seconded colleagues who returned to classrooms and continue to retain membership of the INTO, while the fact that education officers were seconded classroom teachers working (on contract) for the NCCA may have ensured that their parent affiliation exercised more influence over their habitus than would be the case if they were permanent employees. Granville indicates that this point is crucial, and one to which the NCCA was initially oblivious while the INTO, much more than its post-primary counterparts, was astute in realising its significance. Having been politically outmanoeuvred, NCCA personnel acquiesced in this "uncontested development" (Granville, personal correspondence). Bourdieu's framework provides a timely wake-up call that reveals the importance of the structure of power relations, the agency of actors and their habitus as integral to the shaping of the revised curriculum.

AN ARCHAEOLOGY OF THE REVISED CURRICULUM

As already indicated, the authors of the 1971 curriculum were a small group of primary inspectors who consulted with colleagues, some practitioners and colleges of education personnel, while creation of the NCCA represents a major structural alteration to these earlier power relations (see OECD, 1991). It is legitimate to ask, therefore, in what ways are these major structural alternations to the field of power manifest in the revised curriculum documentation, in a changed context where a "partnership" approach is official policy (Ireland, Government of, 1995) and reflected in recent legislation (Education Bill, 1998).

For the purpose of the analysis, it is neither possible nor practical to deal with all of the documents that were disseminated to schools in September 1999. Two subject areas are selected as being both illustrative and representative of the process generally. These subjects are a "traditional" (3Rs) subject and a "new" subject that is an addition to the previous programme: English and Social, Personal and Health Education (SPHE) respectively. The manner in which the process of reform was played out during the decade of the 1990s was through "partnership" representation on a series of (subject) committees. Table 6.2 documents the membership of these committees and individuals' institutional affiliations and the evidence is scrutinised for evidence of the structural shifts in power relations just described.

Two comments are necessary and appropriate as illumination and clarification on the content of Table 6.2. In the case of all committees, chairpersons were elected from within by the membership. Thus, they were answerable to the members in a way that

Table 6.2: Committee Membership: English and SPHE

Players/ Representatives	English	SPHE	Institutional Affiliation
Chairperson(s)	2 (2M)	1 (F)	Irish National Teachers' Organisation (INTO)
Advisers/ Education Officers	2/2* (3M/1F)	2/1** (3F)	NCCA/INTO/Colleges of Education
Inspectors	3 (2M/1F)	2 (2M)	Department of Education & Science (DES)
Teachers	6 (2M/4F)	3 1M/2F)	INTO
Parents	2 (2F)	2 (1M/1F)	National Parents' Council (NPC)
Teacher Educators	2 (2M)	1 (1M)	Irish Federation of University Teachers (IFUT)
Management/ Teacher Educators	2 (1M/1F)	1 (1M)	Management of Colleges of Education
Representative/ Management	2 (2M)	1 (1F)	Church of Ireland Board of Education
Teacher Rep	2*** (1M/1F)	1 (1F)	Association of Teaching Brothers/Primary Teaching Sisters
Representative/ Managerial body	2 (2F)	1 (1F)	Catholic Primary School Managers' Association (CPSMA)

*Two Education officers, two co-opted advisers

** There were two Ed. Officers up to 1996, one thereafter.

*** It is not evident from the information if one of these individuals replaced the other, in which case there would be one rather than two representatives.

might not be the case had they been chosen in another manner and this too may underscore their affiliation. The appointment of Education Officers, on the other hand, "was carried out through a mysterious process of informal consultations, notably with the INTO and the department". Granville reflects that their appointment was "a more independent" process in the days of the CEB.

Nevertheless, he feels that education officers should be distinguished from regular committee members because they possess a "unique non-voting role" and though "part of the NCCA executive" some "remained visibly union-oriented" while "others were more consciously NCCA focused". He notes that with "only a few exceptions" (drawn from Teacher Education) the officers were members of the INTO (Granville, personal correspondence, 2001). The temporary nature of NCCA contracts may have been significant in determining individual stance.

Some committee members were "boundary spanners": individuals nominated as representative of a particular institution or organisation with claims also to particular expertise, thus wearing a number of hats. This may be the case for members of both committees. This table, therefore, does not do justice to the complexity and collective expertise of the committees but it does provide evidence of the representational nature of these groups. It is clear that teachers were very well represented and occupied the key positions of chair and adviser in each case. When the two committees are combined, the number of females marginally outnumbers males: 22 females and 21 males. However, there is considerable variation between the two committees. On the English committee, there were 15 males and 12 females, while on the SPHE committee, this pattern is reversed: 10 females and 6 males. Is this evidence that a "new" and "caring" (Noddings, 1992) subject is perceived as being the domain of females or is it more likely to be an issue of subject status (Goodson, 1994) or the gendered nature of curriculum and reform (Datnow, 2000)? These issues are worthy of further analysis at another time as integral to the dynamics and micro-politics of reform (Blasé, 1998).

Much has been learned in the intervening decades since 1971 about the inadequacies of top-down rational linear planned change that indicates the necessity for teachers to be participants in the reform rather than mere cogs in the implementation process (Fullan, 1991; Tyack and Cuban, 1995; Cuban, 1993). The then leader of the primary teachers' union declared in an editorial immediately after the revised curriculum was distributed to schools that it was "their" (teachers') curriculum, and because it was theirs it would be implemented. He states:

> Unlike the 1971 Curriculum, this one was produced by the NCCA through subject committees that were driven, guided and influenced by working teachers. We are not implementing the new curriculum "for the DES". We are doing it because teachers demanded it, teachers designed it and because teachers have decided that this is the best way forward for their pupils. (O'Toole, 1999, editorial)

In what appears to be an almost complete reversal of roles played prior to 1971, he asks rhetorically: "are there INTO members who really believe that the Department [DES] could ever produce anything as dynamic and as progressive as the revised Curriculum?" Substantiating the claims made in these two short passages is not the purpose of this chapter. Rather, it is to map the route traveled and to identify the major compass readings along the way, from a political, policy and power perspective, in addition to locating the content of the reforms within the curriculum frameworks outlined above. As a first step in this act of archeological reconstruction, it is necessary to begin with the impetus for reform.

Impetus for Reforms

The Primary Curriculum Review Body Report (PCRB, 1990) is acknowledged repeatedly in the introduction to the revised curriculum as a key starting point for the reform process throughout the decade (Government of Ireland, 1999a). It states:

> The Primary School Curriculum marks the development of a process that has evolved since the publication of the Report of the Review Body on the Primary Curriculum through the passing of the Education Act in 1998. (Introduction, 1999, p. 74)

This gives rise to three pertinent questions: what was being said at the time of departure, what has evolved during the decade of gestation, and where have the influences come from? Five years prior to the completion of this report, a Curriculum and Examinations

Board (CEB) publication called for a thorough and systematic review of the primary curriculum, its principles and practices. In the
appendix to its discussion document it states:

> Because of the relatively large areas still unresearched, it is dif-
> ficult to get any overview of actual practices in classrooms, of
> national standards of attainment, of teacher effectiveness, or of
> the suitability of the curriculum. (CEB, 1985, p. 40)

While some additional research became available in the intervening years, these observations are still sustainable, and testify to the
lack of evidence about the system, particularly in relation to the
dynamics of classroom life.

There are two additional reasons why the PCRB report gains
in significance. One of these was provided by an insider to the
process of agreeing the content of the PCRB report. My informant
suggested that there was difficulty finding a common language to
which everyone would subscribe. Consequently, in order to keep
participants on board, it was necessary to state things in rather
general and neutral language. A retelling of this perspective suggests that the nature of power relations were such that finding
agreement meant finding a neutral if not entirely sanitised language. With the benefit of hindsight, my second informant argues
that the report served an important purpose:

> . . . the Quinlan Report[1] on the primary curriculum (1990)
> [PCRB] was the critical moment in the revised curriculum
> process. Not just because of its overall recommendations but
> because embryonic battles were stifled in the course of that re-
> view — "back-to-basics" and all that. The register of curricu-
> lum discourse was established from that point on, one that
> was already the official register of INTO documents and con-
> ferences and so on. (Granville, personal correspondence)

Both comments indicate that the relationships of "domination"
shifted significantly during the process, some controversial discourses were "stifled", while there was general disappointment,
particularly on the part of major players, that there were two reservations attached to the main report. It is necessary to turn to the

report itself and its terms of reference to identify the "battle lines" that shaped the final document, and how power relations were shaped by and shaped the process.

There were three terms of reference that reflect the particular preoccupations at the time:

1. To analyse the aims and objectives of the 1971 curriculum and establish the extent to which they are being achieved with particular reference to Irish, English and Mathematics. This may have some bearing on the "back to basics" comments above and there was concern also about closer alignment between the senior end of primary schooling and the junior cycle of the post-primary curriculum.

2. The committee was asked to identify various means by which specified objectives could be evaluated and students' progress monitored.

3. They were required to identify additional areas for development and possible strategies for their realisation (PCRB, 1990, p. 109).

The wider context of the time had significance also for these deliberations. During this period the term "fiscal rectitude" became commonplace as the public was warned of the dire consequences of failing to put public finances in order. Consequently, the period of the deliberations did not encourage bold imaginings; Colleges of Education graduates were being recruited by various Councils in England, Carysfort College of Education had been closed, and forecasts for teacher requirements were very bleak (see Sexton, 1990, pp. 129–47). The then Minister for Education (Hussey, 1984–1987) provided a grant to facilitate the establishment of a National Parents' Council. Consequently, parents had a voice at the table during the deliberations in relation to the PCRB and this was a significant breakthrough. This period also reflected an increasing trend by Governments of appointing specialist advisers so that Ministerial nominees began to be appointed also to review groups, something that was reflected in the composition of the review committee.

These wider "trends" indicated a loosening-up of traditional "power blocs" in an attempt to engage in wider dialogue about the nature and purposes of primary education. Despite this tendency, there were more reactionary forces also. For example, a subsequent (Fianna Fáil) Government insisted on committee membership that "reinforced traditional power blocs as representative organisations" thus "rolling back the more independent appointees of the earlier CEB regime" (Granville, personal correspondence, 2001).

The OECD (1991) visiting committee singled out existing structural weaknesses for particular comment. It observed that "It is almost as thought there has been in-built resistance to creating any permanent machinery for facilitating the policy-making process" (OECD, 1991, p. 40). The report pointed to the establishment of the NCCA as indicating "a new awareness of the desirability of establishing a semi-independent advisory body, at least for curricular and assessment purposes" as a very positive development, that would democratise the deliberative process, while creating the possibility that the inspectorate, freed from primary responsibility for curriculum design, would have more time available for strategic planning and policy development. The report stated:

> ... strenuous efforts are required to generate sound strategies and seek consensus about both the need and the directions for change in the most intimate areas of professional life — the organization of the school and the practice of pedagogy. (OECD, 1991, p. 61)

Recently, a member of that visiting committee spelled out this perspective more fully in response to a private query as to what they had in mind in relation to building a consensus about educational reform. The response provides an important "outsider" perspective on power relations within the system, as well as indicating the perceived "shift" in such relations deemed necessary for reform. It reads:

> As for the words in question, you might think of them as reference to two broad, long-term strategies generally favoured by OECD types: loosening the reins of central bureaucracies in

a move toward strategic steering ("deregulation" is a quite inadequate descriptor); developing much stronger forms of
teacher professionalism (not to be confused with traditional
union power which in Ireland as elsewhere is often the other
side of the coin whose face is central bureaucracy). So of
course the consensus we had in mind was to be on a different
basis from the old power-sharing carve-up. We also had in
mind the desirability of wider partnerships than the education
clique. (Personal correspondence, 2001)

Collectively, the original and the much more recent elaboration
indicate that structural changes are a necessity in the process of
reform, that existing power relations need to be altered. It may be
suggested, therefore, that embryonically at least, the composition
of the PCRB committee was already beginning to move away
from traditional power blocs, while the key players, the "fish in
water", continued to be inspectors and teachers as represented by
their union, while there were some additional "swimmers" in this
newly created reform pool also.

Two other factors need to be borne in mind when considering
the major recommendations in the PCRB report (1990). The absence of evidence, particularly observational studies on actual
classroom practice, had been identified five years earlier by the
CEB as a major difficulty in making judgements about the system.
Similarly, the OECD (1991, p. 42) report noted "a dearth of policy-
related research" in the Irish context. Additionally, the report continues: "Data on the performance and quality of educational practice at the school level are not as comprehensive as they could be
and such collections and analyses as are made are either not published at all or are issued years after the event" — all of which, it
is reasonable to conclude, is highly unsatisfactory (p. 62). This
dearth of evidence, particularly in relation to the dynamics of
classroom routines and rituals, shapes both the deliberations and
the recommendations of the PCRB as well as the power relations
between the major players.

What the Evidence Says

Despite the absence of observational studies, and the preponderance of survey evidence from teachers that is self-reported, as well as the perspectives of principals and inspectors, the report conflates what it calls "acceptance and implementation"; it equates teachers' intentions with their actions, their "espoused theories" with their "theories in use" (see Sugrue, 1997; Schon, 1983, 1987). The rhetoric of teachers' responses is accepted as coterminous with classroom practice. Consequently, the report identifies considerable discrepancies between the reported perspectives of inspectors and those of teachers. In the absence of any observational evidence, the process of constructing a report becomes primarily an issue of power relations between two competing perspectives on the health of primary education: the views of the primary inspectorate and those of teachers' representatives.

On the basis of four surveys completed over a period of a decade, and presenting significant variation, the report concludes: "The vast majority of inspectors regard the syllabus as being suitable, while the majority of teachers regard it as unrealistic and demanding excessive expertise" (PCRB, 1990, p. 64). As a consequence of the power plays within deliberations, a very definite trend is identifiable in the Report. Whenever even veiled criticism of teachers and teaching is advanced, it is accompanied by ritual condemnation of structural inadequacies such as school architecture, lack of equipment and resources, as well as inadequate provision for professional development. In the absence of more substantial and appropriate evidence, it becomes more of a battle of wills as to whose perspective will hold sway. While these contextual realities have an inevitable and important shaping influence on the nature and quality of teaching and learning provided, the tendency is that both teaching and learning become less visible, if not entirely invisible, parts of the process of schooling, and structural issues alone are represented as being the key to quality.

In such circumstances, finding a general neutral language can become an end in itself. It is significant that the major players signed up to the final document while two participants included a reservation each. Their comments are a useful means of interpreting the report as a whole, and for gaining further insight into the iterative nature of the deliberative process. These reservations are discussed immediately below.

Power Relations and Dissenting Voices

Murphy[2] (1990, pp. 101–4) was unhappy with the English section while "fully agreeing with the main body of the report" (p. 101). His more general comment in relation to "discovery" is particularly instructive and suggests that there was a collective if understated acceptance that there was currently a "looseness" about the manner in which the "radical" reforms advocated in 1971 had been implemented in the intervening years (Sugrue, 1997; Coolahan, 1981). He argued that the most significant of these revisions is the emphasis on "*directed* discovery as distinct from *free* discovery" which he regards as "a fundamental change in the pedagogic philosophy now being recommended for primary schools" (p. 103). While the author may have exaggerated the overall significance of this particular revision, it seems that he was echoing a kind of truth that had gained acceptance within the inspectorate as well as among more discerning teachers. Aligning these comments with the terms of reference that specifically sought to tighten up objectives that may have been implicit in the Teachers' Handbooks (Department of Education, 1971) and to indicate effective means of evaluating their implementation, is testament in itself that there was at least tacit acceptance that a more rigorous approach to teaching and learning was overdue. In the wake of radical reforms in 1971, there was a *laissez faire* period during which there was greater clarity about being against the rigid, lock-step uniformity that characterised much of primary schooling prior to 1971 than being for a very definite set of "progressive" pedagogies (Sugrue, 1997). Evidence for the truth suggested above can be found in the OECD report where the authors were not constrained in the same way as the members of the report committee by internal power relations. Specifically in relation to the primary curriculum, the report asserts:

> Despite the vision and thoroughness of the 1971 primary school curriculum proposals and the many practical innovations since carried through by dedicated teachers, the evidence suggests that emphasis is still largely on a didactic approach and often, in later primary years, in a relatively narrow range of subject matter. (OECD, 1991, p. 67)

One of the reasons cited for this widespread didacticism, despite two decades of official child-centredness, was the "long pedagogical tradition which teachers need a great deal of support and encouragement to enlarge and broaden" (p. 67). As indicated above, however, the necessary curriculum development infrastructure awaited development. Such a significant challenge of building capacity within the system requires both "better co-ordination of existing agencies and the installation of new structures". The report concludes that "the general orientation now gives greater emphasis to a firm, subject-oriented structure for the curriculum and to quantifiable student performance . . ." (p. 66). These general statements are redolent of Granville's comments above about successfully resisting more conservative demands for a "back to basics" curriculum, while informal conversations with some of the players suggest that there was genuine concern (and fear) about clawing back on the spirit of progressivism that had become the dominant rhetoric in the system bolstered by the comments of many parents that "schools are much happier places today than they were in my day".

Despite this general perspective, Murphy's reservation was fundamentally about what counts as adequate evidence, and he reasoned that the language of the report was overly neutral given the evidence available; that there was substantial evidence about inadequate literacy levels among pupils leaving primary school and that while the work of "the majority of teachers [was] highly satisfactory, the inspectors found that this was not the case in respect of a substantial minority" (p. 103). More accustomed to the cut and thrust of academic debate, Murphy's considered view was that the evidence clearly signalled that there were "pedagogic problems" while he readily acknowledged that in some instances these could be explained by contextual constraints "beyond the control of teachers" and a more general lack of "provision for in-service education". His reservation, therefore, appears to hinge on the manner in which evidence was being used as part of debate, and in this instance he felt strongly that the conclusions needed to be drawn in a more specific and targeted manner. However, power relations effectively marginalised his interpretation of the evidence. Significantly, a decade later, with the benefit of a policy on Adult Education (Ireland, Government of, 2000) and a study of Remedial Education in primary schools (Ireland, Government of, 1999f) there is much more acceptance for the position espoused by Murphy. The nature of power relations and a struggle for domination of the reform agenda between inspectors, the architects of the 1971 curriculum, and the voices of teachers' representatives who, if not seeking hegemony over the process, asserted a powerful voice in shaping field relations and the agenda of reform.

The reservations entered by parent representatives are less relevant to questions of curriculum and can be summarised briefly. There was concern about the length of the school day and year and the erosion of instruction time, and disappointment that the report would not recommend the inclusion of a European language in the senior years of primary schooling, a decision that may have been shaped by the pervasive rhetoric of fiscal rectitude at the time. There are suggested additions to strengthen the "assessment and evaluation" section, the need to prioritise the use of resources for reduction of pupil–teacher ratios, and to extend remedial services to all children who require them. Finally, there was concern that parental involvement in the implementation of reforms did not receive adequate and more detailed attention. This last point is an important political statement from the fledgling NPC that as partners in education they no longer wished to play a subordinate role, that having a seat at the table is only a first step in constructing more democratic processes and of breaking up traditional "power blocs".

Concern about time has intensified considerably in the intervening decade, and primary principals in particular increasingly recognise that without some negotiation on the length of the school day, many aspects of the increasingly collaborative endeavours of teachers cannot be completed during "regular" school hours (Sugrue, 2003; Sugrue et al., 2001). The parents' reservation regarding early "diagnosis" of literacy problems has become a new orthodoxy in the revised curriculum. While NPC advocated the inclusion of a statement to the effect that "comprehensive diagnostic assessment should take place throughout the primary years, and not focus only on older children" (PCRB, 1990, p. 105), the Teacher Guidelines (Ireland, Government of, 1999b, p. 20) in English specifically state that "it is essential that children with language and reading difficulties are identified as early as possible and given the necessary remedial support".

On the basis of evidence provided and argument advanced above, the stance of significant players around the PCRB table can be summarised in the following terms. Since 1971, teachers had come to enjoy the relative autonomy and discretionary judgement that a child-centred policy conferred on them; they had made heroic efforts to implement progressive principles against enormous constraints; and they recognised that erosion of any of this hard-won autonomy and discretion would be to the detriment of the nation's children. Even if there were some inadequate teaching in places, this could be explained by lack of resources, poor school facilities and professional development support. The power plays that helped to construct the PCRB report ensured that structural inadequacies were the major if not the only constraints on the quality of teaching and learning, while teaching became invisible and silenced, the silent discourse of the reform process. The absence of research evidence, particularly observational research documenting classroom practice, made the process a more blatantly political exercise of power in shaping the contours of the reform agenda.

From the 1980s, the inspectorate may have been less certain of its role, and less secure about the degree of accountability in the system, while the creation of the NCCA with responsibility for curriculum increased uncertainties and insecurities.[3] Parents too were rapidly gaining appropriate recognition as "partners" in education, though this was a term that did not enjoy widespread currency until the Convention report (Coolahan, 1994) and subsequent policy orthodoxy in the White Paper (Ireland, Government of, 1995, p. 9) where it states: "The parental role confers on them . . . rights as individuals to be consulted and informed on all aspects of the child's education and their right as a group to be active participants in the education system at school, regional and national levels." The symbolic significance of the NPC stance, therefore, and its reservation on the PCRB report, gains enormously in importance; it was a very clear declaration that the voices of parents were going to be heard, and that increasingly the field of power in education would have to be shared more equitably, from their perspective. Constructing the report, therefore, apart from its symbolic significance, was important for "the *division of the work of domination*" (Bourdieu and Wacquant, 1992, p. 76) and the process may be understood as "the distance, the gaps, the asymmetries between the various specific forces that confront one another" (p. 76). In such circumstances, the deliberations among the participants in the process of curriculum review are indicative of the "struggles to transform or preserve these fields of forces".

Recommendations

The general drift of the report has already been captured in the preceding discussion. In relation to principles, full and harmonious development is retained as a laudable aim that is translated into a broadly based but balanced curriculum. The principle of discovery has already been dealt with at length, and the report contains a significant drawing back from more *laissez faire* pedagogical tendencies, reflecting more conservative times, as well as the emergence of constructivist research. However, Appendix Four clearly signals that pedagogy revolves around specified goals and this is the case with learning of "basics" or with genuine effort to develop self-esteem, independence of thought and activity, creativity and imagination as well as self-reliance.

Significantly the principle of integration is downgraded to the status of a pedagogical principle and this may amount to a more "fundamental" revision than that claimed by Murphy in relation to reduced status of free discovery to a guided version. Though it is not stated explicitly, the recommendations concerning environment-based learning may also be said to be reduced to a pedagogical principle captured in the following: "In this sense, the principle could be related to the well established practice of explaining the unfamiliar in terms of experiences and encounters that are already part of the child's experiences" (p. 21), as well as the immediate environment being a resource for teaching.

In every subject-matter area except Mathematics, the report calls for greater specification of objectives, substantial revisions in areas such as Music and PE with a complete overhaul of primary Science being deemed necessary, and the benefit of specialist teachers being advocated in some curricular areas, such as Music and PE, but not in others such as Art and Craft, with more attention paid in every area to assessment and monitoring of student progress (see Summary pp. 97–100). The scene was set, therefore, for more detailed specification of objectives in all subject areas, and greater attention also to assessment, with more structure in teaching generally, and with a return to more traditional subjects (p. 19).

Within Eisner's framework, and without wishing to be reductionist, the rhetoric of child-centredness is to be retained, but a more conservative and less extravagant version of it that will have greater evidence of subjects (academic rationalism), more structured teaching and more evidence also of ongoing assessment (cognitive processing and increased technology of teaching) with increasing emphasis on social adaptation rather than transformation, reflecting a lack of optimism and fiscal rectitude. Other voices in the report hinted that parental participation and issues about evidence would, henceforth, be raising their heads with greater alacrity, frequency and determination. With the completion of this report, the field of power relations shifted from the report committee to the structures and processes of reform created by the NCCA.

Constructing the Revised Curriculum

Within the NCCA, an elaborate committee system was created, typically two for each subject-matter area. As already indicated, teachers rapidly gained control of pivotal positions. This proliferation of committees had the benefit of maximising the number of teachers involved in the process and, as the period of gestation became elongated, this enabled teachers to become the key insiders in the process. As an extension of the power play that has been discussed at length above in relation to the PCRB report, what follows is a description by an NCCA insider of the power relations. These comments are an elaborate response to a query in relation to dominant characteristics of the NCCA:

> I'd say you're right in respect of the primary teachers seconded to NCCA — they were able from an early stage to engage with the rhetoric of reform, the language of curriculum . . . [and] while the NCCA rhetoric was indeed quite distinct from the language of the staffroom, most primary teachers would have been blooded in the curriculum principles and approaches of the 1971 curriculum, imbued with the aspirations if not the operations of "progressive" educational ideals etc. The primary Education Officers presented a much more coherent cohort of experience and disposition than did their second-level counterparts. In particular, they were greatly influenced by the INTO, both in its overall cultural influence on that primary constituency and also in the specific "whip" that the INTO placed upon the Education Officers. (That's putting it a bit strong, but there was at the very least a parental guidance influence exerted by INTO on "their" Ed. Officers — significant initial contacts as to the "soundness" of potential appointees, pre-appointment briefings, etc.) (Personal correspondence, 2001)

It may be argued therefore, that the longer the process continued, the greater the extent to which teachers gained a dominant influence over the substance as well as the process of revisions. However, power relations alone were not the only consideration. There was a necessity to build expertise, as the challenge was a new

experience for virtually all concerned. The entire process, therefore, was a critical learning experience for participants and this
educative process takes time — "real-time" learning (see Bridges,
1992). What emerged in the course of the decade therefore is a
kind of "educational entrepreneur" or what Tyack and Cuban
(1995) refer to as a "policy elite" (p. 8) "who acquire formidable
powers to set the agenda of reform, to diagnose problems, to prescribe solutions, and often to influence what should *not* be on the
agenda of reform". This elite group of entrepreneurs has been extended significantly with the further secondment of a whole cohort of practitioners to facilitate professional learning through a
five-year planned programme of professional support for implementation. Collectively, these are an elite group of teachers, so
that not only has curriculum development become the domain
and province of practitioners but the delivery of a significant proportion of professional development programmes is increasingly
also becoming the responsibility of teachers themselves.

From completion of the PCRB report (1990) to the launch of
the revised curriculum (1999) and its complementary professional
learning programme, the evidence suggests that teachers have
consolidated their "domination" of the field of curriculum development and increasingly also, their position in the allied field of
professional learning. Paradoxically, in the absence of a more differentiated career structure in teaching, organisational sponsorship and affiliation have come to dominate reform, and are primary vehicles for career advancement, even if this is temporary
through the process of secondment.[4] Additionally, while the
NCCA during this period relied primarily on seconded staff
(teachers) to conduct its business, it is both more difficult and
takes much longer to create an appropriate institutional culture,
and to build and retain capacity and expertise in the system, both
of which were deemed essential structural requirements for reform by the OECD more than a decade ago.

The process of negotiating the content of the PRCB report
(1990) was a critical moment that indicates a significant shift in
power relations in the field of primary education. In the ensuing

decade, the emergence of an "entrepreneurial elite" has enabled teachers to consolidate a dominant position in curriculum reform and professional learning. Both of these responsibilities traditionally have been important dimensions of the inspectorate's role. However, the OECD report suggested that it was necessary for this group to shed "certain existing duties" (p. 44) in order to focus on "the overall accountability of the system". This more clearly defined role and function is a timely reminder of the issue of accountability and assessment. Attention is now focused therefore on the actual documentation of the revised curriculum with a particular emphasis on principles, teaching and evaluation, to subject the content of the introductory text, English and SPHE guidelines and curriculum documents to close analysis.

Revision or Reform?

The documentation begins with a statement that indicates its conservative stance; no "radical" shift on this occasion, unlike 1971. Rather, its purpose is "evolutionary and developmental" but whether this stance is a recognition and understanding of the gradual nature of school reform, one of "continuous adaptation" (see Tyack and Cuban, 1995) or the conservatism of those involved is not made explicit. While the introduction is careful to retain the distinction made by the PCRB report between a curricular and a pedagogical principle, by the time the introductory document is finished elaborating on both, this distinction has been obscured, thus rehabilitating the more expansive rhetoric of 1971 in a somewhat modified language.

Rhetoric plays an important function affectively, in terms of reassurance, motivation and orientation, but the multiplicity of terms — vision, aims, principles (pedagogical, curricular, and learning), features, issues, general aims, specific aims, general objectives, all of which are used without the benefit of a glossary or definition — tend to confuse rather than to clarify. However, in a more general sense, this much more elaborate introductory document (than its 1971 predecessor) seeks to capture and to communicate a sense of the much more complex and diverse educational landscape that teachers must learn to navigate with increasing sophistication if the aspirations implicit and explicit in the rhetoric are to be achieved. Yet, if principles — curricular, pedagogical and learning — are to serve as guides to action, as the term implies, the text is stronger on progressive sentiment and much more vague on what this would look like in practice. Nevertheless, the documentation repeatedly indicates the necessity for a more expansive repertoire of pedagogical skills and expertise to embrace more collaborative group work, individualisation, etc., albeit within a more subject-oriented curriculum. However, due to the general nature of this rhetoric, a premium has been placed on professional development as the major vehicle for enabling teachers to imagine a different, revised pedagogy that is in tune with the aspirations of the documentation.

The new language extends also to the structuring of content in the curriculum — areas, strands and units. If the purpose of this new language was to communicate greater need for continuity, coherence and challenge across the primary age range, its initial impact is to obscure rather than make this meaning explicit. Similarly, use of the phrase "the seven curricular areas" hides, even temporarily, the reality that there are now more subject areas than ever before in the curriculum, SPHE being a subject in its own right, with Drama becoming a "subject" very late in the process of reform for reasons that are not entirely clear. This is particularly surprising since the PCRB (1990, p. 69) report recommended that Drama become "a pedagogic resource and focus for integrating various aspects of the curriculum". This is primarily what the revised curriculum documentation reflects, particularly in SPHE where a lengthy section is devoted to declaring the virtues of drama as a pedagogical practice as the nature of the subject matter lends itself to such an approach. It appears that Drama became a subject rather than a pedagogical principle at a very late stage in the process, too late to revise other subject documents to reflect its new status. The power plays that elevated it to the status of a subject remain to be scrutinised at another time.

Comments concerning the language of the revised documentation notwithstanding, when it comes to curriculum guidelines faith is kept with the requirement of the PCRB report to provide greater specification of aims and objectives, while they continue to be of a general rather than a specific nature. Darling-Hammond (1997, p. 227) argues that specification of objectives needs to be:

> clear enough to help teachers develop curricula pointed in a common direction, but they are not so voluminous and prescriptive as to require superficial content coverage or to limit teachers' inventiveness in bringing ideas to life for their students.

While general impressions are that the guidelines have proved useful in the hands of many teachers, particularly when preparing school-based planning days,[5] the documentation does not address the issue of standards. It is important to point out that it is possible to have standards without standardisation (see Darling-Hammond, 1997). This lacuna places a further burden on professional support for in addition to planning the curriculum at the level of the school, teachers must also invent context-sensitive but authentic standards to be attained by their pupils. This identification of appropriate standards is made more onerous in a context where there is an absence of research evidence and documented detail of current practice.

One of the continuities throughout this entire decade of reform is that teaching has continued to remain somewhat invisible as the silent but critically important discourse of the process. Even where exemplars are provided, and there is significant variation from one subject area to the next, they are rather general so that the real goals of the revisions continue to be somewhat intangible. Even when illustrations of children's work are included, which is done as a matter of course throughout the documentation, its impact (if not its intent) is primarily aesthetic when its inclusion provided an important opportunity to illustrate the kind of standards that can be achieved had the ages and school contexts of the creators been included.

One of the surprising features of this work, despite the fact that its architects have been primarily teachers, is that practice is very much underrepresented throughout. In the absence of a research base on the nature of teaching in the system, setting, attaining, and improving standards is much more challenging and may prove elusive. Without such a base, it will be impossible also to determine the success or otherwise of current reform efforts. The documentation is disappointing also in terms of reflecting what is already well documented elsewhere about the knowledge base of teaching (see for example, Darling-Hammond, 1997) and this literature is noticeably absent from the limited range of references that are included in the sources cited in the documents.

Another area in which the documentation keeps faith with recommendations in the PCRB report is the frequency with which "assessment" is mentioned and its centrality to teaching and learning asserted. By 1998, when the launch of the revised curriculum had been postponed on a number of occasions, it was being reported at INTO education conferences that it would be necessary for teachers to become more "assessment literate" and that the over-arching impact of revisions would be to "stress new approaches and methodologies . . . [and] put assessment at the heart of the learning and teaching process" with emphasis also on "the importance of school planning". These assertions gain in significance from the fact that they were being made by members of the organisation who are "boundary spanners" as members of the union's education committee as well as playing important roles within NCCA structures (*In Touch*, 1998, December). There is growing consistency therefore between the official message of the NCCA and the leadership of the teaching profession; in addition to a greater stress on planning, there is recognition also of a necessity for more continuity and coherence of programmes at the level of the school. Although a more rigorous focus on teaching and aspects of assessment continue to be oblique, the documentation does suggest a significant shift in thinking in relation to the importance of assessment among the "educational entrepreneurs" at least, if not yet a shared and ubiquitous element of thinking and practice among the generality of teachers.

As emphasis shifts from planning to implementation, the issue of assessment and evaluation will increase in importance and significance. The cause of assessment was not helped by the dissemination of materials to schools on pupil profiling by the DES just as teachers were getting to grips with the volume of reading material in the revised curriculum.[6] The timing of this suggests that the DES and the NCCA continue to work as semi-detached organisations rather than develop the kind of infrastructural coherence that the OECD indicated was a necessity for reform. Despite these continuing power plays within the system, it is appropriate to mark this development as an important milestone as teachers take greater responsibility for pupils' learning rather than being content to "cover the course" or "deliver the curriculum". The documentation certainly seeks to connect teaching and learning in a more explicit and intimate manner than previous policy statements.

One of the consequences of the committee structure has been a proliferation of documentation as part of the revised curriculum — 23 texts in all. This results in a significant and unnecessary amount of repetition and redundancy, and this is particularly the case in relation to assessment. Each set of guidelines deals with this issue with some relatively minor variations tailored to the specifics of the subject matter being discussed, but repetition is no substitute for a more in-depth treatment of an element of the curriculum that is accepted as critically important. It is not too late yet to consider a teachers' handbook that deals with this topic as an important element of professional support, thus enabling teachers to become more "assessment literate".

There is a more expansive rhetoric that indicates the significance of critical thinking, higher order thinking, imagination and creativity, and a pervasive use of a constructivist language that indicates the necessity for scaffolding, and hands-on work with students, etc. However, the increase in the number of subjects has considerable potential for overloading an already crowded school day that may lead to more superficial coverage of content and increased vocationalisation of the curriculum. This latter potential is evident in the pervasive referencing of the importance of ICT skills throughout the texts while greater emphasis on skill development generally speaks to a more ubiquitous phenomenon of preparing people to compete for market share in the global economy. Time for teacher learning too is a crucial matter that has to be faced. However, in the absence of evidence about the nature of teaching and current standards of attainment in the system, it will be impossible to determine the success or otherwise of this important initiative. Whether this new departure amounts to revision or reform depends to a significant extent on the eye of the beholder. My own view is that use of the term "reform" presents the system with considerably more challenge and reflects more accurately the ambition of those who laboured in the vineyard of curriculum development for the past decade.

POWER, POLICIES AND POSSIBILITIES

The accumulated wisdom and research evidence of three decades or more of curriculum reform indicates clearly that dissemination of documentation is only a beginning and not the final phase of reform (Fullan, 1991; Cuban, 1993). On this occasion, there is a five-year plan for gradual implementation in an effort to avoid curriculum overload and with considerable professional support that is growing in sophistication, but still requires greater coherence and continuity across a variety of agents and agencies (see Sugrue et al., 2001). While the publication of the documentation is undoubtedly an important historical moment in the evolution of Irish primary education, it is merely a beginning. Although a new class of educational entrepreneurs may have their feet firmly planted underneath the top table of curriculum development, this hardly matters to the generality of the teachers who encounter the documentation for the first time after its publication. Nevertheless, perhaps the more important milestone is the relative position of the major players at the end of this process.

International researchers who have visited these shores in recent years, such as Hargreaves, Fullan and Fink, have remarked on the generally positive education climate in Ireland in comparison with other jurisdictions, particularly, they say, Ontario, the US and England. They identify and speak positively of teacher participation in policy formulation and decision-making and contrast this "partnership" approach with the loss of power and influence experienced by teachers in many other jurisdictions. There is little doubt that the partnership approach espoused and practised in Ireland is different from a more adversarial, often negative and hostile educational climate reported in other countries. However, rather than interpret such comments and realities complacently, it is important to recognise the strengths and limitations of this different approach.

It was indicated above that the visiting OECD team in 1991 wished to see old "power blocs" and "cliques" give way to more democratic decision-making and policy formulation in Irish education; the creation of structures and processes that would be more open, inclusive and democratic. My analysis indicates that as the locus of power shifted from the DES to the NCCA, the latter has been colonised by teachers whose primary affiliation is to their "sponsoring" organisation, the INTO. It would appear, therefore, that power continues to be concentrated at the centre. What has changed is that the locus of control has shifted from DES personnel in general and the inspectorate in particular, to a newly emerging policy elite or group of educational entrepreneurs. This group has increased in number significantly with the secondment of teams of teachers with responsibility for designing and delivering professional support, both in relation to the revised curriculum and whole school planning. As more permanent positions within the NCCA are created and filled, it will be interesting to document the manner in which existing power relations are shaped, the kind of "professional culture" that is created within this fledgling organisation, as well as the extent to which the inspectorate focuses its energies and expertise on policy, accountability and evaluation. Recent announcements regarding a "radical shake-up" in the DES suggest a major refocusing of priorities (see *Irish Times*, 2003; Flynn, 2003).

As a consequence of the emerging and ongoing "state of play" in power relations within the field of primary education, combined with the evidence adduced from the analysis presented here, the following is a summary of the more salient issues in the field and its related sub-field, curriculum reform.

- The revised curriculum (1999) rehabilitates, reiterates and elaborates a rhetoric of child-centredness, albeit in modified form, within a language of constructivism and with greater emphasis on the need for assessment across the primary age range.

- Paradoxically, the absence of a comprehensive body of research evidence in the setting concerning the realities of teaching and learning, along with the power plays within the process of negotiation, have been complicit in silencing a discourse around issues of quality and standards.

As a consequence of these forces at play, the system is poorly positioned to monitor the process of implementation, to provide focused professional support for teachers as they struggle with the new curricular and pedagogical realities. Lack of evidence will also continue to limit possibilities of more comprehensive and coherent policies. Without substantial "baseline" evidence regarding children's levels of achievement, and the dominant characteristics of teachers' pedagogical routines, implementation of the revised curriculum will continue to be primarily a matter of perception and power relations.

Current realities provide possibilities also for extending partnership while simultaneously making gains for policy and practice. Comments above suggest that teachers occupy a privileged position within the Irish education system when compared with their counterparts internationally. However, this position also carries responsibilities; and, it is not an end in itself. Consequently, one of the major challenges facing the system immediately is how to build on this reality. It is necessary to build systematically the knowledge base of teaching and this agenda necessitates collaboration between teachers and researchers as well as DES and NCCA personnel. Issues concerning standards and accountability will have to be balanced with the needs of individual learners, as well as with the professional needs of teachers, their career stage and learning trajectories that challenge the education community to create new forms of "professionalism" (Hargreaves, 2000; Hargreaves and Goodson, 1996). The Education Act (1998) is likely to provide important leverage in the system in terms of how power relations evolve when dealing with this agenda. There is an immediate need to provide systematic evidence of practice up close so that the knowledge base of teaching can be built from the ground up: this is the emerging frontier in the power relations in the field of education.

The manner in which this game is played will shape both policy and practice in significant ways in the immediate future as the implementation process gathers momentum. It is by the quality of teaching and learning, rather than the quality of the documentation, that the success or failure of the reform will ultimately be tested. There is a collective onus on all of the players to work towards securing that future now.

References

Beck, U. (2000), *What Is Globalization?* Cambridge: Polity Press.

Berger, J. (1972), *Ways of Seeing*, London: Penguin.

Blase, J. (1998), "The Micropolitics of Educational Change", in Hargeaves, A., Lieberman, A., Fullan, M. and Hopkins, D. (eds.), *International Handbook of Educational Change, Part One*, Dordrecht/Boston/London: Kluwer, pp. 544–57.

Bourdieu, P. (1982), *Leçon sur la Leçon*, Paris: Editions de Minuit; translated as "Lecture on the Lecture" in P. Bourdieu (1990), *In Other Words: Essays towards a Reflexive Sociology*, Cambridge: Polity Press; Stanford: Stanford University Press.

Bourdieu, P. (1989), *The State Nobility: Elite Schools in the Field of Power*, Cambridge: Polity Press; first published in France as *La Noblesse d'État: Grandes Écoles et Esprit de Corps*, 1988.

Bourdieu, P. and Wacquant, L.J.D. (1992), *An Invitation to Reflexive Sociology*, Chicago: University of Chicago Press.

Bridges, E. (1992), *Problem-Based Learning for Administration*, Oregon: University of Oregon.

Chambers Dictionary (1993), Edinburgh: Chambers Harrap Publishers Ltd.

Coolahan, J. (1981), *A History of Irish Education*, Dublin: IPA.

Coolahan, J. (ed.) (1994), *Report on The National Education Convention*, Dublin: Government Publications.

Cuban, L. (1993), *How Teachers Taught: Constancy and Change in American Classrooms 1890–1990*, London and New York: Teachers College Press.

Curriculum and Examinations Board (1984), *Issues and Structures in Education*, Dublin: CEB.

Curriculum and Examinations Board (1985), *Primary Education A Curriculum and Examinations Board Discussion Paper*, Dublin: CEB.

Darling-Hammond, L. (1997), *The Right To Learn*, San Francisco: Jossey-Bass.

Datnow, A. (2000), "Gender Politics in School Reform", in Hargreaves, A. and Bascia, N. (eds.), *The Sharp Edge of Educational Change*, London and New York: Routledge/Falmer, pp. 131–55.

Department of Education (1971), *Primary School Curriculum, Teacher's Handbooks Parts 1 and 2*, Dublin: Government Publications.

Eisner, E. (1979), *The Educational Imagination*, New York and London: Collier Macmillan Publishers.

Eisner, E. (1992), "Curriculum Ideologies", in Jackson, P. (ed.), *Handbook of Research on Curriculum*, Washington DC: AERA, pp. 302–26.

Flynn, S. (2003), "Department of Education Facing Radical Shake-up", *Irish Times*, 7 February, p. 7.

Fullan, M. (1991), *The New Meaning of Educational Change*, London: Cassell.

Giddens, A. (1991), *Modernity and Self-Identity: Self and Society in the Late Modern Age*, Stanford: Stanford University Press.

Goodson, I.F. (1994), *Studying Curriculum*, New York and London: Teachers College, Columbia University.

Hargreaves, A. (1994), *Changing Teachers, Changing Times*, London: Cassell.

Hargeaves, A., and Goodson, I.F. (1996), "Teachers' Professional Lives: Aspirations and Actualities", in Goodson, I.F. and Hargreaves, A. (eds.), *Teachers' Professional Lives*, London: Falmer Press, pp. 1–27.

Hargreaves, A. (2000), "The Four Ages of Professionalism", *Teachers and Teaching, Theory and Practice,* Vol. 6, No. 2, pp. 151–82.

In Touch (1998), "The Revised Curriculum: A Background Paper", *In Touch,* No. 9, December, pp. 14–15.

Ireland, Government of (1990), *Report of the Primary Education Review Body,* Dublin: Government Publications, December.

Ireland, Government of (1992), *Education For A Changing World: Green Paper on Education,* Dublin: Stationery Office.

Ireland, Government of (1995), *Charting Our Education Future: White Paper on Education,* Dublin: Stationery Office.

Ireland, Government of (1998), Education (No. 2) Bill.

Ireland, Government of (1999a), *Primary School Curriculum Introduction,* Dublin: Government Publications.

Ireland, Government of (1999b), *English Language Teacher Guidelines,* Dublin: Government Publications.

Ireland, Government of (1999c), *English Curriculum,* Dublin: Government Publications.

Ireland, Government of (1999d), *Social, Personal and Health Education Curriculum,* Dublin: Government Publications.

Ireland, Government of (1999e), *Social, Personal and Health Education Teacher Guidelines,* Dublin: Government Publications.

Ireland, Government of (1999f), *Study of Remedial Education in Irish Primary Schools,* Dublin: Department of Education and Science.

Ireland, Government of (1999g), *White Paper on Early Childhood Education: Ready To Learn,* Dublin: Stationery Office.

Ireland, Government of (2000), *Learning for Life: White Paper on Adult Education,* Dublin: The Stationery Office.

Irish Times (2003), "Education Shake-Up", Editorial, 7 February, p. 17.

Lynch, K. (1989), *The Hidden Curriculum: Reproduction in Education, A Reappraisal,* London/New York: Falmer Press.

McDonagh, K. (ed.) (1969), *Reports on the Draft Curriculum for Primary Schools,* Dublin: Teachers' Study Group.

McNeil, L.M. (2000), *Contradictions of School Reform: educational costs of standardization*, New York: Routledge.

Murphy, D. (1990), "Reservation on English", Reservation No. 1 (in *Report of the Review Body on the Primary Curriculum*) Dublin: NCCA, pp. 101–4.

National Council for Curriculum and Assessment (1990), *Report of the Review Body on the Primary Curriculum*, Dublin: NCCA and Department of Education Primary Branch, May.

Noddings, N. (1992), *The Challenge to Care in Schools An Alternative Approach to Education*, New York: Teachers College Press.

O'Toole, J. (1999), "Whose Curriculum Is It Anyway?" *In Touch*, Dublin: INTO, Editorial.

OECD (1991), *Reviews of National Education Policies for Education: Ireland*, Paris: OECD.

PCRB (1990), *Primary Curriculum Review Body Report*, Dublin: Department of Education.

Riley, K. (2000), "Leadership, Learning and Systemic Reform", *Journal of Educational Change*, Vol. 1, No.1, pp. 29–55.

Schon, D. (1983), *The Reflective Practitioner*, New York: Sage Publications.

Schon, D. (1987), *Educating The Reflective Practitioner*, New York: Sage Publications.

Sexton, J.J. (1990), "The Supply and Demand Position for Primary Teachers 1989–2000", Report commissioned from the Economic and Social Research Institute Annex, in Government of Ireland, *Report of the Primary Education Review Body*, Dublin: The Stationery Office, pp. 129–47.

Stenhouse, L. (1975), *An Introduction to Curriculum Research and Development*, London: Heinemann.

Sugrue, C. (1997), *Complexities of Teaching: Child-centred Perspectives*, London: Falmer Press.

Sugrue, C. (2003), "Irish Primary Principals' Professional Learning: Problems and Possibilities", *Oideas, 50*, pp. 8–39.

Sugrue, C., Morgan, M., Devine, D. and Rafferty, D. (2001), *The Quality of Professional Learning for Irish Primary and Secondary Teachers: A Critical Analysis*, Dublin: A Report commissioned by the Department of Education and Science.

Tyack, D. and Cuban, L. (1995), *Tinkering Toward Utopia: A Century of Public School Reform*, Cambridge, Massachusetts: Harvard University Press.

Endnotes

[1] The Report of the Review Body on the Primary Curriculum (PCRB) is commonly referred to as the "Quinlan Report" as the chairperson of the committee that produced it was Moya Quinlan.

[2] Dan Murphy was an esteemed member of the Department of Higher Education and Research at Trinity College Dublin. He had particular interest and expertise in English language and literature. As an academic, familiar with the cut and thrust of intellectual debate, something he enjoyed enormously, he had limited tolerance for political posturing and sought to vindicate his perspective on the basis of available "evidence".

[3] In the early 1980s, the period of probation for beginning teachers was reduced from two years to one year, thus reducing the work of inspectors dramatically in this area, particularly when the number of beginning teachers in the system was declining dramatically after a period of expansion since the mid-1960s. Additionally, the resuscitation of the "Tuairisc Scoile" (school report) which began in 1982, was greeted with hostility by the teachers' union and the process was quickly reformed to prevent inspectors from naming individual teachers in school reports and the emphasis shifted to reporting in general terms on the work of a "whole school".

[4] A significant structural issue is the lack of career opportunities for teachers. Additionally, the vast majority of those involved in working with either the NCCA or the national implementation committee are seconded from their school employment and continue to retain membership of the primary teachers' union.

[5] The general pattern of professional learning opportunities provided as integral to the implementation process of reform includes six days per annum, two days out of school followed by a day in school, or in a cluster of small schools with a particular focus on planning curricula.

[6] Just as teachers were getting to grips with the "curriculum box" containing the 23 texts of the revised curriculum, their principals received (unannounced) considerable documentation concerning student profiling — important documentation that irritated many, while the timing of its delivery displays a lack of awareness of school realities.

Chapter 7

MAKING THE IRISH:
IDENTITY AND CITIZENSHIP IN THE
PRIMARY CURRICULUM

Fionnuala Waldron

INTRODUCTION*

On the occasion of the first meeting of parliament of the newly unified Italian state, Massimo d'Azeglio declared, "We have made Italy, now we have to make Italians" (Hobsbawm, 1990, p. 44). While few would argue that Ireland has, in any final sense, been "made", the idea that Irish identity is work-in-progress resonates through much of the socio-cultural critique of the past decade and stands in stark contrast to the cultural certainty characteristic of Irish education from Independence to the 1960s. The modernising influences of economic expansion, changes in education, membership of the EU and the ongoing process of globalisation on Irish society in the second half of the twentieth century have been analysed elsewhere (see, for example, Breen et al., 1990; Clancy, 1995; Kirby et al., 2002). In recent years, public interest in ethnicity and diversity, sparked by new patterns of immigration, highlight the

* I would like to thank my colleagues Mark Morgan, Pauric Travers, Mary Shine Thompson, Philomena Donnelly and Bernie Collins for their comments on an earlier draft of this chapter.

extent to which Irish society thought of itself as homogeneous, ignoring indigenous forms of cultural and ethnic difference. The new plurality brings with it tensions and concerns about identity and belonging. In the private sphere, these tensions find expression in the opposing ideas of racism and solidarity. In the public sphere, the state responds with its own contradictory *mélange* of exclusionary impulses in terms of citizenship and inclusionary educational initiatives.[1] While the recent economic and socio-cultural phenomenon of the Celtic Tiger has added its own bleak mix of individualism and materialism to the melting pot, the idea that there is no longer a blueprint for Irish identity is, in many ways, a liberating one. Perhaps we can mix a little of the traditional "craic" with some free-wheeling capitalist energy, add some multicultural chic and come up with the quintessential Irish person for the twenty-first century. If we want a sense of social solidarity and a commitment to a just and equal society to feature somewhere in that heady mix, however, there is a need to take control of that emergent identity, to name, discuss and debate its characteristics and its consequences.

The recognition of identity as a fluid and somewhat contested space is paralleled by a belief that the practice of citizenship is in crisis. Much of the concern about voter turnout at elections, referendum overload and corruption-induced cynicism is targeted at the young, who are seen as increasingly alienated from the polity. This preoccupation with the practice of citizenship is not confined to Ireland, however. Within the EU, concerns about tensions between national and supra-national institutions and between the need to build a sense of shared purpose and an increasingly diverse community have led to calls for an educational focus on European citizenship.[2] That this concern is also felt on a national level within the European Union and beyond can be seen in the flurry of reports, research projects and publications relating to citizenship[3] which have emerged in the past decade.

This chapter examines the response of the primary school curriculum in the Republic of Ireland to these fundamentally related questions of citizenship and identity and explores the model of citizen and the idea of Irish identity implicit in it. While issues of identity and citizenship permeate all aspects and areas of the curriculum, this critique does not propose to offer a comprehensive analysis.[4] Instead, there are preliminary comments on what is implied by the term citizenship education in the context of child education and on the relationship between identity and citizenship. These are followed by an exploration of the representations of identity and the ideas and processes of citizenship embedded in the areas of History, Geography and Social, Personal and Health Education within the Irish primary school curriculum documents (Ireland, Government of, 1999a–g) for each subject area. Where appropriate, the continuities and discontinuities over time between the *Primary School Curriculum* (Ireland, Government of, 1999a) and earlier guidelines are also examined. An analysis of curriculum documents can reveal much about the ideological project of education at any given historical moment. It is, however, at the interface between theory and practice that the fault lines appear — those gaps and contradictions which allow one to evaluate the integrity of that project. In conclusion, some of the constraints — systemic, ideological and practical — which make the implementation of these curricula problematic are identified.

CITIZENSHIP, IDENTITY AND CHILD EDUCATION

Since the launch of *Curaclam na Bunscoile/Primary School Curriculum* (Department of Education, 1971a, 1971b) in 1971, the dominant ideology in child education in Ireland has been that of child-centred education. Characterised by its commitment to experiential and environment-based learning, to the holistic development of the child and to the idea of the child as active learner and constructor of knowledge, and premised on a view of the educative relationship as democratic, child-centred education appears to offer the ideal context for the development of the concepts, skills, attitudes and dispositions of democratic citizenship. While an explicit and sustained focus on political education as a separate subject area is generally associated with second-level education,[5] the appropriateness of primary school as a site of citizenship education is widely accepted. White (1999, p. 63), for example, sees primary school — the first public institution that most children experience — as uniquely suited to developing the civic dispositions needed for the maintenance of a democratic society. Many of these attitudes, skills and understandings will be developed in an integrated way across a range of subject areas and as part of the general organisation of the school. Morgan (2002, p. 114) notes the tendency in Ireland to see the solution to societal fears and problems in the creation of educational packages which may not only be counterproductive but also serve to paralyse primary education through curriculum overload. However, while an integrated approach to citizenship education may be the most appropriate one, this should not rule out providing space for a more focused exploration of issues relating to citizenship which a dedicated programme might allow. It is easy to underestimate the capacity of children to reflect in an open, thoughtful and critical way on concepts such as identity, justice and power (Howard and Gill, 2000; Pike, 2001). The extent to which the primary curriculum provides such opportunities will be one measure of the seriousness of its intent in the area of citizenship education. The nature of those opportunities and the educational contexts in which they are embedded will also help to reveal the conception of citizenship underlying the curriculum as a whole.

It seems obvious that if education is to have an impact on the practice of citizenship, it must go beyond a concern with procedures and institutions and include the development of attitudes, values and dispositions (Kymlicka, 2001, p. 293). In his perceptive and well-argued examination of the kind of political education needed to maintain democracy, Callan (1997, p. 11) identifies the development of autonomy as one of those dispositions. The reciprocity and empathy needed to maintain mutual respect in a pluralist democracy requires an ability to stand outside the limits of one's own cultural beliefs and certainties and take on the perspective of the other. Predicated on a view of the citizen as capable of making independent and informed choices, it seems axiomatic that such an education must also hold within it the ideas of critique and action, that is, the ability to think critically, to question received tradition, to evaluate evidence coupled with the imperative to action, which an acceptance of democratic responsibility brings. Because of this potential to challenge inherited values and traditions, Callan (1997, p. 13) sees education for democratic citizenship as inherently transformative both at societal and personal levels. One could argue that such an education could shatter the social bonds and the sense of common purpose which are also necessary to the maintenance of democracy and which a celebratory rather than a questioning approach to tradition and culture might promote. Indeed, the need to develop a collective sense of purpose, solidarity and a commitment to justice and care is seen by Callan as central to education for citizenship. Education, then, needs to develop in children the ability to think for themselves, while at the same time remaining open to and respectful of the views of others. And it needs to do so in a context which promotes the ideal of a common purpose, a shared sense of belonging aligned "with the claims of justice" (Callan, 1997, p. 90). What is the basis of that shared sense of belonging?

There is a strong argument that a common allegiance to political principles and institutions is unlikely to provide sufficient basis for social unity in a pluralist democracy (Honohan, 2001, p. 21; Kymlicka, 2001, p. 311). A sense of shared membership is also needed. National identity can provide one source of that shared membership. The model of a generic democratic citizen, uncontaminated by national identity, seems neither tenable nor desirable. We are all creatures of context, time and place. A sense of national identity can be seen as both a constitutive part of identity (Dunne, 2002, p. 72) and an integrative force in society (White, 1997, p. 16). The relationship between social solidarity and national identity is not without its tensions, however. To the extent that national identity can be reduced to questions of a common language, ethnicity or culture, it offers an exclusionary version of solidarity that can bring ethnic and cultural conflict in its wake. The construction of a shared identity in a pluralist society is a difficult and complex project[6] which includes recognition of a multiplicity of communities and diverse ways of belonging. In a pluralist society, then, the question becomes: how does one construct a shared identity which is socially cohesive and promotes a sense of belonging and affiliation while at the same time recognising difference? And what role does education have to play in the creation of that shared identity?

HISTORY

Traditionally, History is one of the school subjects most associated with the formation of national identity. Leaving aside the arguments of theorists who reject the idea that education should play any role in nation-building (Enslin, 1994, cited in White, 1997, p. 16), there remains the question of whether history teaching and learning should be used in a democracy to promote identification with the state. The idea of national histories as myth,[7] imagined stories of "imagined communities" (Anderson, 1991), has enough resonance to trouble most tellers of the national story, whether historians or educators. White (1997, p. 21), however, defends the place of national myths as part of a democratic education and makes the point that attachment to a national community is one of a number of communal affiliations which make us what we are — "without histories, no communities". He argues for a critical and questioning approach to the teaching of national history. His defence of the place of national myths in education is balanced by recognition that the version of the national story embodied in the myth is contestable. This tension between the promotion of national identity and a critical appropriation of national history is also evident in Kymlicka's argument that while schools should teach history truthfully, they should also promote "an emotional identification" with the nation's history, a sense of pride in its accomplishments and shame in its injustices (2001, p. 315). Callan, however, cautions against an approach which is overly critical and suggests that, rather than promote a shared identity, it may lead to political alienation. He argues instead for a pedagogy rooted in critical reasoning which looks for "the best of the tradition" (1997, p. 98).

Despite Callan's caution, it is arguable that none of the theorists mentioned go far enough in their recognition of the need for a critical appropriation of the past as part of the educational project. Presenting the national story as an already constructed narrative suggests a view of history as static and reified rather than something that is open to interpretation, partial and the source of multiple stories. The thrust of history education in recent decades has been towards a re-conceptualisation of the child's relationship with the past. Rooted in the Brunerian (1977, p. 4) idea that "the schoolboy learning physics *is* a physicist", the concept of the child as historian places the learner at the centre of the discipline rather than at the periphery. Through a process of active engagement with historical sources, the child is inducted into the attitudes, skills, concepts, modes of thinking and doing of history as a discipline. While this approach is not necessarily incompatible with the development of national pride or national sentiment, responsibility for the development of such aspects of identity belongs elsewhere. What history teaching and learning have to offer are the tools and context for a critical understanding of our collective stories.

History and sentiment make a powerful and potentially destructive combination, a fact that has been recognised in Irish educational circles for a long time. A recurring educational debate in nineteenth- and early twentieth-century Ireland centred on the potential of Irish history and Irish history textbooks to promote nationalist feeling and to subvert allegiance to the crown (Fitzpatrick, 1991). With the establishment of the Free State in 1922, the teaching of history in primary schools became an important part of the wider project of Gaelicisation. This construction, or reconstruction, of a national identity that was thought to be truly Irish was premised on a national story characterised by "a noble tradition of heroism, and persistent loyalty to ideals" (Department of Education, 1933). Callan (1997, pp. 100–8) argues that an approach to the teaching of history which fosters a sentimental and unquestioning form of patriotism can lead to an inability to imagine alternative historical outcomes, the demonising of opposing causes and the mystification of sectional power interests in the society in question.

It is certainly the case that the decades after Independence wit-
nessed an institutionalising of class, denominational and gender
interests that were rarely openly challenged and an acceptance
within education of the nationalist narrative as the national story.

The crisis which erupted in Northern Ireland in the late 1960s
and early 1970s brought with it serious concerns about the way in
which history was being taught in Irish primary schools. The
celebration of nationalist heroes, which reached its apogee in the
1966 commemoration of the 1916 Rising, was seen to provide the
context within which physical force nationalism could survive
and flourish. With the advent of pedagogic and curriculum reform in 1971, significant changes were envisaged in the teaching
of history. While children's characters were still to be fired by
"habitual visions of greatness" and exposed to "sublime examples
of patriotism, courage, self-sacrifice and devotion to noble ideals",
Curaclam na Bunscoile (Department of Education, 1971a, p. 88)
cautioned against telling the national story in ways which might
develop prejudice and against "the distortion or the suppression
of any truth which might seem to hurt national pride". History
teaching should, moreover, be true to the facts and avoid special
pleading, as well as ensuring that the contributions of all "creeds
and classes" to the making of modern Ireland was recognised. The
idea that the development of national pride and identity was one
of the purposes of school history is, however, common to both the
pre- and post-1971 curricula. This role of history is even more explicitly named in the 1971 civics programme.

> History, more than any other aspect of the curriculum, helps
> to develop pride of race in the child but it is essential that this
> pride should be rational and balanced. Anything which sa-
> vours of chauvinism or any form of excessive nationalism,
> tends to blur the child's awareness of the common bond of
> humanity. (Department of Education, 1971a, p. 117)

What is also characteristic of both curricula is the conceptualisation of identity predominantly in national terms. Thus, while the
1971 curriculum promotes the investigation of the local environ-

ment, the rationale for this focus is firmly based in learning theory rather than in any commitment to the idea of local identity. Yet, involvement in multiple collectivities, even at local levels, suggests that each of us negotiates a plurality of identities which overlap, fluctuate and sometimes conflict. The exploration of our manifold identities and how they relate to each other is, or should be, part of the educational project. One should not underestimate the shift in thinking which the 1971 curriculum embodied. In its move away from an uncritical acceptance of the national story, it signified an opening up of cultural categories to critical scrutiny and extended the healthy scepticism of the historian beyond the academy. The most significant shift, however, was not the suggestion that the national story was open to interpretation, but the new emphasis placed on the history of ordinary life and the idea of everyday life as a site of civic virtue. The category of patriot was expanded to include both the noble and the ordinary. One no longer had to be a dead hero to be an Irish patriot (Bennett, 1994, p. 27).

The *Primary School Curriculum* (Ireland, Government of, 1999a) continues this commitment to social history present in the 1971 curriculum and the vast majority of the units focus on the experience of ordinary people across time rather than on the actions of elite groups. While an emphasis on social rather than political history will inevitably weaken the dominance of the national story in school history, what is remarkable about the Revised Curriculum, as it is colloquially called, is the extent to which the idea of national identity itself is rendered devoid of sentiment. There is no mention of heroic self-sacrifice or of patriotic virtue in this relentlessly post-nationalist document. It is striking that the words "Ireland", "Irish" or "country" do not appear at all in the aims of the History curriculum (Ireland, Government of, 1999b, p. 12) while in the named objectives (Ireland, Government of, 1999b, p. 13) national identity itself is cited as only one of a number of identities which the child will explore and interrogate. Mirroring the pedagogical principle of starting from the known world of the child, the History curriculum begins with an exploration of personal and family history in the infant classes, moving progressively outwards to investigate the local, national, European and world contexts. Through this exploration, the History curriculum will "develop a sense of personal, local, national, European and wider identities through studying the history and cultural inheritance of local and other communities" (Ireland, Government of, 1999b, p. 13). Throughout the documents, there is an overwhelming emphasis on history as a means of interrogating identity rather than building it. Thus, history is seen as a way of revealing the cultural and social underpinnings of our multiple identities (Ireland, Government of, 1999b, p. 9; 1999c, p. 29). In telling the political story, the emphasis is on critique rather than celebration, on perspective and balance rather than identification with the narrative, on recognising the contribution of different traditions to the construction of national identity rather than co-opting all children into the dominant one. The danger of oversimplifying complex periods and issues is balanced against the need for children to contextualise current issues.

> If children begin to appreciate the power which people's interpretations of the past can have on their perspectives and actions today then history will have achieved one of its fundamental purposes and will have contributed towards the resolution of many of the issues facing present and future generations of Irish people. (Ireland, Government of, 1999c, p. 22)

Given the traditional dominance of the Irish patriot as a central motif in school history and the institutionalisation of cultural nationalism as the dominant ideology informing Irish curricula prior to 1971 (Coolahan, 1981, p. 38), it is significant that the recurring theme in the most recent curriculum is the celebration of diversity. The recognition of difference embodied in the History curriculum is underpinned by a commitment to the exploration of the historical contribution of different ethnic groups in local, national and international contexts and to the development of tolerance, appreciation and respect for other groups and cultures. Care is taken to expand children's experience of other cultures beyond the European context and teachers are reminded to include a range of perspectives across gender, age, class, culture, ethnicity and religion in their exploration of units of study at national and international levels (Ireland, Government of, 1999c, p. 37).

So what view of Irish identity underlies the History curriculum? Recognising the nested identities of multiple communities and characterised by openness and inclusiveness, it is outward-looking and generous in its disposition. But is it Irish? If one removed the units which relate specifically to Irish political history, there would be little left to identify its origin. Having called earlier in the chapter for a distinction between the teaching of history and the development of national sentiment, it may seem churlish to criticise a curriculum which painstakingly eschews any such association. Yet, in avoiding the dangers of sentimental patriotism, it may have missed the opportunity to create a situated pedagogy. While the idea of story itself, both as content and methodology, is well represented here, the relegation of the rich heritage of Irish myth and story to a single bullet point is regrettable.[8] It is both desirable and necessary to provide children with the opportunity to explore the myths and stories of other European and world cultures. One would, however, expect more than a passing reference to our own. Leaving aside questions of intrinsic value, the central role which story has traditionally played in Irish culture makes the interrogation of the motifs, ideas and values embedded in our ancient myths and legends an essential part of the critical appropriation of cultural heritage. Of even more import, perhaps, is the tendency to recreate engines of social cleavage and inequality as benign categories. While it encourages multiple perspectives on events and periods, the History curriculum fails to problematise the historical roots of either class or gender relations. The inclusion of nomadism as a suggested topic through which to explore continuity and change over time in fifth and sixth classes (Ireland, Government of, 1999b, p. 71) simply highlights the failure to name our largest ethnic minority, namely Irish Travellers, and to engage in a meaningful way with Travellers as a historic community.

In terms of citizenship, the History curriculum is not explicit in its focus. One could lament the absence of a strand or strand unit focusing on democracy, suffrage or human rights. It is, however, replete with opportunities to develop the type of skills, attitudes and dispositions on which the practice of citizenship relies. Skills of analysis, of deduction and evaluation are developed through an engagement with the past which promotes the idea of historical empathy, an appreciation of perspective, a rigorous understanding of the role of evidence and the ability to recognise causal relationships. Children who have experienced such an approach to the past will have gone a long way towards developing the reciprocity and skills of critical reasoning which necessarily underpin the modern concept of democratic citizenship.

GEOGRAPHY

Whatever one may think about the History curriculum, a reluctance to problematise is not evident in the Geography documents in which issues such as homelessness, pollution, fair trade and famine are identified as areas to be investigated and discussed. While focusing more explicitly on the child as proto-citizen, the geography curriculum continues to develop children's understanding of communities and their role within them. From infant classes (4–7 years) on, there is an emphasis on the child's increasing awareness of belonging to collectives, beginning with the family, school and the local community. What is the nature of those communities and the child's relationship to them? Again, diversity is given a strong positive value locally, nationally and internationally. While the development of a "sense of place" is central to the curriculum, the idea that, at a local level, locality and community are not coterminous and that a locality can contain a number of communities is implicit throughout (Ireland, Government of, 1999d, p. 54). This "sense of place" includes the idea of security, of belonging and of the child's affective relationship with places and their communities (Ireland, Government of, 1999e, p. 18). Whereas in History, the educational justification for environment-based learning remains rooted predominantly in the requirements of child learning, in Geography there is room for attachment to place, and for a recognition of what makes a place special or a locality distinctive. The specificity of experience is underlined in the approach to the wider world which is based on the exploration of identifiable locations and named communities (Ireland, Government of, 1999e, p. 119). The curriculum cautions against simplification and over-generalisation in children's exploration of other places implicit in the idea of the generic South American or Italian. Within local places and communities, there is an emphasis on the civic spaces where people interact as social, cultural, economic and political beings and on exploring children's relationship to and responsibility for those spaces. Community groups and associations, leisure and interest clubs, voluntary and commercial or state service providers are conduits for investigation. The potential of involvement in civil society for the promotion of solidarity (Dunne, 2002, p. 83; Walzer, 1995, p. 170) is amplified by the extent to which the communities and places explored through this curriculum are also characterised by their interdependence. Opportunities to acknowledge, identify and analyse interdependent relationships are integrated into the curriculum from the earliest years. Where this interdependence tilts into dependence, the relationships are problematised (Ireland, Government of, 1999d, p. 77; 1999e, pp. 16-17). There is a very definite emphasis on developing in the child a critical understanding of issues of global concern. Using content such as this in social studies programmes has been associated with developing feelings of international solidarity in children (Albala-Bertrand, 1997, p. 6). At the very least, a focus on the interdependent nature of human communities, the interaction between economic, social and cultural spheres and the physical, social and economic links between places builds a sense of belonging to a wider global community (Ireland, Government of, 1999d, p. 7).

Like History, the Geography curriculum also offers many opportunities for the development of attitudes of respect and tolerance and skills of analysis, evaluation, collaboration, debate and discussion, all of which are an essential part of the procedural knowledge of democratic citizenship. There are two particular dispositions, however, which are characteristic of this curriculum and which are constitutive elements in the concept of active citizenship, namely a sense of responsibility and an inclination to action. The emphasis on participation in civic society evident in the curriculum has already been mentioned. This is complemented by the strand "Environmental Awareness and Care"[9] which is concerned with fostering a sense of individual and collective responsibility for the environment at a local, national and global level. The idea of an individual and collective role as custodian of the Earth's environment and resources is embedded in the text (see, for example, Ireland, Government of, 1999d, pp. 8, 9, 14, 15 and 84). Allied with this sense of responsibility is the imperative to act. From the earliest years, there is a definite emphasis on going beyond critique to action. In infant classes, for example, strategies aimed at improving the home and school environments are identified and implemented. By the senior classes, children are focusing on identifying and, where possible, participating in the solution of problems relating to pollution, issues around sustainable development and the idea of renewable and non-renewable resources. Children's awareness of environmental problems is tied to the understanding that they can effect change. While there is some attempt to critique issues of social concern, however, when it comes to action, the locus is the immediate environment of the child and the focus for action is exclusively environmental rather than social or political. One gets the sense of comfortable and safe parameters being drawn around the concept of action, a sense in which the idea of action upon the world is itself domesticated.

SOCIAL, PERSONAL AND HEALTH EDUCATION

The idea of action is also integral to the Social, Personal and Health Education (SPHE) curriculum, a recent addition to the primary curriculum in Ireland. Characterised by a pedagogical perspective which uses active and collaborative teaching strategies, SPHE seeks to foster the "personal development, health and well-being of the child and to help him/her to create and maintain supportive relationships and become an active and responsible citizen in society" (Ireland, Government of, 1999g, p. 2). Of the three areas, SPHE has the most explicit focus on citizenship education and includes among its aims and objectives a commitment to active and participative citizenship, an appreciation of the democratic way of life and a recognition of the rights and responsibilities associated with living in a democracy (Ireland, Government of, 1999f, pp. 9–10). While skills and attitudes relevant to the practice of democratic citizenship are found in all strands, my comments are confined mainly to the unit "Developing citizenship" which is part of the strand "Myself and the wider world". In this unit, the school and the classroom become sites where citizenship skills are practised and honed. Involvement of the child in making classroom rules, participating in decision-making at class and school level, representing the school in events and celebrating a sense of belonging through school assemblies and events are seen as ways of inducting the child into the world of participatory citizenship. Here the child is also introduced to the workings of democracy at state level. The meaning of democracy, the organisation of representative democracy within the Irish state, the role of the Constitution are explored in a context that acknowledges the idea of individual rights as a constitutive concept in modern democracies. The importance of civil society as a site of participative citizenship is underlined by a structured exploration of local organisations, clubs and community groups, which begins in the infant classes.

In common with both History and Geography, the child is characterised as belonging to multiple collectivities, a series of nested and interlinked communities beginning with the child's own family and moving outwards to the school community, local communities, national, European and global communities. The idea of belonging, of sharing a sense of commitment to these communities, goes hand-in-hand with valuing the multiplicity of identities they confer. Here one finds the celebration, the affirmation of identity which was conspicuously absent from the History curriculum. National, regional and local accomplishments, traditions, folklore and festivals are to be celebrated for their distinctiveness, and as a source of pride and identification. The national flag and the national anthem become symbols of belonging and deserving of respect (Ireland, Government of, 1999f, pp. 50–65).

These communities are not imagined as homogenous groups, however, and the focus on collective identities is balanced by a recognition of diversity at all levels of human society and an affirmation of the contributions of different groups to the local, national and international communities. One would be concerned if this celebration of diversity did not acknowledge the faults and cleavages in Irish society and internationally which turn difference into deficit. This is not the case. The SPHE curriculum has a strong justice and equality perspective. Children are provided with opportunities to explore unequal structures and relations in the school and local communities as well as at national and international levels. Prejudice, racism, gender inequalities and poverty are subjected to critical scrutiny. Experiences such as immigration and discrimination are sensitively explored through drama and collaborative activities. To a significant extent, SPHE incorporates both the content and pedagogical strategies of Peace Education, Anti-Racist Education and Anti-Bias Education. Add to this a strand focused on a critical engagement with the media, pedagogical approaches which foster collaborative skills, conflict resolution and decision-making, the willingness to listen to and take on board the views of others while retaining a capacity for independent thought and one is fairly close to describing a model education for citizenship curriculum.

POSSIBILITIES

It is plausible to argue that a combination of history, geography and SPHE as envisaged in these documents provide primary education with a coherent and well-balanced blueprint for citizenship education in the twenty-first century. The nuanced and inclusive approach to identity and community balance the virtue of solidarity with a respect for different cultures, ethnicities and traditions.

While one might wish for more recognition of the affective dimensions of identity in the History curriculum and a greater sense of the value of belonging to a storied community, the focus on a critical appropriation of history at local, national and international levels is to be welcomed. History teaching has its own ghosts to lay in Irish education and it is appropriate that celebration be located elsewhere. Across the subjects, the idea of multiple, overlapping identities and of interlinked and interdependent communities releases the child into the wider world while holding on to the idea of belonging.

A sense of the magnitude of the changes that have occurred in Ireland is conveyed when the ideas of identity and community implicit in the 1971 civics curriculum are examined. While there is some evidence of continuity in a recognition of "shared membership of various groups" (Department of Education, 1971a, p. 115) in the 1971 curriculum, that is where the similarities end, for it is a membership that is both defined and confined by a sense of responsibility and duty and the "cultivation of good habits" (Department of Education, 1971a, p. 118). Indeed, the idea of citizenship itself is seen as less important than the inculcation of "acceptable social and moral attitudes which take into account the rights of other members of society" (Department of Eudcation, 1971a, p. 115) and a "fair measure of freedom within the school" is justified by the need to instil self-discipline rather than the opportunity to develop the practice of democracy. What is most striking, however, is the extent to which civics is seen as an offshoot of religious education (Department of Education, 1971a, p. 116). The assumption of a shared Christian ethos, characteristic of the curriculum as a whole,[10] is at its most explicit here. The family as a community is modelled explicitly on the "Holy Family"; Christ is presented as the model which the child is urged to emulate (Department of Education, 1971a, p. 122). The "National Community" is seen as an extension of the family, a site for the practice of "patriotic virtues" consistent with "duty to God and to the moral law". Overall, it presents an exclusive concept of identity and a model of the citizen as the good and dutiful son/daughter who neither questions nor challenges the status quo. The *Primary School Curriculum* (Ireland, Government of, 1999a), on the other hand, is premised on an inclusive concept of identity and on the idea of the citizen as informed and critical, ready and able to accept the "burdens of judgement" (Rawls, 1993, p. 54) which accompanies an acceptance of, and respect for, the other. The emphasis on taking the perspective of the other, on listening to and taking account of the opinion of others is coupled with the promotion of respect for evidence and the capacity for independent thought. For the child informed by a knowledge *of* the world, a sense of responsibility *for* the world and a readiness to act *in* the world, her/his environment becomes the site for the practice of civic virtue.

And yet, there is the suspicion that, stripped of its more liberal context, the conception of action implicit in the Geography and SPHE curricula has its roots in the dutiful concerns of the earlier child/citizen. Is this inevitable in a citizenship programme aimed at children? While there are legitimate questions to be asked about the ethical limits of action in child education, the right of all citizens to participate in a democracy should not be limited by age. Parental or professional support cannot be assumed for a concept of participation that could be seen as political. Few, however, could quarrel with a field of action whose boundaries are those of the school, home and community. The idea of action in SPHE includes participation in democratic procedures within the school. The opportunity to participate at school level in itself brings with it many benefits. There is evidence, for example, that involvement in school activities is a good predictor of civic commitment and that the opportunity to engage in concrete action on reality promotes later involvement in civic life (Albala-Bertrand, 1997, p. 7). Moreover, one could argue that limited and appropriate action on wider community issues could be negotiated.[11] There is also, however, a strong case for recognising the rights of children to participate on a broader scale at regional, national[12] and global levels. While the appropriate form of participation may require some lateral thinking (Shine Thompson, 2003), one needs to be careful that it remains authentic and real and avoids the dangers of tokenism.

Certainly, as a blueprint for citizenship education, there is much of value here. It holds within it a concept of the good society which is democratic in its practices and inclusive in its membership, where justice is taken seriously, where solidarity extends beyond local or national communities and where membership brings with it not only the *freedom from* embodied in individual rights, but the *freedom to* of participatory citizenship. Despite the limitations already identified, the emphasis on civic engagement and agency, allied with the recognition of interdependent and diverse communities characteristic of this curriculum, suggests a serious commitment to the ideals of republican citizenship. Given the deep-seated inequities which characterise Irish society, it seems fair to say that what is being posited here is a society not yet in existence and the educational project of creating citizens for an imagined future. It is, in this sense, a campaigning curriculum. Imagined futures, however, must take account of the constraints of the present if they are to be realised.

CONSTRAINTS

The role of education within Irish society is replete with contradictions, not least of which is the contradiction between education as giver of life-chances at the individual level and the generative role it plays in limiting those same chances through the reproduction of inequality at societal level. In a society where advancement is premised on the accumulation of credentialised knowledge, access to that knowledge can both determine and be determined by one's position in the social hierarchy. That such a role in the distribution of privilege is at odds with the impulse towards social solidarity and social cohesion required of citizenship education in a pluralist democracy seems self-evident. This is not the place for a lengthy critique of the relationship between education and society and the role which education plays in the reproduction of inequality (see Lynch and Lodge, 2002; Drudy and Lynch, 1993; Breen et al., 1990). However, in seeking to outline the nature of the constraints with which education for democratic citizenship is forced to engage, it is important to draw upon some points in that critique. The following arguments, consequently, are necessarily selective and suggestive, and do not seek to give a comprehensive account of these complex relationships.

In her analysis of the hidden curriculum in Irish secondary schools, Lynch (1989) highlights the extent to which potentially equalising forces in Irish education are subverted by particularistic tendencies within the system. The equalising or universalistic potential of state examinations, for example, is offset by the ability of the wealthy to buy access to extra educational knowledge in the form of private tuition and by particularistic practices such as streaming within schools themselves. This particularism is an inevitable by-product of a system which is segmented along the sectional lines of class, ethnicity,[13] gender and religion. The denominational nature of the Irish education system raises questions in relation to other capacities and dispositions. There is a tension between comprehensive doctrines that are used as the arbiters of fundamental truths and the development and exercise of autonomy, between the rights of traditional communities to recreate themselves and the needs of a pluralist democracy (Callan, 1997, Chapter 7). From a class perspective, segmentation along class lines, whether between schools through geographical segregation and greater middle-class access to the mechanisms of school choice, or within schools through streaming and tracking, leads, at the very least, to issues of distributive justice (Lynch and Lodge, 2002, p. 35). A system which colludes in institutionalising sectional interests to this extent is unlikely to promote a commitment to social solidarity.

Schools are also highly complex institutions in which intricate and interwoven patterns of relations can be defined by issues of authority, power and control (Lynch and Lodge, 2002; Lynch, 1989). While school climate and organisation, involvement of students in decision-making, pedagogical style and democratic classroom practice all play an important part in the development of citizens (Kymlicka, 2001, p. 292; Emler and Frazer, 1999, p. 269; Albala-Bertrand, 1997, pp. 6, 7), the extent to which schools can be considered to be centres of democratic practice is questionable.[14] Despite its stated commitment to child-centred education, Irish primary education has been characterised as teacher-directed and traditional (O'Rourke and Archer, 1987, p. 77), highly structured and teacher-controlled (Burke and Fontes, 1986, p. 72). In his 1990 review of child-centred education in Ireland, Sugrue highlights the extent to which the principles of child-centred education are open to wide interpretation and can indeed be stretched to accommodate a range of practice from the traditional to the progressive. There are those who would argue that this ideological elasticity is sustained by the inadequacy of its central concepts which are seen as vague and superficial and lacking in rigour.[15] When one examines the introduction to the 1999 curriculum, there is evidence to suggest that same tendency to ideological weakness and a failure to explicate its philosophical underpinnings beyond the superficial.[16] Based on a view of the relationship between education and society as unproblematic (Ireland, Government of, 1999a, p. 6), and a conception of equality confined to issues of opportunity and fairness of access (Ireland, Government of, 1999a, p. 28), it is unlikely to provide a basis for genuine critique or a solid foundation from which to challenge existing classroom practice.[17] While it may be prudent to have reservations about the rigour and coherence of child-centred education as an ideology, it is possible to argue, however, that it offers a place from which to start the journey towards democratic education and that it is legitimate to look to "the best in the tradition" (Callan, 1997, p. 98) as a way of moving forward.

CONCLUSION

The creation of a curriculum which offers opportunities for the development of democratic citizenship has to be welcomed at any time. The affirmation of diversity at the heart of its conception of Irish identity represents a significant ideological shift from one bounded by ideas of a common culture and a shared religious ethos to one which recognises the multiplicity of identities and the permeability of those boundaries. In the context of a society which is engaged in an uncertain and potentially transformative process of change, such a curriculum is more than welcome, it is essential. There is, however, a legitimate concern that in its determination to embrace cultural pluralism, the curriculum neglects the shared meanings and traditions which give Irish identity its historical roots. Moreover, despite its commitment to a conception of citizenship which is participatory and inclusive, there is no guarantee that this intent will have any practical outcome. An expectation that a change in curriculum and pedagogy in schools will lead to a wider transformation in society is plainly naïve. To succumb to the opposite view, however, that the structural role which education plays in the reproduction of existing social relations makes curriculum reform irrelevant, is deterministic and overly pessimistic. To do nothing is to do something and a belief in the inability to affect change allows existing practices to continue unchallenged. Central to that change will be the preparedness of schools to provide the necessary context for the development of the skills of active citizenship through the democratisation of relations. There is a tension within education between control and agency which needs to be confronted honestly. It seems highly improbable that one can educate children towards their full participation in a democratic society through a system of education whose social relations are determined by power. Paulo Freire argued that "it's impossible in a truly liberating praxis for the educator to follow a domesticating model". (1985, p. 105). Martin Buber put it even more succinctly when he said "No way leads to any other goal but to that which is like it" (1979, p. 50). Nor can the creation of opportunities within primary education for children to engage with issues of identity and citizenship be divorced from the need to create a wider forum for debate and dissent in Irish society as a whole. In an Ireland that strives to balance the recognition of diversity with the ties of solidarity, finding a space for children's voices should be a priority.

References

Albala-Bertrand, L. (1997), "What Education for What Citizenship? Preliminary Results", *Educational Innovation and Information*, Vol. 90, pp. 2–8.

Anderson, B. (1991), *Imagined Communities*, London: Verso.

Beiner, R. (ed.) (1995), *Theorising Citizenship*, Albany: SUNY Press.

Bennet, J. (1994), "History Textbooks in Primary Schools in the Republic of Ireland, 1971–1993", in *Oideas 42*, pp. 5–22.

Blenkin, G.M. and Kelly, A.V. (1981), *The Primary Curriculum*, London, Harper and Row.

Bowles, S. and Gintis, H. (1976), *Schooling in Capitalist America*, New York: Basic Books.

Breen, R., Hannan, D.F., Rottman, D.B. and Whelan, C.T. (1990), *Understanding Contemporary Ireland*, London: Macmillan.

Bruner, J. (1977), *The Process of Education*, Cambridge: Harvard University Press.

Buber, M. (1979), *Between Man and Man* (trans. Smith, R.G.), London: Fontana.

Burke, A. and Fontes, P.J. (1986), "Educational Beliefs and Practices of Sixth-Class Teachers in Irish Primary Schools", *The Irish Journal of Education*, Vol. xx, No. 2, pp. 51–77.

Callan, E. (1997), *Creating Citizens: Political Education and Liberal Democracy*, New York: Oxford University Press.

Coolahan, J. (1981), *Irish Education: Its History and Structure*, Dublin: Institute of Public Administration.

Clancy, P. (ed.) (1995), *Irish Society: Sociological Perspectives*, Dublin: Stationery Office.

Department of Education (1933), *Notes for Teachers*, Dublin: Stationery Office.

Department of Education (1971a), *Curaclam Na Bunscoile: Primary School Curriculum 1*, Dublin: Government Publications Office.

Department of Education (1971b), *Curaclam Na Bunscoile: Primary School Curriculum 2*, Dublin: Government Publications Office.

Dewey, J. (1961), *Democracy in Education*, New York: Macmillan.

Drudy, S. and Lynch, K. (1993), *Schools and Society in Ireland*, Dublin: Gill and Macmillan.

Dunne, J. (2002), "Citizenship and Education: A Crisis of the Republic?" in Cronin, M., Gibbons, L. and Kirby, P. (eds.), *Reinventing Ireland: Culture, Society and the Global Economy*, London: Pluto, pp. 69–88.

Dunne, J. and Kelly, J. (eds.) (2002), *Childhood and its Discontents: The First Seamus Heaney Lectures*, Dublin: The Liffey Press.

Egan, K. (1997), *The Educated Mind: How Cognitive Tools Shape Our Understanding*, Chicago, London: University of Chicago Press.

Egan, K. (1978), *Teaching as Storytelling: An Alternative Approach to Teaching and the Curriculum*, London: Routledge.

Emler, N. and Frazer, E. (1999), "Politics: The Education Effect", *Oxford Review of Education*, Vol. 25, Nos. 1 and 2.

Enslin, P. (1994), "Should Nation-Building be an Aim of Education?" *Journal of Education (Natal)*, Vol. 19, No. 1.

Fitzpatrick, D. (1991), "The Futility of History: A Failed Experiment in Irish Education", in Brady, C. (ed.), *Ideology and the Historians*, Dublin: Lilliput Press.

Freire, P. (1972), *Pedagogy of the Oppressed*, Harmondsworth: Penguin.

Freire, P. (1985), *The Politics of Education: Culture, Power and Liberation*, London: Macmillan.

Hobsbawm, E. (1990), *Nations and Nationalism since 1780: Programme, Myth, Reality*, Cambridge University Press.

Hogan, P. (1986), "Progressivism and the Primary School Curriculum", *Oideas*, Vol. 29, pp. 25–40.

Honohan, I. (2001), "Freedom as Citizenship: The Republican Tradition in Political Theory", *The Republic*, Issue 2, Spring/Summer, pp. 7–24.

Howard, S. and Gill, J. (2000), "The Pebble in the Pond: Children's Constructions of Power, Politics and Democratic Citizenship", *Cambridge Journal of Education*, Vol. 30, No. 3, pp. 357–78.

Ireland, Government of (1999a), *Primary School Curriculum: Introduction*, Dublin: The Stationery Office.

Ireland, Government of (1999b), *Primary School Curriculum: History*, Dublin: The Stationery Office.

Ireland, Government of (1999c), *Primary School Curriculum: History, Teacher Guidelines*, Dublin: The Stationery Office.

Ireland, Government of (1999d), *Primary School Curriculum: Geography*, Dublin: The Stationery Office.

Ireland, Government of (1999e), *Primary School Curriculum: Geography, Teacher Guidelines*, Dublin: The Stationery Office.

Ireland, Government of (1999f), *Primary School Curriculum: Social, Personal and Health Education*, Dublin: The Stationery Office.

Ireland, Government of (1999g), *Primary School Curriculum: Social, Personal and Health Education, Teacher Guidelines*, Dublin: The Stationery Office.

Ireland, Government of (2002), *Promoting Anti-Racism and Interculturalism in Education: Draft Recommendations towards a National Action Plan.*

Irish National Teachers Organisation (1996), *Primary School Curriculum: An Evolutionary Process*, Dublin: INTO.

Ignatieff, M. (1995), "The Myth of Citizenship", in Beiner, R. (ed.), *Theorising Citizenship*, Albany: SUNY Press, pp. 53–77.

Kenny, M. (2000), "Travellers, Minorities and Schools", in Sheehan, E. (ed.), *Travellers: Citizens of Ireland*, Dublin: The Parish of the Travelling People, pp. 139–47.

Kirby, P., Gibbons, L. and Cronin, M. (eds.), (2002), *Reinventing Ireland: Culture, Society and the Global Economy*, London: Pluto.

Kymlicka, W. (2001), *Politics in the Vernacular: Nationalism, Multiculturalism, and Citizenship*, New York: Oxford University Press.

Lentin, R. and McVeigh, R. (eds.) (2002), *Racism and Anti-Racism in Ireland*, Belfast: Beyond the Pale Publications.

Lynch, K. and Lodge, A. (2002), *Equality and Power in Schools: Redistribution, Recognition and Representation*, London: Routledge Falmer.

Lynch, K. (1989), *The Hidden Curriculum: Reproduction in Education, a Reappraisal*, New York: Falmer Press.

Morgan, M. (2002), "Too Much Knowledge, Too Much Fear: Curricular Developments in Irish Primary Schools", in Dunne, J. and Kelly, J. (eds.), *Childhood and its Discontents: The First Seamus Heaney Lectures*, Dublin: The Liffey Press, pp. 107–21.

Murphy, D. (1986), "The Dilemmas of Primary Curriculum Reform", *Oideas*, Vol. 29, pp. 7–24.

National Children's Strategy (2000), Dublin: The Stationery Office.

O'Rourke, B. and Archer, P. (1987), "A Survey of Teaching Practices in the Junior Grades of Irish Primary Schools", *The Irish Journal of Education*, Vol. XXI, No. 2, pp. 53–79.

Osler, A., Rathenow, H. and Starkey, H. (eds.) (1995), *Teaching for Citizenship in Europe*, London: Trentham Books.

Oxford Review of Education (1999), Vol. 25, Nos. 1 and 2.

Pike, S. (2001), "Ideas about being Irish", *Primary Geography*, No. 45, October.

Qualifications and Curriculum Authority (1998), *Education for Citizenship and the Teaching of Democracy in Schools* (Crick Report), London: QCA.

Rawls, J. (1993), *Political Liberalism*, New York:

Shine Thompson, M. (2003), Republicanism and Childhood in Twentieth-Century Ireland, *The Republic*, Issue 3, Spring/Summer.

Sugrue, C. (1990), "Child-Centred Education in Ireland since 1971", *Oideas*, 35, Spring, pp. 5–21.

Sugrue, C. (1997), *Complexities of Teaching: Child-Centred Perspectives*, Washington, DC: Falmer Press.

Waldron, F. (2002), *"A Nation's Schoolbooks Wield a Great Power": How the Romans are Depicted in Irish History Textbooks*, paper delivered at History Textbook Conference, Bath University, 7 February.

Walzer, M. (1995), "The Civil Society Argument", in Beiner, R. (ed.), *Theorising Citizenship*, Albany: SUNY Press, pp. 153–74.

White, J. (1997), "National Myths, Democracy and Education", in Bridges, D. (ed.), *Education, Autonomy and Democratic Citizenship: Philosophy in a Changing World*, London: Routledge, pp. 15–22.

White, P. (1999), "Political Education in the Early Years: The Place of Civic Virtues", *Oxford Review of Education*, Vol. 25, Nos. 1 and 2, pp. 59–70.

Endnotes

1 For an analysis of individual and institutional racism in Ireland see Lentin and McVeigh (eds.) (2002). In early 2003, the Irish Supreme Court delivered a majority judgement which denied immigrant parents of children born in Ireland the expectation of residency on the basis of their child's citizenship (see *Irish Times*, 25 January 2003). For an overview of the state response to racism from an educational perspective see Department of Education and Science (2002) *Promoting Anti-Racism and Interculturalism in Education: Draft Recommendations towards a National Action Plan.*

2 See for example, A. Osler, H. Rathenow and H. Starkey (eds.) (1995), *Teaching for Citizenship in Europe,* London: Trentham Books

3 The Crick Report (1998), for example, stimulated debate and curriculum development in the UK In 1999, the *Oxford Review of Education,* Vol. 25, Nos. 1 and 2 was devoted to the topic of citizenship education. See also the books, reports and initiatives in the bibliography.

4 While it is arguable that all subjects, both in their content and pedagogy, contribute to the construction of identity and the practice of citizenship, some contributions are more explicit than others. It seems obvious, for example, that the Irish language plays an important, if sometimes ambiguous role, in the construction of Irish identity within education. Sport, music, literature also play a part in the construction of identity and in the development of citizenship. The 1999 curriculum introduces drama to the primary curriculum both as a discrete subject and as a cross-curricular approach. In its exploration of self, of community and interdependence, drama has the potential to contribute significantly to individual and group identity and relations. Its participative and collaborative methodology and the opportunities it provides for children's voices to be heard have obvious implications for the practice of citizenship.

5 At second level, students study Civic, Social and Political Education to Junior Certificate level. This is a dedicated citizenship programme which focuses on concepts, skills, attitudes and knowledge around the themes of the individual and citizenship, the community, the state and the global community. The 1971 primary curriculum also included a dedicated civics programme which is discussed elsewhere in the chapter.

6 Notwithstanding the impossibility of an ahistorical generic citizen, the ideals of liberal democracy are unapologetically universal in impulse. The inherent tensions in a pluralist society between the universal and the particular have been teased out by Beiner (1995), Callan (1997) and Kymlicka (2001), among others.

7 The Platonic commitment to the telling of "myth" as a way of promoting loyalty to the state suggests that this instrumental use of history has a long tradi-

tion. My use of the term "myth" in this section is informed by Ignatieff's (1995, p. 53) distinction between the "noble conception of myth as ancient story" which he characterises as a bearer of truths about the universe and our place in it and a more modern conception of myth which sees it as an ironic synonym for untruth. I believe both conceptions to be relevant to national stories.

[8] The following appears in different forms in the curriculum from first and second class onwards as part of the story strand: *The child should be enabled to*

- *Listen to, discuss, retell and record a range of myths and legends from different cultural, ethnic and religious backgrounds in Ireland and other countries.*

[9] This strand is common to the Geography, Science and SPHE curriculum. From fourth class on, the notion of agency becomes even more explicit with the creation of two strands, one focusing on awareness and the other on care.

[10] The position accorded to religion in the *Primary School Curriculum* (Department of Education, 1971) is problematic in a number of ways. Not only does it assume a consensus of belief amongst the community at large (1971, p. 12) but by its insistence on the integration of religion with "secular instruction" (p. 19) it seeks to conflate knowledge-as-belief with knowledge-as-construction. That the nature of religious knowledge is antithetical to the epistemological perspective endorsed by the child-centred model, i.e. that of pragmatic empiricism, becomes even more problematic when religious beliefs and practices are accorded the status of "transcendent values" through which all other knowledge is to be interpreted and evaluated (p. 23).

[11] Most people, for example, would have no objection to teachers involving children in a letter-writing campaign to the local council seeking a pedestrian crossing on a local road; while making posters in support of a campaign for a halting site in the local area, however rooted in concepts of justice, respect and equality, might not be viewed with the same equanimity. Participating in debate and discussion around the issue, however, and exploring attitudes underlying different standpoints in the area could be construed as action in this case.

[12] In this context, one must welcome the provision in the National Children's Strategy for giving children a voice through the formation of a *Dáil na nÓg* or National Children's Parliament as a forum for debate and raising concerns and for the representation of children's views on other national and local forums. The following goal is identified: "Children will have a voice in matters which affect them and their views will be given due weight in accordance with their age and maturity". See National Children's Strategy (2000), Dublin: The Stationery Office.

[13] While the cultural and social apartheid experienced by Irish Travellers within the education system though the provision of separate provision in the form of special schools and special classes in the initial period of provision (see Kenny, 2000) has given way to a policy of integration with learning support, a visiting

teacher scheme and a national co-ordinator, there are currently three special schools for Travellers, six Junior Education Centres and 28 Senior Training Centres supported by the Department of Education and Science (Department of Education and Science Statistical Report, 2002).

[14] The idea of democratic education has a long history and wide literature. For classic statements of the case, it is difficult to surpass John Dewey's (1961) *Democracy in Education* and, from the perspective of critique, Paulo Freire's (1972) *Pedagogy of the Oppressed* and Bowles and Gintis (1976) *Schooling in Capitalist America*.

[15] The ideas underlying child-centred education have been subjected to periods of sustained questioning over the years, both from a traditional and from a critical perspective. In an Irish context, debate has been sporadic and never allowed to disturb the calm waters of educational consensus. The mid-1980s saw an interesting if brief flurry of debate on child-centred education in the exchange of views between Hogan (1986) and Murphy (1986). Sugrue (1990; 1997) and Blenkin and Kelly (1981) provide a good overview of the classic arguments around child-centred education. An interesting and thought provoking alternative to the child-centred model is offered by Egan (1997; 1998).

[16] See, for example, the failure to provide any elaboration of the concept of agency (Ireland, 1999, p. 14) and the reduction of the need for a positive school climate in which individuals are "valued, cared for and respected" to the requirements of effective learning and communication (Ireland, 1999f, p. 22). Moreover, the tendency to reduce critical thinking to the level of problem-solving (Irl., 1999, p. 16) reinforces the proclivity already identified to domesticate the concept of action.

[17] One of the contradictions in practice consistently found to be characteristic of Irish primary classrooms is that between a commitment to active learning and the reliance on textbooks as a method of teaching. Research into classroom practice in the 1970s, 1980s and 1990s suggest that the thoughtful and nuanced conceptualisation of identity embedded in the History, Geography and SPHE curricula may well be hijacked by the traditional commitment of Irish teachers to the textbook as a method of both planning and teaching (Irish National Teachers Organisation, 1996). Children's understandings of the world can be shaped indirectly by the materials they use, the images they are exposed to and the books they encounter. Textbooks bring with them their own assumptions about the nature of Irish identity, some of which are antithetical to the idea of a pluralist Ireland (Waldron, 2002).

Chapter 8

THE PRIMARY CURRICULUM IN NORTHERN IRELAND: APING BIG BROTHER OR FINDING ITS OWN VOICE?

Margaret Reynolds

INTRODUCTION

The Northern Ireland curriculum was introduced as a common curriculum in 1989 and the next six years were spent modifying contents, and planning, piloting and setting in place a process of assessment. In 1995, the then Department for Education for Northern Ireland (DENI) promised teachers a five-year period of continuity when no further changes would be introduced. Since 1999, however, the Council for Curriculum, Examinations and Assessment (CCEA) has been engaged in reviewing the curriculum. Their current proposals took as their starting point a series of conferences held in 1998 and 1999 (CCEA, 1999a) and suggest a radical departure from the current curriculum which is structured in cognate subject areas. CCEA's current view of the curriculum not only marks a change in curriculum structure, however; it also seems to herald a change in the tradition that the curriculum in Northern Ireland schools should largely reflect the curriculum in schools in Britain.

The history of curriculum development in Northern Ireland schools has been described as "aping big brother" (Gallagher,

2001). As successive changes were introduced in the system of education in Britain they were eventually visited on schools in Northern Ireland. Thus, to understand the forces that have shaped the curriculum in Northern Ireland schools, it is essential to look at what was happening at that time "across the water", particularly in England and Wales.

There were several essential pressures which informed the curriculum debate and the establishment of a prescribed curriculum in Britain and Northern Ireland. According to Lawton (1989), these were: an increasing consumerisation of education, a preoccupation with value for money, a desire to raise standards and the need to ensure that the curriculum was not manipulated by politically motivated activists. Underpinning and informing these influences is a web of beliefs about the nature of education, its relationship to benefits for society and the personal development of pupils. Individual curricula are expressions of the ideology of the education system to which they belong. This implies that the structure of a curriculum does not merely mirror objective states of affairs. It contains underpinning assumptions about knowledge, action and the nature of the educated individual that crucially affect the form that the curriculum and its assessment take. It also reveals central values conveyed in the selection of the curriculum contents and assessment adopted by those with legislative power.

This chapter first outlines the development of the primary curriculum in Britain which was introduced in 1988 and discusses the influences that shaped it. Second, a critical analysis of "official documentation" is undertaken to reveal and lay bare its underlying assumptions. Third, it examines the implicit views of knowledge, learning and values that underpin the curriculum and have influenced the form it takes. This examination includes an analysis of the forms of assessment adopted in the Northern Ireland curriculum and deconstructs the assessment process itself to lay bare the tacit values therein. In the concluding section, the implications of the analysis for the immediate future of primary curriculum and schooling are summarised and an outline sketched of an alternative vision.

ANATOMY OF TEACHER AUTONOMY AND
CURRICULUM PRESCRIPTION

It is a truism to say that the primary curriculum and how it is taught is a significant political issue. With the introduction of compulsory schooling in Britain and Ireland in 1870, the history of education has been one of increasing state intervention. Whilst compulsory schooling was introduced in Britain largely because of fears that other nations were pulling ahead in terms of industrial and technological development (Musgrave, 1968), it was introduced in Ireland principally as a means of social control (Coolahan, 1981). However, the approach to curriculum content was largely consistent within both jurisdictions. Initially, there was central control over what should be taught in schools and a largely traditional curriculum was imposed that was dominated by the 3Rs. By 1926, however, curriculum prescription had ceased in Britain and by the 1950s the "golden age" of teacher control over curricula had begun (Lawton, 1989). Nevertheless, the curriculum in the majority of primary schools remained largely unchanged in its emphasis on reading, writing and arithmetic. One reason for this was the need for primary schools to prepare children for the 11+ examination, which governed access to grammar schools. By the late 1960s in Britain, the effects of the 11+ were greatly reduced by the gradual introduction of comprehensive schooling and the resulting reduction in selection which began in the early 1970s. This had significant impact on primary schools which no longer had to stream pupils by ability to create homogeneous groups for examination drilling. The curriculum was no longer influenced by an examination syllabus and schools could concentrate more on tailoring curriculum content to perceived needs rather than to the exigencies of external assessment.

Government policy also appeared to confirm that schools should have autonomy in what they taught when in 1967 the Plowden Report (CACE, 1967) was published. This report made a strong policy statement about the need for education to take account of the uniqueness of each child and to individualise the teaching and learning process. Taken to its logical conclusion, it would mean that schools would no longer plan a formal curriculum. Rather, teachers would respond to the needs and interests of the children in their classes. There is much debate about the impact that the "progressive" views voiced in the Plowden Report had on actual classroom practice (Bennett, 1976). However, the report certainly contributed to the progressivist *zeitgeist* and for that reason it is a seminal document in the history of curriculum reform in Britain. It gave official credence to the belief that what was done in schools should reflect the needs and interests of the children themselves rather than the interests of society. It also provided a target for those who were critical of the progressive ideal and seemed to galvanise critics of progressivism into active opposition to its main precepts. Throughout the late 1960s and early 1970s, a series of Black Papers, such as that of Cox and Dyson (1969), consistently criticised progressive methods and school curricula.

By the late 1960s, precisely at a time when teachers had most autonomy, the curriculum had become an issue of contention and debate. This debate was brought specifically to the attention of the British nation at large in 1976 when James Callaghan, the then Prime Minister, called for a public debate on education. This debate was not confined to those professionally concerned with education but gave full opportunity for employers, trade unions and parents as well as teachers and administrators to make their views known. The results of this investigation were published in 1977 (DES, 1977): the educational system was criticised for producing school-leavers who had not learned the basic skills required by industry and this was linked to the perceived failure of schools to define curriculum content precisely. Schools were reminded that the role of education should be to contribute to Britain's economic survival which, it was claimed, could only be assured through the efficiency of British industry and commerce.

In terms of general education, the review begun by Prime Minister Callaghan resulted in the suggestion that a core curriculum that would emphasise certain basic skills should be established (DES, 1977). It also aimed to narrow the gap between the worlds of education and work by stressing the skills which would be of use in an occupational context. The perceived skills gap between what industry required and the kinds of learning promoted in schools was claimed as one of the main factors affecting the economic wealth of the nation. A closer liaison between education and employment was also encouraged. By the 1980s, the Government's main educational objective (DES, 1985) was to equip pupils for work by helping them to acquire the necessary skills for effective employment; furthermore, the emphasis on skills was expected to influence the curriculum in all schools, not merely at secondary level. Thus, market ideology with its focus on economic pressures and the needs of consumers became a major influence on education and schools (Jonathan, 1997).

Throughout the next decade, the question of curriculum content was keenly debated and the notion of a common curriculum which would be broad and balanced in terms of the range of subjects it covered was eventually distilled. In 1988, the Education Reform Act was passed in Britain outlining the arrangement for a National Curriculum for all schools. In parallel, the Northern Ireland Curriculum was introduced in 1989 in the Education Reform Order. Both the curricula in Britain and Northern Ireland contain details of the subjects that should be included in the curriculum, their content and assessment arrangements. In Northern Ireland, the common curriculum was introduced in primary schools against a background of curricula still heavily influenced, at least for those pupils preparing for it, by the demands of the 11+ examination. Whilst there is a common curriculum in Northern Ireland, much of the time in primary six and seven is spent preparing for the 11+ examination. Only after that examination finishes do teachers turn their attention fully to common curriculum contents.

The Northern Ireland Curriculum

In Northern Ireland, English, Mathematics and Science and Technology are central to the curriculum and English and Mathematics are formally assessed. Other subjects, for example History, Geography, Music, Art and PE also form part of the curriculum but they are not assessed formally. There are also four cross-curricular themes: Education for Mutual Understanding; Cultural Heritage; Health Education; and Information Technology. The subjects of the Northern Ireland Curriculum are defined in programmes of study which give details of subject content, learning objectives and attainment targets. Attainment targets outline the standards in terms of pupil performance in particular aspects of a subject. For example, in English the attainment targets are reading, writing, talking and listening. They form the basis for judging pupil attainment. There are eight levels in each attainment target and level descriptors indicate the range and type of behaviour expected at each level. By the end of the primary phase it is expected that the majority of children should be working at level three or four. The programmes of study supply lists of the activities in which pupils should engage but it is the attainment targets that provide the detailed content for each subject because they contain the standards against which pupils will be assessed.

PERFORMANCE AND SKILLS AS OBJECTIVES IN THE NORTHERN IRELAND CURRICULUM

The structure of the Northern Ireland Curriculum displays, consistent with its sister curriculum in Britain, an emphasis on performance, skills and objectives. Its structure reflects the influence of skills-oriented education and training advocated by Government since the middle of the 1970s. It was also influenced by the objectives approach to curriculum planning introduced in British schools because of the raising, in 1973, of the school leaving age to sixteen. Schools at that time were faced with the potential prospect of teaching large numbers of disenfranchised teenagers who, normally, would have left school at fifteen. The traditional academic curriculum was thought to be inappropriate for these pupils because of their poor level of ability. The solution was thought to be the construction of objectives-based courses that would clarify expectations. It was assumed that clarification of expected outcomes would motivate pupils and also ensure success. The approach was individualised; emphasis was placed on individual achievement and the correct pacing of learning for each pupil (Gordon and Lawton, 1978). Performance was stressed and objectives were constructed to give a precise statement of what was to be achieved. Objectives were preferred to aims because, unlike the latter which are broad statements of purpose and intention, objectives list the expected outcomes of a lesson or a course of study in terms of what the individual should be able to do on completion of the lesson or course (Taba, 1962). The importance of skills within this objectives framework is evident. Skills are checklisted, taught and lists ticked (Fletcher, 1991) as the skills are displayed in performance.

The Northern Ireland Curriculum reflects a performance-based approach to curriculum planning by listing skills and setting performance targets for both primary and secondary education. It seems to reflect the assumption that skills can be promoted by concentrating on defining subject content in behavioural terms and assessing desired performance by relating it to behavioural descriptors. For example, in English it is the skills of writing and reading that are highlighted rather than the development of understanding or the disposition to read. Emphasis in assessment is currently given to evaluating the underlying skills, for example decoding and sentence construction. However, complete specification of outcomes is not a comprehensive framework for specification of curriculum content. The inadequacy is exemplified in assessment where Wolf (1993) claims that an individual test item relies ultimately for its effectiveness on factors which lie outside the test. Assessment of a literacy skill, for instance, cannot be independent of the context in which the test is set and the context cannot be reduced to the constituent elements, or descriptors, of the test itself. In assessing the skill, the context in which the assessment is set, including the way the question is asked, will influence to a large degree the efficacy of the test. Prescription of objectives or learning outcomes alone provides an insufficient basis for the curriculum.

THE AIMS AND VALUES UNDERPINNING THE NORTHERN IRELAND CURRICULUM

The history of the development of the national curricula in Britain and Northern Ireland demonstrates increasing emphasis on performance and the relevance of education to economic prosperity and the needs of the market. Current curriculum in Northern Ireland seems to be a response to this drive by concentrating on promoting practical competence. Although this emphasis is particularly evident in the secondary sector, the primary curriculum is also influenced by similar goals. It might seem self-evident that some kind of competence has always been the aim of education. Any system of education could be said to have the aim of promoting competence in learners. Liberal education, for example, promoted effective performance in rational thinking. O'Hear (1981) claims that the aims of a liberal education would also include promoting autonomous decision-making, helping pupils to develop the skills to provide for themselves and educating them morally. The development of personal competence in a range of fields would be essential for the achievement of these goals. However, the kind of competence promoted by liberal education is contextualised within a range of intrinsic goals that are largely personal; the development of practical competence is not an end in itself. Where competence is only linked to practical application of skills, however, it takes on a distinct character consistent with a very narrow view of the role of education in personal development. The nature of the performance displayed by the individual becomes the focus for attention rather than the nature of the person performing. Whereas liberal education has the general aim of developing the educated person, the curriculum now seems to have the general aim of simply providing for skilful performance by individuals within specific areas.

The primary curriculum in Northern Ireland then, whilst appearing to be constructed on the basis of traditional subjects, reveals many of the premises of competence-based education. These are that desired performance is itemised precisely, knowledge and understanding required is listed and assessment of competence is focused solely on completion of task. It is a system which depends on objectives rather than longer-term aims: if the task is completed successfully, the learning has been successful. Education, on the other hand, has traditionally been linked to longer-term goals, such as the development of the moral person. Such aims can be criticised for being associated with the kind of liberal education which focused on the development of the individual rather than concern also for the social role of the individual. Pring (1995), for example, claims that a major shortcoming in traditional views of liberal education has been the omission of any reference to the context of individual's lives and the roles they fulfil. O'Hear (1981) also argues that any view of liberal education must take account of the needs of the person as a member of society. The Northern Ireland curriculum is superficially structured in line with a traditionally liberal content but it reflects such an emphasis on behavioural objectives that the wider goals associated with education are largely neglected. Thus, a rhetoric that it should provide for the development of the whole person is not reflected coherently in the structure and expectations of the current curriculum.

From CCEA statements about the purposes of education (for example, CCEA, 2001), it appears that personal and social development are major aims of the curriculum. However, the history of the development of the Northern Ireland curriculum and the underpinning purposes of promoting the foundational skills necessary for effective practical competence indicate a preoccupation with current societal needs. This betrays an instrumentalist approach to values. In an instrumentalist view, "good" is what relates to current interests. Something is of value if it satisfies immediate purposes and helps achieve current goals. The achievement of the current goal or goals is the means to gain the next goal. In this view, the ends of action become the means to achieve success in subsequent actions. Ends therefore are largely subsumed under means and thus the distinction between means and ends is obscured (MacIntyre, 1993). Value lies in the means as ends and it is, therefore, associated with the immediate; value is not linked to consideration of what the final goal of a process such as education might be. In this approach to values, decisions about goals are claimed to be objective because they appear to concern the pragmatic requirements of the situation only; they are grounded in observations about the world as it is. For example, the needs of industry are surveyed and the results fed into our determination of the objectives of curriculum planning. It is also assumed that by surveying social needs or the needs of the consumer, we can achieve a totally objective account of what education should provide: if there are too many teenage pregnancies, for example, we should be providing more sex education in schools.

The view that we can make evaluations based on empirical survey and can thus guarantee that resultant decisions are totally objective has a fundamental flaw. Objectivity cannot be guaranteed by "taking a look" (Lonergan, 1970) at what actually exists. For instance, when someone has hallucinations, their first reaction is to think that what they see is real. However, afterwards they can evaluate their experience and determine if it was real or illusory by weighing it against a range of commonly agreed standards of what is "real". Experience alone, without a process of evaluation, tells us very little about the real world. Objectivity is characterised by a mediating intelligence that evaluates data using agreed standards. Similarly, values can be said to be objective to the extent that they are based on objectively established and interpersonally operative standards. Something is of value or can be considered a legitimate goal if the reasons for claiming it as such have a basis in reality. Crucial to any determination of goals is an evaluation of how they meet the standards of the field involved. Thus, the curriculum as it stands appears perhaps to reflect the objective needs of society such as the need for sex education, but in fact it is grounded in the evaluations that policy makers have made about the relative value of a range of possible subjects and skills to meet certain targets. It would be possible, in response to the increasing number of teenage pregnancies, to decide that more personal and social education rather than more sex education is what is necessary.

Values then are reflected in the judgements that are made about goals and the means to achieve them. The aims of education are encompassed in the standards that we set for the educational process. Currently these standards in the primary curriculum in Northern Ireland relate to learning outcomes which can be assessed in the immediate term. However, the traditional goals associated with benefits of education, such as autonomy, are not necessarily verifiable through empirical study, nor are they immediately demonstrated. Assuming that the goals and standards of quality education are quantifiable is to misunderstand the nature of the education process. It largely neglects the standards we traditionally identify with education. Education is normative in nature and thus it tends to reflect social and cultural mores and the implicit values and system of morality underpinning these. In turn, these mores and values reflect enduring views about what is good for human beings and society. Unless we base education on values that are more enduring, we risk moving to a system which cannot cater for the development of the person but merely the promotion of what society needs now. Because it would have few long-term goals, such a system would be subject to the vagaries of current trends and would tend towards constant obsolescence. The current curriculum then reflects a deficit in understanding of the foundational role that values play in education. It also shows a lack of awareness of the way in which knowledge and understanding are integral to learning and the demonstration of meaningful learning outcomes.

KNOWLEDGE, UNDERSTANDING AND LEARNING IN THE NORTHERN IRELAND CURRICULUM

CCEA states that the programmes of study "set out the opportunities which should be offered to all students . . . in terms of the knowledge, skills and understanding at each key stage" (CCEA, 2001, p. 1). In effect, the programmes of study take the form of lists of activities and expected outcomes. Purpose is also indicated in terms of the skills that contribute to effective performance. For example, in the programme of study for English, some indication is given that pupils should write to express their thoughts and feelings but the focus rests firmly on the skills of writing for effective performance. There is little indication that through the English curriculum children would be introduced to ways of understanding, knowing and acting that help them develop an understanding of their cultural role, a function that MacIntyre (1981), claims is central to any form of narrative. Where links between reading and cultural heritage are indicated in the programme of study they are expressed in terms of the opportunity reading gives pupils to find out "about people from other cultures, religion, race or social backgrounds" (DENI, 1996, p. 6). At best, this is a short-sighted view of the links between reading and cultural heritage and it indicates clearly the approach to learning implicit in the curriculum. This approach neglects the role that English plays in developing personal identity. The curriculum also shows no appreciation of the link between subject study and the development of pupils' understanding and perception of the world around them. Neither does the programme indicate that storytelling is a means of helping children to "organise, evaluate and transform" experience and to "read the signs between the lines" (Pirrie, 1999, p. 348).

The Northern Ireland Curriculum, as a whole, reveals an approach to learning that is consistent with a system which is preoccupied with the development of performance on task. It concentrates on the skills and knowledge that are required for performance and it focuses on process within the context of each subject. Therefore, it takes the form of a criterion-referencing of desirable knowledge and skills. This has the advantage of appearing to state content unambiguously, of making outcomes seem clear. However, criterion-referencing has the disadvantage that Mill noted with any system of reduction: it is a "security for accuracy, but not for comprehensiveness" (Mill, 1987, p. 144). Itemisation aids clarity but it is of little help in defining the more general constructs into which the items are grouped and thus whilst the programmes of study are comprehensive they lack any real link to the wider aims of the curriculum to promote the "spiritual, moral, cultural, intellectual and physical development of pupils" (CCEA, 2001, webpage). In focusing on skills and process, the Northern Ireland Curriculum has the advantage of promoting the ability to transfer learning into a range of situations. However, the relationship between knowledge and performance is not clear. Knowledge content seems to have been reduced to facts and information and outcomes seem to be largely interpreted as performance using skills and the accrued information. For example, two attainment targets for Science and Technology are: "knowledge and understanding" and "investigating". There is no indication that there is a link between these attainment targets or that successful investigation crucially involves the knowledge required to make sense of the problems under investigation. There is little realisation that performance is the successful combination of knowledge, experience and executive ability. This lack of coherence has potentially dysfunctional ramifications for how the curriculum is taught. If the curriculum appears to indicate an approach to learning which stresses process on the one hand and knowledge as facts and information on the other, this could lead to children memorising facts and engaging in activities but making perhaps few connections. Without the links, understanding is sacrificed because the implied key to competent performance in the curriculum is the process of using informational knowledge rather than valuing or internalising the understanding involved.

Concentration on skills and factual information in the Northern Ireland Curriculum is on the task rather than the person. It betrays a view of knowledge as dissociated from the knower, thus implying that knowledge is in some way part of the objective conditions of the environment. The programmes of study that prescribe subject content seem to imply that only the kind of knowledge which refers to physical or environmental circumstances would be considered relevant for subject content. Thus, in the programmes of study for English, emphasis is given to fact-finding, decoding and learning skills. Where children are called upon to reflect on an issue, there is no evidence that anything other than the facts of the situation and the personal experience of the pupils is required to be brought to bear. Knowledge, however, has a crucial role in perception and action (Polanyi, 1969). It informs personal judgement which directly feeds into the kinds of decisions which lead to effective performance. It enriches the viewpoint of pupils and mediates their perception of reality. Objective conditions are mediated by personal judgement and a framework of understanding rather than belonging to the realm of the merely empirical (Lonergan, 1970). There is little recognition in the curriculum documentation that the complexity of the learning process has been grasped by curriculum planners.

ASSESSMENT IN THE NORTHERN IRELAND CURRICULUM

It is a truism to say that assessment has a crucial influence on what is taught in schools. Different forms of assessment reflect different priorities for learning and thus assessment has been an important factor in facilitating educational reform (Broadfoot, 1989). Changes in education and training, such as the introduction of the National Curriculum, have led to changes in assessment which has become more closely focused on performance and learning outcomes. The Northern Ireland Curriculum reflects this trend and each programme of study is accompanied by sets of attainment targets and levels of attainment which are cast in behavioural terms. The performance of pupils is assessed against these targets and levels and forms the basis for recording pupil achievement. The levels are then used by teachers to plan learning activities for their classes.

This is a very different form of assessment from the norm-referenced approach to testing traditionally employed in examinations such as A-level. In norm-referencing, the grades awarded to candidates refer to a general level of quality to be achieved. Norm-referenced assessment has long been associated with courses that provide a general education: the focus is not vocational. One criticism of norm-referencing is that it only indicates comparative achievement (Darling-Hammond, 1994) rather than providing a comprehensive description of pupil performance. Thus it is criticised for a lack of precision that creates difficulty in objective analysis of pupil achievement, diagnosis of need and planning further learning for the individual, particularly where overt performance is the goal.

Criterion-referenced assessment, on the other hand, measures a person's performance against a set of criteria rather than against the performance of others. Thus, it gives precise details on each element of pupils' performance. Criterion-referenced tests, unlike norm-referenced tests, document successes: the assessor knows precisely the criteria by which assessment is to be made and the pupil knows what he/she has achieved. One reason for the increased popularity of criterion-referenced tests is that they hold the promise, through clarification of outcomes, of making education accountable and open to analysis in terms of cost-effectiveness and efficiency (Helsby and Saunders, 1993). This is because criterion-referenced tests stipulate exactly what the pupil is to do in order to gain accreditation. The assumption is that, if a clear definition is given to teachers and pupils, everyone concerned will know exactly what is to be taught and learned. Those engaged in assessment will have a precise statement of what the candidate should be able to do and stakeholders or consumers will have a clear statement of achievement.

The structures of criterion-referenced testing depend upon a specification process (Lindvall and Nitko, 1975). The behaviours expected for each item or level are specified as clearly as possible; each behaviour is defined by a set of test items or test tasks in which the behaviours and all their important aspects are displayed. A "standard", which is described in terms of performance on task, is used as a measure or criterion by which candidates are assessed. Thus, the performance of the candidate is measured against some independent definition of what should be achieved and the performance is reported on in relation to this criterion. Criterion-referenced systems of testing have become increasingly popular in recent years (Wolf, 1993) and the Northern Ireland Curriculum, although not conforming strictly to the process of criterion-referencing, which demands detailed specification of outputs, displays many of the characteristics of this form of testing. This emphasis is evident on grading the skills element of behavioural outputs and the drive to make the assessment process transparent by basing judgements on precise behavioural descriptors.

Despite the possibilities for describing performance which criterion-referencing offers, there are problems associated with this form of testing. One problem is that the attempt to specify exactly what a person should be able to do has led, in some cases, to a narrowing of expectations. Problems arise because of the attempt to offer unambiguous and comprehensive descriptions of exactly what the person can do. The inevitable result of attempting to state standards unambiguously seems to be that what is tested becomes trivialised. Thus, only certain kinds of processes — those that reveal a restricted set of behavioural criteria — are accessible in any meaningful way to strict criterion-referencing. Furthermore, individual test items rely for their effectiveness as assessment items on factors that lie outside the test. Assessment of a literacy skill cannot be independent of the context in which the test is set and the context cannot be reduced to the constituent elements, or descriptors, of that test. In assessing the skill, the context in which the assessment is set, such as the manner in which a question is asked, will influence to a large degree the efficacy of the test. To attempt to take every context into account in constructing a test would lead to an infinite expansion of descriptive conditions.

Initially, a narrow approach to criterion-referencing was adopted in curriculum assessment in Britain. Faith was placed in the transparency of the criteria to ensure accuracy in assessment. However, this faith was found to be misplaced. In English testing, for example, Broadfoot and Abbott (1991) found that different grades were being awarded for similar kinds of work. Furthermore, it was found that providing levels for each child in each attainment target in each subject told little about the overall ability of the child in relation to curriculum subjects. This kind of reporting was eventually abandoned: teachers have been asked to make a professional judgement about the child rather than fill in checklists (Dearing, 1993). Although teachers need to know the child's level of achievement in various skills, it is more important to gain a more general view of the child's ability which other teachers can understand and build on. In addition, Dearing indicated the importance of professional judgement in the assessment process. The importance of the evaluative element in assessment Cronbach (1971) claims is crucial because "interpretation of data arise from a specified procedure" (p. 447). Hambleton (1978) suggests that professional judgement is an essential foundation for testing and in standard setting there is no totally objective means of selecting cut-off scores to differentiate between pass or fail, competent or not competent. Someone has to use their judgement to decide on the thresholds. In curriculum assessment, therefore, the decisions which teachers have to make about an individual's performance require that they determine whether the pupil is competent or not. It is the kind of judgement which Dearing (1993), for example, stresses in outlining desirable modes of curriculum assessment. This kind of evaluation gives an overview of pupil learning rather than a set of scores indicating each child's ability to perform discrete tasks. The need to interpret performance criteria is particularly relevant in assessment situations where outputs cannot be described exactly and where flexible response is required in areas such as poetry and writing.

The system of assessment devised for the Northern Ireland Curriculum took account of the early failings of the British system and, unlike England and Wales, it relies solely on teacher assessment. There are no checklists of achievement and teachers provide an assessment based on their judgement of the level that each pupil has reached in each attainment target in English and Mathematics. There is a moderation process whereby portfolios of pupils' work are submitted with teacher commentary and estimated level of achievement for each. As in any moderation process, the salient aim is to achieve reliability and validity of the assessment process. In a norm-referenced system of examinations such as A-Level, examiners achieve a high level of reliability in their marking (Murphy, 1982) although they do not specify

exactly in behavioural terms the outcomes desired. A-Level asses-
sors are socialised into the assessment model during joint meetings where standards are debated. Through this process the
examiners seem to internalise the standards expected from the
students and they share an understanding of levels of performance; holistic judgement forms an important part of the final
grade awarded. The process of moderation at A-level indicates a
possible framework that could be generalised across the four
stages of the Northern Ireland curriculum. However, this form of
moderation has not been adopted for moderating pupils' work in
the curriculum. While teachers meet to discuss and compare levels awarded to individual pieces of work, their discussion of the
completed tasks takes the form of direct reference to the level descriptors provided for each attainment target in each subject.
Typically, the kind of commentary on pupils' work used as exemplary material for training teachers in assessment makes reference
in the main to the skills involved. For example, in story-writing,
typical comments would make reference to: conveying information clearly; using generally accurate spelling and punctuation;
writing legibly; and using appropriate form. Thus, implicitly the
kind of assessment standards being applied are those which refer
to competent task completion; there is little reference to the depth
of understanding or creativity displayed. The limitations in this
kind of assessment are demonstrated in the degree of difficulty
experienced by teachers in grading poetry against the level descriptors for writing.

The system of assessment then in the Northern Ireland curriculum reflects many of the assumptions of criterion-referenced
assessment, whilst not providing the precise prescription for performance which generally accompanies criterion-referencing. The
assessment process has the advantage of focusing teaching and
pupil effort on the skills that are crucial for effective performance
in English and Mathematics, although at a rather instrumental
level. However, it offers an impoverished interpretation of what it
means to be educated in those subjects. It does not indicate how
new learning is integrated into the pupil's existing framework of

knowledge which is an important indicator of learning (Mayer, 1990). Nor does it assess sufficiently the extent to which this learning will influence understanding of, and performance on, related tasks. Mayer claims that it is not the ability to reproduce learning faithfully but the extent to which pupils have made sense of the learning in relation to their existing knowledge and beliefs which is crucial in order to ensure progression.

The current form of testing in the Northern Ireland Curriculum presents problems for the assessment of other subjects of the curriculum which depend even more crucially on the development of attitudes and values. CCEA plans to introduce personal education and citizenship into the curriculum in Northern Ireland. An objective approach to testing, as attempted in the current process, which ignores the fact that achievement and assessment are "heavily context and culture dependent" (Gipps and Murphy, 1994, p. 276) and crucially involve values and ways of understanding would be problematic for the assessment of these areas of study. Yet if the inclusion of these areas of study is to be guaranteed they must be accompanied by appropriate forms of assessment because it is commonly recognised that teachers and pupils tend to concentrate on those subjects that they know will be tested. There are indications that the Qualifications and Assessment Authority (QCA) in Britain has realised the shortcomings of the assessment process employed in the National Curriculum and is actively seeking ways to broaden its approach to assessment in citizenship education (Holmes and McCarthy, 2001). Recognition of similar problems with the Northern Ireland assessment process is also indicated in the current curriculum review undertaken by CCEA. However, there is no guarantee that the process of assessing learning that is currently employed in existing curriculum subjects will be reviewed.

CHALLENGES TO THE CURRENT CURRICULUM

The above discussion challenges the Northern Ireland curriculum in several respects. It questions the general approach to the curriculum which emphasises overt performance rather than integrating this with the personal development of the individual. It challenges the lack of connection between the overt aims of the curriculum and how the curriculum is manifested in the programmes of study; and finally it criticises the impoverished approach to the purposes of education reflected in curriculum documentation. The present curriculum in Northern Ireland has also been criticised by the CCEA who manage it: Gallagher (2001) claims that the curriculum concentrates on what is easily assessable, is deeply conservative in its structure, concentrates on information transmission and could be more relevant to the needs and interests of young people.

In response to criticisms of the existing curriculum, CCEA have developed plans for a curriculum which centres around processes and transferable skills. CCEA surveyed pupils in secondary schools (Gallagher, 2001) and this informed the direction of the proposed changes, at both primary and secondary levels. It is hoped to increase relevance by concentrating on the promotion of personal development, citizenship and employability. Personal development in this approach refers largely to the promotion of the ability to contribute to society, the economy and the environment. The new curriculum also aims to emphasise learning rather than teaching (Gallagher, 2001) and places discovery learning to the fore in the classroom. "Creativity, innovation, enterprise, alternative thinking, adaptability, resilience and responsibility" are to be the "skills at the heart of the curriculum" (Gallagher, 2001, p. 22). Rather than subject-based, the proposed curriculum will be organised into five cross-curricular aspects: Literacy, Numeracy, Creativity, Personal Development and The World Around Us. The subjects currently in the Northern Ireland Curriculum will act as contexts for the development of skills. Generic skills, such as self-management and communication skills, will be the focus for learning.

The proposed changes to the curriculum are wide-ranging and ambitious, requiring teachers to go beyond subject boundaries to foundational processes such as thinking and discovering. They also recognise the crucial role of aspects of personal development, such as education of the emotions, largely omitted from the current curriculum in schools. However, the proposals also share some of the presuppositions of the current curriculum. They appear to ignore or take for granted the complexity of the learning process and the extent to which learning is internalised and influences perception and interpretation of the data of experience. The proposals do not reflect an understanding that we use the subjects of the curriculum to help pupils make sense of the multifarious nature of their experience, developing a coherent structure for that experience (O'Hear, 1981). Because of this lack of appreciation of the role of subject knowledge, links are not made in current proposals between the development of subject knowledge and the development of skills such as problem-solving. Gallagher (2001) claims that by 2020, subjects may no longer form part of the curriculum and she sees the main obstacle to this as the degree of subject loyalty among teachers. There is no indication that the relationship between existing knowledge and the process of knowledge accretion is appreciated or that this must be taken into account if we decide to abolish subject study *per se*. Thus, although a major and valuable aim of the proposals is to enable pupils to become more active in their learning, there is little evidence that the learning process has been analysed. A more far-reaching analysis is required on the part of our curriculum planners of the role of subjects and their effect on the promotion of processes and skills underpinning the education process.

The new proposals have also attempted to take into account a range of needs of society and of pupils. In a study of pupil perceptions of current curriculum contents, for example, Gallagher (2001) claims that pupils do not make links between what they learn in school and their lives. Pupils also feel that the work they do in schools is disjointed and compartmentalised. As indicated in my discussion of the current curriculum, there is a lack of vision of the purposes of education which can only lead to a lack of coherence in approach to the contents of learning. The current curriculum, I have argued, is oriented in the longer term towards practical competence, concentrating on the skills that are developed in subject learning and the information necessary for the performance of those skills. CCEA seem to have attempted to remedy these omissions by directly appealing to pupils. For example, changes in Art, Music and PE have been aimed at "a shift in emphasis of study towards popular culture and forms of expression, sport and dance to which young people relate" (CCEA, 1999b, p. 22). Thus, the curriculum in these areas is to refer to the interests of young people, an advance on curriculum development involving only the needs of employers, for example. However, it has not been recognised that what pupils are interested in is not necessarily the same as what is in their interests. Also, in many ways, education involves creating interest in pupils as much as responding to their existing interests. Developing an interest in a subject frequently involves foregoing the instant gratification that immediate interest provides and substituting this with a more distant pleasure that only hard-won understanding can facilitate.

Making the curriculum more appealing to pupils may not indeed lead to its fulfilling the needs of pupils, other than in a superficial way. The instrumental approach adopted by CCEA has the virtue of itemising precisely the skills that pupils need to learn. However, it concentrates almost exclusively on immediate needs and interests. It neglects that dimension of education that transcends the immediate and recognises that learning to be a good citizen or an effective adult involves the promotion of attitudes and dispositions. These can be fostered through the education process but such an education needs to be grounded in principles that reflect more than a survey of the needs and interests of stakeholders, such as employers and parents.

The new proposals also emphasise competence, as does the current curriculum. There is, however, a distinct shift in emphasis. Whereas currently the curriculum places greatest emphasis on the skills of performance within subject context, the proposals focus on the skills required for citizenship and employability. Life in the family and the community is also stressed and the general well-being of pupils appears to be a major concern. The problem with the goals outlined in new curriculum proposals is that they seem to have been taken from research findings concerning societal needs, theories of intellectual and emotional development and a survey of student views. Thus, the basis for selection of curriculum contents has been derived from largely empirical evidence. This demonstrates continuity in approach in both curricula and evaluation. Although the range of evidence taken into account is much broader in the new proposals, the basis for selection seems to be grounded still in the expectation that data alone can provide the basis for selection of goals and content of the curriculum. The extent to which this approach can fully accommodate the development of longer-term goals that seem to be indicated in the proposals is questionable.

Like the existing curriculum, the proposed curriculum changes also place emphasis on performance and skills. Whereas it is proposed that personal education should form a crucial part of the new curriculum, the importance given to the promotion of the less tangible aspects involved, such as values and attitudes, will depend very much on how it is assessed. In the current curriculum, priority in assessment is given to quantifying overt performance on task. CCEA intend to construct new forms of assessment to facilitate the promotion of new emphases in the curriculum. However, this assessment seems to be seen in terms of "more effective assessment of a range of thinking skills; the demonstration of creativity . . ." (Gallagher, 2001, p. 23) and other transferable skills. Whilst this form of assessment is intended to map processes, it shows an enduring emphasis on the demonstration of skills associated with assessment in the current curriculum. A curriculum that aims principally to produce competent performance takes little or no account of longer-term goals. Rather, it concentrates on objectives which are realisable in the short term. Current concern for citizenship and vocational education may indicate concern mainly for the group, for the functional and the productive, depending on the way in which these areas of study are realised in a curriculum. It may be very difficult to broaden the goals of these areas of study if teachers and pupils have been socialised into the kind of schooling which has practical ability as its predominant goal.

CONCLUSION

Current proposals for changing the curriculum in primary schools in Northern Ireland display an attempt to go beyond the prescriptions of British curriculum requirements. The National Curriculum in Britain has pragmatic goals that indicate increasing demands of the marketplace and of competence-based education and training. There have been attempts to broaden the curriculum in England and Wales by introducing citizenship and health education. However, the seemingly broader curriculum which has resulted shows the same lack of coherence as its predecessor. Subjects such as citizenship require the promotion of central values consistent with being a competent citizen, yet the framework of curriculum development shows reference to the values of the market and the instrumental values of societal demand. This is an inadequate framework for citizenship or health education. Furthermore, the assessment system and the importance of skilled performance it reflects are also of limited relevance to wider dimensions of education.

In Northern Ireland, there has been an attempt to address the perceived inadequacies of the existing curriculum. This has been done by prescribing the skills to be developed and by broadening reference to process and the personal aspects of education. However, the ideology of the marketplace and the exigencies of consumerism are evident in the proposals. A lack of coherence can be seen here too in the direction of the intention to satisfy the need to develop the more personal aspects of the curriculum whilst sustaining the emphasis on skilful performance and behavioural outcomes. The planned changes to the Northern Ireland Curriculum demonstrate an awareness that the current curriculum is narrow and neglects the personal education of primary school children. However, this inadequacy cannot be remedied by change of content alone; a new framework for understanding the curriculum must be developed that transcends current market ideology. We need to investigate more thoroughly the integrative principles that need to operate to bring into equilibrium the knowledge, skills, needs and values associated with the personal and social aspects of human living. On this it could be claimed rests the possibility of coherent curriculum planning.

The proposals for education recently developed by CCEA show independence on the part of educational planners here and a move to construct a rationale for the curriculum that is based on Northern Irish needs rather than those of England and Wales. There are indications of a growing self-confidence and an awareness that if we are to solve the educational and social problems that exist in Northern Ireland, solutions must be sought here. Ready-made measures drawn from the "mainland" have proved, at best, incomplete. Despite attempts by CCEA to develop a curriculum that is tailored to local needs, proposals for a new curriculum continue to be influenced by an instrumental view of the curriculum that is a dominant framework for educational planning in Britain. We need to step beyond a curriculum that is grounded in what is immediately empirically verifiable. Rather than merely reorienting the curriculum from emphasis on subject content to concentration on process, we need to examine the evaluative principles on which our curriculum should be based. We need to recognise that the effects of the educational process are not definitive in terms of a strict causal relationship: that many of the aims of education cannot be guaranteed by prescription of curriculum content. There is a need to look to the interrelationships between knowledge and understanding and underpinning processes and skills. Crucially, there is also a need to consider the pedagogy that supports the curriculum, ensuring that teachers are encouraged to develop a critical pedagogy that allows for flexibility of practice rather than prescription of methodology. This could be challenging in a framework of teacher education which in Northern Ireland is currently focused on competences. Furthermore, a radical review of assessment is required to take account of more than predetermined behavioural outcomes. Finally, a coherent network is required that can take account of social needs, both pragmatic and cultural, and the personal needs of pupils. The direction that curriculum planning seems to be taking in Northern Ireland holds out much promise but we need to go further in examining the factors that underpin our educational needs and in drawing up the educational principles on which the appropriateness of curricula depend.

References

Bennett, S.N. (1976), *Teaching Styles and Pupil Progress*, London: Open Books.

Broadfoot, P. (1989), *The Significance of Contemporary Contradiction in Educational Assessment Policies in England and Wales*, Bristol: University of Bristol.

Broadfoot, P. and Abbott, D. (1991), "Look Back in Anger?" Findings from the PACE project concerning primary teachers' experiences of SATs.

Central Advisory Council for Education (CACE) (1967), *Children and Their Primary Schools* (The Plowden Report), London: HMSO.

Coolahan, J. (1981), *Irish Education*, Dublin: Institute of Public Administration.

Council for the Curriculum, Examinations and Assessment (CCEA) (1999a), *Key Messages from the Curriculum 21 Conferences and the Curriculum Monitoring Programme 1998*, Belfast: CCEA.

Council for the Curriculum, Examinations and Assessment (CCEA) (1999b), *Developing the Northern Ireland Curriculum to Meet the Needs of Young People, Society and the Economy in the 21st Century*, Belfast: CCEA.

Council for the Curriculum, Examinations and Assessment (CCEA) (2001), Northern Ireland Curriculum http://www.ccea.org.uk/curriculum.htm, accessed 16/07/01.

Cox, C.B. and Dyson, A.E. (eds.) (1969), *Fight for Education: A Black Paper*, London: Critical Quarterly Society.

Cronbach, L. (1971), *Essentials of Psychological Testing*, New York: Harper and Row.

Darling-Hammond, L. (1994), "Performance-Based Assessment and Educational Equity", *Harvard Educational Review*, Vol. 64, No.1, pp. 5–30.

Dearing, R. (1993), *The National Curriculum and its Assessment*, Final Report to the Secretary of State for Education, London: School Curriculum and Assessment Authority.

Department of Education and Science (DES) (1977), *Education in Schools: A Consultative Document*, London: HMSO.

Department of Education and Science (DES) (1985), *Better Schools: A Summary*, London: Department of Education and Science/ Welsh Office.

Department of Education for Northern Ireland (DENI) (1996), *The Northern Ireland Curriculum: Programmes of Study and Attainment Targets*, Bangor: DENI.

Fletcher, S. (1991), *NVQs, Standards and Competence*, London: Kogan Page.

Gallagher, C. (2001), *Education 2020*, Belfast: The Blackstaff Press.

Gipps, C. and Murphy, P. (1994), *A Fair Test? Assessment, Achievement and Equity*, Buckingham: Open University Press.

Gordon, P. and Lawton, D. (1978), *Curriculum Change in the Nineteenth and Twentieth Century*, London, Hodder and Stoughton.

Hambleton, R.K. (1978), "On the Use of Cut-Off Scores with Criterion Referenced Tests in Instructional Settings", *Journal of Educational Measurement*, Vol. 15, No. 4, pp. 277–90.

Helsby, G. and Saunders, M. (1993), "Taylorism, Tylerism and Performance Indicators: Defending the Indefensible?" *Educational Studies*, Vol. 19, No. 1, pp. 55–77.

Holmes, E. and McCarthy, K. (2001), "Citizenship: Just Do It!" *Education Matters*, 2, March, London: The Stationery Office, pp. 5–7.

Jonathan, R. (1997), *Illusory Freedoms: Liberalism, Education and the Market*, *Journal of Philosophy of Education*, Special Issue, Vol. 31, No. 1, pp. 1–220.

Lawton, D. (1989), *Education, Culture and The National Curriculum*, London: Hodder and Stoughton.

Lindvall, C.M. and Nikto, A.J. (1975), *Measuring Pupil Achievement and Aptitude*, New York: Harcourt, Brace and Jovanovich.

Lonergan, B. (1970), Insight, 3rd edn., New York: Philosophical Library.

MacIntyre, A. (1981), *After Virtue*, London: Duckworth.

MacIntyre, A. (1993), *A Short History of Ethics*, London: Routledge.

Mayer, M. (1990), "Assessing and Understanding Common-Sense Knowledge", in Bell, C. and Harris, D. (eds.), *World Yearbook of Education 1990: Assessment and Education,* London, Kogan Page, pp. 188–99.

Mill, J.S. (1987), "Bentham", in Mill, J.S. and Bentham, J. *Utilitarianism and Other Essays,* Harmondsworth: Penguin Books, pp. 132–76.

Murphy, R. (1982), "A Further Report of Investigations into the Reliability of Marking the GCE Examinations", *British Journal of Educational Psychology,* Vol. 52, pp. 58–63.

Musgrave, P.W. (1968), *Society and Education in England since 1900,* London: Methuen.

O'Hear, A. (1981), *Education, Society and Human Nature,* London: Routledge and Kegan Paul.

Pirrie, A. (1999), "Supposing: Reading between the Lines: An Allegorical Account of Contemporary Debates on Literacy Acquisition", *British Journal of Educational Studies,* Vol. 47, No. 4, pp. 348–63.

Polanyi, M. (1969), *Personal Knowledge,* London: Routledge and Kegan Paul.

Pring, R. (1995), *Closing the Gap,* London: Routledge.

Taba, H. (1962), *Curriculum Development: Theory and Practice,* New York: Harcourt Brace and World.

Wolf, A. (1993), *Assessment Issues and Problems in a Criterion-Based System,* London: Further Education Unit.

SECTION FOUR

IRISH EXPERIENCES:
INTERNATIONAL PERSPECTIVES

Chapter 9

SIGNPOSTS AND SILENCES: SITUATING THE LOCAL WITHIN THE GLOBAL

Ciaran Sugrue and Jim Gleeson

INTRODUCTION

This concluding chapter, as its title suggests, deals with some of the major emergent signposts evident in, and emanating from, analysis and argument in the previous chapters. It deals also with some significant systemic silences that we feel strongly should be part of future dialogue and debate wherever ideology and policy reform are under scrutiny. The inclusion of systemic silences gains in significance as they are deeply embedded in current educational structures and processes, some of which have their origins in nineteenth-century political power struggles, but are sustained in many instances by contemporary currents in Irish society, the silences and silencing that surround them. We are mindful of Said's (1993, p. 47) perspective, of "the power to give or withhold attention", of the fact that we too are "fish in water" (Bourdieu and Wacquant, 1992, p. 128). Consequently, it is necessary to bring to the surface the structured silences surrounding reforms in the Irish setting, to question the "taken for granted" and, by doing so, provide a "contrapuntal" (Said, 1993, p. 49) reading of contemporary discourses on curriculum reforms, the change forces, global and local rhetorics that shape and surround them. In setting such an agenda for ourselves, we recognise the partial, subjective nature of the task, its "oppositional nature" and "critical vocation" (Said, 1993, p. 49). We are mindful also that "past present and future are fundamentally ambiguous . . . that there [is] no single right or correct interpretation of the world around us, no single answer . . . no single definitive arrangement" (Homer-Dixon, 2001, p. 389).

We begin with prevailing international currents identified in the first section of the book as a means of situating more focused discussion on signposts and silences, of illustrating and illuminating connections between national (internal) discourses and prevailing currents of debate and international (external) global forces. This brief discussion of "social movements" such as lifelong learning helps to situate a more sustained agenda-setting discussion that is at two levels. First, we identify three concerns that emerge from analysis of issues presented in sections two and three of the text — three signposts that both pave and point the way for ongoing debate on the re-forming of Irish schooling and curricula. We are less preoccupied with the mindsets of the most powerful players, with taking on "the shape of their imagining" and more concerned "to conjure with [the] . . . readers' sense of what is possible or desirable or, indeed, imaginable" (Heaney, 1995, p. 1), and, in the process, to set new parameters for debate beyond current norms. For this reason, we also identify three major silences in the system and seek to include them in the educational discourse as a means of moving beyond "the normative authority of the dominant language" (p. 5) of more typical discourses of educational reform in the Irish context, to "redress" perceived inadequacies. We are cognisant also of the extent to which terms such as "reform" and "change" are used interchangeably in the setting and regard this as problematic as well as providing some evidence of continuing essentialist thinking and possible "co-option" through partnership (Ball, 1994).

By addressing both signposts and silences, our intention is to raise pertinent matters for critical scrutiny and, in the process, to provide focus and purpose without seeking to circumscribe future ends or pre-determine means. As signposts and silences are inextricably linked, two sides of various coins that have gained currency and prominence within the educational system, we see them as issues to be addressed as part of a more democratic and open discourse on reform that is more mindful of the manner in which power is distributed and refracted within the national system of education.

GLOBAL AND LOCAL FORCES: RECOGNITION AND RESISTANCE

At a recent theme conference on "Curriculum Contestation" that was jointly hosted by the NCCA and the Educational Studies Association of Ireland (ESAI), and at which we both contributed, there was remarkably little dissonance. On a number of occasions throughout the conference, phrases such as "this little island of ours", and "this great little place" tripped from individual's tongues with a sense of ease and "contentment" (Galbraith, 1992). Simultaneously, language was occasionally peppered with terms such as "risk", new "departures" and "horizons", and while there were some dissenting voices, much of the dialogue also could be described as "safe simulation" (Hargreaves, 1994) or "ritual performance" (McLaren, 1993) rather than sustained engagement.

There were voices raised in defence of partnership: that Ireland, for some years, has been pursuing a unique trajectory that has largely inured it, if not entirely, then provided some protection from the harsher forces of educational change — Change Force without the "Vengeance" (Fullan, 2003)! However, there were other voices too that could see greater evidence in the language if not yet in the actions of reformers, of the global rhetorics of educational reform. This was evident particularly around such issues as re-centralisation, assessment and the performativity of teachers and accountability mechanisms and processes. There was at once, therefore, recognition and resistance, a tendency perhaps to construct partnership within a protectionist mindset whereby it becomes a protective cocoon against the worst features of global forces. This protective cocoon of partnership becomes a hiding-place where those who work in the system can be protected from the flow of international currents and ideas, and in a somewhat paternalistic manner.

In the introduction to this book, Beck's (2000) notion of the "glocal" was identified as a means of capturing the degree of interdependence between these competing and conflicting forces, the anarchic tendency to seek refuge in the "local" and the equally anarchic and potentially destructive inclination to capitulate to the market, to surrender to the values of materialism, conspicuous consumption and self-indulgence. Barber captures these competing tendencies within an educational frame of reference when he states that:

> To grow into our mature better selves, we need the help of our nascent better selves, which is what common standards, authoritative education and a sense of the public good can offer. Consumption takes us as it finds us, the more impulsive and greedier the better. Education challenges our impulses and informs our greediness with lessons drawn from our mutuality and the higher goods we share in our community of hope. (1996, p. 117)

He concludes that public education and indeed any sustainable version of the "common good" is in jeopardy when Governments promote and privilege the market and the privatisation of the public sphere and, in the process, cease to take responsibility for promoting and/or defending the common good. Yet, as Logan and O'Reilly (1985, p. 475) indicate, the purpose of partnership and the assumptions that underpinned the establishment of the CEB were "to broaden the social base of decision-making so that the process of selecting knowledge, skill or experience for inclusion on the national curriculum will address the common good". The extent to which market forces are a subterranean player in Irish education circles is best understood against the manner in which the socio-economic terrain has altered during the past decade.

In *Ireland Unbound* (Corcoran and Peillon, 2002), Peillon argues that "in the contemporary world, it would be difficult to find an example of such deep, intense and rapid transformation as has occurred in Ireland" (p. 1). He argues that Irish society appears to have skipped a developmental stage, but from a pre-industrial order has "managed to establish itself as a post-industrial enclave within global capitalism" and, he adds, with an apparent mix of amazement and alarm, that "despite the speed and the structural violence of such a process, this transformation has taken place without major social upheaval" (p. 1). Perhaps one survival strategy for these changing times has been a "circling of the wagons", and, through the rhetoric of partnership, a continuing rhetoric of inclusion and continuity; however, below surface "spin" there is growing evidence of fragmentation, marginalisation and exclusion, some of which was evident in earlier chapters. It is timely therefore to question the extent to which global forces have already impacted on the education system, particularly at primary and post-primary levels.

In general, there is recognition, acknowledgement and even celebration of the presence and impact of global forces in our midst — multinationals, particularly in the electronics and pharmaceutical industries, and their transformation of individuals' lives and lifestyles. Their presence has been a catalyst for a more prosperous Ireland generally. In less than a decade, they have helped to transform the populace from being self-effacing and lacking in bravura to a younger set of mobile-phone wielding, loud, brash, unapologetically avaricious consumers of the proliferating toys that are the products of material values and wealth and perceived as their entitlement. In the opening chapter of this book, Goodson warns of the asymmetrical relationship between these forces and their impact at national, regional and local levels; they create unrivalled opportunities for some while increasing instability and precariousness for all. In such circumstances, he argues, collective anamnesis rather than cultural and historical amnesia become vital as a means of finding continuity and creating stability. Goodson's penetrating analysis of the impact of market forces invites the question: how have these global forces been refracted within power relations and decision-making mechanisms in the Irish system? Each of the chapters in this book signals in its own way that there are various means of interrogating existing policies and the manner in which such policies are formulated, and how such forces are refracted within education systems. As Goodson himself has asserted elsewhere: "it is high time that the historical facts with regard to the . . . Curriculum were known, and known in connection with the social forces which brought them into the educational curriculum" (1994, p. 116). According to this perspective, it is necessary to create an "invented tradition" of curriculum studies, a task that is ideally suited, in part, to the National Council for Curriculum and Assessment (NCCA) as well as the wider education community. We are in agreement with Goodson (1994, p. 118) when he argues that by ignoring the "history and social construction of curriculum" the task of re-inventing the status quo through "the reproduction of 'traditional' curriculum form and content" is rendered both much easier and more likely (Goodson, 1994, p. 118). Debates that seek to divide participants, therefore, into opposing camps of "recognisers" and "resisters" become increasingly futile. What is necessary is greater recognition of the "glocal" nature of reform agendas, and the necessity to trace the trajectories and influences of ideas as they are "refracted" within national and local curriculum debates.

Skilbeck (Chapter Two) lends further legitimacy to this agenda when he identifies lifelong learning as a new "horizon" with enormous consequences for how schooling and its attendant curricula are currently construed. The underlying assumption is that the combination of rapid change and the creation of the "knowledge society" necessitate continuous learning across the lifespan. This scenario is far removed from the realities of many individuals' lives who, until relatively recently, left school at the age of thirteen to enter the world of work. This emerging reality and its attendant rhetoric is captured in recent EU documentation that states:

> The knowledge, skills and understanding we learn as children
> and as young people in the family, at school, during training
> and at college or university will not last a lifetime. Integrating

learning more firmly into adult life is a very important part of putting lifelong learning into practice, but it is, nevertheless, just one part of the whole. Lifelong learning sees all learning as a seamless continuum "from cradle to grave". (EU Commission, 2000, p. 7)

This seamless robe of learning needs to be "lifewide", to capture elements of formal, informal and non-formal learning and, as Skilbeck asserts, such reconceptualisations of learning pose considerable challenges to more traditional and deeply embedded notions of school-learning and prescribed curricula. If it is no longer a necessity to have "mastered" a corpus of knowledge, a content that is rapidly on its way to redundancy, by the end of compulsory schooling, is it necessary to persist with a "prescribed" curriculum, and to continue to privilege a style of learning that is largely cognitive in orientation with a premium on syllabus content rather than generic skills. Additionally, is the continued perpetuation of a nineteenth-century conveyor-belt model of learning by "age cohort" an organisational strategy that has outlived its usefulness?

Significantly, in the Irish context, the language of lifelong learning has been "sponsored" more by Enterprise, Trade and Employment and included in successive partnership programmes rather than mainstream education. This general "theme" has been taken up more recently in the White Paper on Adult Education (Ireland, Government of, 2000, p. 30) where the main concern is with those not well served by the formal education system, and which marked the adoption "of a commitment to lifelong learning as the governing principle of Irish education policy, and as having a pivotal position in the overall Irish economic and social strategy". In the most recent Strategy Statement 2003–2005 (DES), lifelong learning is presented as applicable primarily to second-chance education. Consequently, there is little evidence thus far that the concept has been extended to formal schooling. The general tendency is for adult education and vocational education and training to be positioned as peripheral to mainstream education (see Gleeson, 2003), while focusing on the need for basic skills as an essential element of an individual's participation in the knowledge society and underpinning equality of access and participation by prioritising those with special needs and disadvantaged students. An integrative approach to lifelong learning challenges both primary and post-primary education to promote holistic learner-centred approaches to learning and teaching while adhering to a core objective of preparing the student for a life of learning rather than for a terminal examination. Apart from the White Paper on Adult Education therefore, the sectoral interpretation of lifelong learning, which is the dominant meaning in most Irish policy statements, is concerned with second-chance education.

Despite an increasing diversity of school types in the Irish context, there is remarkably little diversity of school architecture, or a tradition of experimentation in terms of curriculum content or pedagogy (see OECD, 1991). Consequently, it may be argued, there is an unhealthy degree of homogenisation in Irish schooling that runs counter to the spirit of "lifewide" learning, that harbours potential also to perpetuate privilege through reproducing the "cultural capital" enjoyed by the middle classes, while privileging control and conformity over creativity and critical thinking (Lynch and Lodge, 2002). Will the newly emergent secular elite in Irish education, which is currently replacing or filling the power vacuum created by a diminishing religious presence at all levels within the system, take up the challenge of lifelong learning in ways that recognise and disrupt the perpetuation of the status quo? Or will such tendencies towards reform be resisted in the interest of perpetuating their own positions, their own "cultural capital" and that of their offspring? These considerations provide a significant challenge that warrants creative and imaginative responses; a spirit of diversity and experimentation rather than more of the same. Business as usual is no longer adequate.

These questions reinforce Goodson's perspective that "social movements" or "global forces" are invariably refracted in different ways within national boundaries. Global forces may be refracted within internal discourses in ways that re-form existing elites rather than trans-form the educational landscape into forms of learning that are recognisably different, more democratic and inclusive. They also reinforce the necessity to articulate deeply embedded silences in the system, as a first step towards creating more democratic modes of learning in the ongoing project of re-forming teaching, learning and a curriculum of life. Despite the pervasive tentacles of globalising tendencies therefore, there is much to play for in *Charting Our Education Future* (Ireland, Gov-ernment of, 1995). Our approach here is to take up the dominant international "forces" and to indicate and argue their influences, both potential and actual, on reform discourses and trajectories as they are refracted through prevailing signposts and silences in the Irish educational system. We begin with emergent signposts from the analysis in earlier chapters.

Signpost One: Partnership as Ideology

It is a commonplace of the Irish education system in recent years that "partnership" is espoused as one of the "principles of ap-proach" that underpins "the formulation and evaluation of educa-tional policy and practice" (Ireland, Government of, 1995, p. 3) and the National Education Convention (NEC) is seen as a proto-type of this "model" (Coolahan, 1994). It is frequently asserted also that the trajectory of this approach is distinct and signifi-cantly different from more ideologically driven top-down central-ised reforms that are dominant in very visible ways in England, Australia, the US, Canada and elsewhere. However, this "model" tends to conflate "consensus building", which was advocated by the OECD (1991) as being necessary in the Irish system, with pol-icy formulation. Emphasis on, if not preoccupation with, eco-nomic growth during the past decade, apart from a tendency towards vocationalisation of school curricula, has occasionally also informed and "framed" the question: "Are we closer to Bos-ton or Berlin?" This is an ideological question that asks Irish citi-zens to position themselves within global rhetorics — do we favour neo-liberal economic agendas, the "free" market, more than an ideological comfort with, or pre-disposition towards central and northern European norms and values of welfare-statist social security "nets", health care and pension entitlements? These questions are posed here to indicate that what is sometimes asserted as a "principle" in practice can become a "mantra", a rhetoric with potential to degenerate into an ideological stance that may actually serve to fudge dispositions within an ideological Irish mist intended to render less visible value stance, commitment, power relations as well as the capacity to co-opt "the partners" into pre-determined Government policy.

In Chapter Four, Gleeson cited evidence of the continuities of anti-intellectualism, essentialism and pragmatism both within the education establishment and in Irish society since the foundation of the state. The White Paper on Education (Ireland, Government of, 1995, p. 3) asserts the need to "continue the search for further consensus" but this may be a continuing ruse to stifle dissent, to control contestation by privileging consensus over dissonance that respects rather than seeks to deny difference with an abiding emphasis on continuity and conformity rather than diversity and individuality. There may be a central paradox therefore at the heart of an ideology of partnership that homogenises through consensus-building when elements of the global rhetorics suggest that diversity, creativity and "thinking outside the box" of conformity are vital. Homer-Dixon captures the consequent "ingenuity gap" for policy-makers and education elites when he states:

> As our world becomes more and more complex, and as the political and cognitive tools that our leaders bring to this world become, relatively, less and less adequate, our leaders hunker down. They eschew boldness, because anyone who makes bold decisions will be thrown out of power. They tend to become tinkerers and managers — and not particularly good managers, at that, because the systems they seek to manage are full of non-linearities and unknown unknowns. In sum, they become less able to make their critical contribution to the supply of the social and technical ingenuity that our societies need. (2001, p. 330)

Granville too (Chapter Three) indicates that the "power of the provisional" nature of the pioneering CEB paradoxically gave its personnel the "freedom" to be bolder in their imaginings than more recent conformist or orthodox behaviour since the NCCA has become a more "permanent" fixture within the education establishment or hierarchy. Significantly, as he indicates, the transition from "provisional" CEB, which had a representative membership, to a permanent NCCA that is representational, seems to have increased orthodoxy. Similarly, the work of the Curriculum Development Centres in Dublin (Trinity) and Shannon, was innovative precisely because it tended to be conducted on the margins, on the periphery of the education system (Gleeson, Chapter Four). It may well be the case, therefore, that an ideology of partnership has significant strengths in terms of maintaining and perpetuating existing power and control within the system but is much less adept in dealing with the challenges presented increasingly by rapid change and the increasing number of "unknown unknowns" that continue to emerge.

Earlier analysis also suggested that a partnership based on representation also tends towards creating a dialogue of sectoral interest rather than a more open-ended discourse that eschews power and privilege in favour of educational concerns. Sugrue's analysis (Chapter Six) of the manner in which key players from the primary teachers' union came to occupy gate-keeping roles within the NCCA committee structures is particularly instructive in this regard.

Our argument here is that partnership has become little more than an ideological predisposition of key stakeholders in the Irish educational system who use it as a strategy to legitimate their interests and policies. As currently played out, it is flawed and suspect, particularly from the perspective of maintaining and perpetuating power relations, and a generally cautious and conservative approach to reforms that tend to (re-)produce rather than trans-form existing social relations. It is necessary, therefore, to keep partnership under review, not just in some informal manner but in a sustained and systematic way. In a climate of greater accountability, transparency and quality assurance, a more vibrant culture of educational research and awareness among teacher educators of their roles and responsibilities as public intellectuals have significant potential to address the following questions in an ongoing and systematic manner: partnership for what purpose and for whom? The OECD review (1991) indicated that there was need to build consensus as a means of breaking up traditional monopolies between centralised state machinery and the power of teacher unions, and lauded the creation of the CEB/NCCA as a major step forward in this regard. However, the "representational" nature of ensuing partnerships may have largely re-enforced or created an alternative kind of centralised hegemony that may be equally intolerant towards diversity, dissent and experimentation.

There is an enduring paradox at the centre of these power partnership relationships: while the rhetorics of market and globalising tendencies argue for unfettered creativity and experimentation, efforts to contain and control these forces have tended to lead to rigid conformity, standardisation and homogenisation, forces that in practice become anathema to life-wide learning, the recognition of difference and the fostering of creativity and imagination. An important measure of partnership therefore may be the extent to which it cultivates a climate and a context that leads to greater curriculum diversity rather than less. Such a climate would support more autonomy for teachers to develop individual talents and abilities rather than applying the dead hand of high-stakes testing that is increasing alienation from learning even among middle-class students. In these circumstances, professional judgement would have a key role in teaching rather than the more technical application of tried and tested formulae that guarantee examination success. These criteria may be a more realistic and important measure of partnership arrangements. It is important to recognise that how such partnerships are played out in the policy and practice arenas and how they impact on the life chances of learners are more critical than the level of satisfaction expressed by the partners themselves with current arrangements.

Creating spaces and opportunities for the voices of students and their parents to be heard in this ongoing debate becomes crucial if some enduring silences are to be avoided. It is necessary to recognise that "different types of collective decision-making processes yield different kinds of outcomes" (Stone, 2002, p. 354). The current pervasive presumption that "partnership" is either the "best" or the "only" means of framing policy and curricula needs to be continuously open to question and reform also. Since the framing of the Education Act (1998), what has effectively happened is that the power to control a sphere of policy has been conferred on a particular group of individuals. A review of partnership therefore is a call to account of the manner in which such powers are exercised, with the possibility also that such power be reallocated. In the absence of appropriate accountability measures and appropriate mechanisms to question and to hold to account, these partnership arrangements become monopolistic with a tendency to perpetuate existing power relations. For this reason, the following questions raised by Stone (2002, p. 356) need to be applied consistently to current partnership arrangements:

1. Should the *membership* of the decision-making body be changed?

2. Should the *size* of the decision-making body be changed? or

3. Should there be a shift in the *locus* of decision-making?

In the case of all three questions, the consistent sub-text is about the distribution and exercise of power. The first question recognises implicitly that the current representational nature of the NCCA committee system, for example, confers power on teachers unions in particular. The second question, concerning the number of "representatives" is about how the power dynamic may be altered depending on the number of persons involved. Chapter Six, in particular, indicates the manner in which primary teachers engineered a controlling influence on the NCCA primary committee system. The final question raises concerns about the locus of decision-making and the allocation of resources. Although the NCCA, for example, has gained status since the enactment of legislation (Education Act, 1998), the locus of decision-making continues to reside with the DES, but if regionalisation were to become more of a reality within education, something that has already occurred within the Inspectorate and advocated for the system in the Government White Paper on Education (Ireland, 1995), such centralised decision-making might become more controversial and contested. At a minimum, these scenarios indicate clearly that current constructions of partnership are problematic and contested, and should be subject to ongoing review and, where necessary, re-form also.

Signpost Two: Curricula for the Knowledge Economy or Knowledge Society?

There is systematic and sustained evidence that, through the 1990s, as the Irish economy prospered, there was a corresponding tendency for rhetoric and policy alike to advocate further vocationalisation of the curriculum; to prepare students for the world of work, to develop skills and competencies that would increase Ireland's competitive edge in the global economy (Gleeson, Chapter Four; Lynch, 1992; O' Sullivan, 1992). It is important to understand how this global rhetoric, so far, has been refracted within internal national debates. Before turning attention to this however, it is important to the argument that distinction be made between the knowledge "economy" and the knowledge "society". This distinction also enables us to situate national reform efforts and initiatives within international perspectives.

In his most recent book, *Teaching in the Knowledge Society*, Hargreaves (2003, p. *xvi*) distinguishes one from the other when he states: "The knowledge economy serves the private good. The knowledge society also encompasses the public good." Consequently, as part of public service and some continued communitarian sentiment and commitment to civil society, the continued existence of which is also related to our proximity to Boston or Berlin, "our schools have to prepare young people for both of them" (p. *xvi*). Paradoxically, therefore, a strong market forces ideology requires an equally determined commitment to the public sector, to social capital and to what the OECD (2001) describes as a "nation's well-being" (Healy, 2002; Sennett, 1998). It is no longer therefore an old cold war dichotomous either/or choice between the free market and a command economy. Hargreaves sums up the challenge in the following terms:

> The challenge . . . is not to attack globalization or destroy the knowledge economy. Its economic benefits are too great for that. Instead, we have to commit more resources and pay better global attention to the other social needs. In preparing the generations of the future, state education is in pole position to teach a set of values, dispositions and senses of global responsibility that extend beyond the bounds of the knowledge economy. (p. *xix*)

The "both/and" rather than "either/or" approach poses particular challenges in the Irish context due to more recent social change as well as more deeply embedded traditions. For example, Gleeson (in Chapter Four) has already indicated the extent of anti-intellectualism, essentialism and pragmatism that have characterised if not entirely dominated public life in Ireland since independence, and the manner in which these continue to "play out" within curriculum reform debates and policy initiatives. This intellectual malady is confounded by an inter-generational dynamic that has been shaped by as well as continuing to shape Irish public discourse.

It is frequently said of the 1960s generation, who are now a dominant force within the educational community, that, as a "cohort", we are much clearer about what we are against rather than what we are for. For much of the first fifty years of independence, Ireland was largely a failed economic entity where emigration was the constant social safety valve until the 1980s when it was construed by prominent politicians as an opportunity to go abroad to acquire skills and expertise that one could bring back, thus enhancing the Irish economy. Throughout this period, the authority of the dominant Catholic Church held sway in a coercive and overbearing manner, and this was particularly evident in education, including the professoriate. Key positions such as school principalships, particularly in the secondary sector, were the exclusive purview of religious orders and Diocesan clergy. The dominant values officially subscribed to in the educational arena were conformity and conservatism; maintaining continuity rather than fostering change was paramount; and a defensive mindset became apparent from the 1970s onwards as vocations went into decline. As a generation of teachers and educators, we were against this controlling authority, its monopoly on power and control without necessarily identifying what this "power" was for. A combination of anti-intellectualism and conformity induced by coercive authority conspired in such a manner that the values of the controlling individuals and their institution largely remained unexamined — as did the values, beliefs and attitudes of those who sought to shake off the yoke of the "ruling class" in education. This set of scenarios is summarised by O'Carroll as follows:

> The seminaries and novitiates were the growth industries of the times and the volunteers for the foreign missions reached unimaginable proportions. Instead of considering measures to reverse the processes that marginalized large sections of society, the establishment struggled incessantly to ward off the forces of change. (2002, p. 38)

There were other social movements afoot nationally also. The period of the past thirty years has borne witness to major urban re-settlement (*tréigint na tuaithe*) with a corresponding increase in urbanisation that, in itself, generates a kind of internal exile or alienation. Massive migration from west to east coast has created significant "dislocation" and has contributed to a rupture with the past. A generation ago, Irish society was the place of the "squinting windows" (of McNamara) from which many wished to escape, either by emigration (largely for the least educated) or internal urbanisation (for the rural educated "class"). Urbanised Ireland has now become to a significant degree a series of "gated communities" where volunteerism is in retreat (O'Donoghue, 2002). Yet, the spirit of community and the traditional *"meitheal oibre"* so abundantly evident for the Special Olympics indicates clearly that with appropriate leadership and policy-making, this residual but crucially important resource can be harnessed in very productive ways for the common good.

However, our consumerist hedonism is being increasingly recognised. The Irish President recently described it as the darker side of the Celtic Tiger, speaking of the "newly prosperous, whose main concern appears to be the acquisition of a prestige address [in one of those gated communities] and a rural nostalgic retreat" (O'Carroll, 2002, p. 146). It is ironic that, until recently, it was this rural Ireland that many wished to escape from as an all too stark reminder of poverty and backwardness (see for example, Scheper-Hughes, 2001). It is largely this newly prosperous group whose offspring have taken like "ducks to water" to the high-octane consumption that has become an integral part of Ireland's recent economic miracle.

Recent developments in Ireland, therefore, are the very antithesis of teaching in and beyond the knowledge society and capitulation to market forces seems to be the dominant influence. The particular confluence of global, social and economic forces as they are refracted within the Irish milieu is summed up in the following:

> The current ideology, banal though it may be, conflates society with nation and economy, and fails to identify and discriminate between the nature and appropriate functions of community, public sphere and the state. Society itself has been largely neglected. (O'Carroll, 2002, p. 148)

O'Carroll concludes that there is "a failure to recognise the importance of the public sphere, a key component of modern democracy in which communities articulate their differences, attempt persuasion and ensure enforcement of legal entitlements" (p. 148). His analysis suggests that we are closer to Boston than Berlin, and that we have privileged economy to the neglect and detriment of civil society. Dunne (2002, p. 83) captures this capitulation very succinctly when he states: "integration of the education system into the economy all too easily means its colonisation" and this results in "the loss of any sense of the intrinsic value or integrity of different subject areas and the triumph of a managerialist ethos". We narrow the focus of this debate to determine, even in a preliminary manner, the extent to which this more general analysis is sustained in the educational context, and what might be necessary or appropriate by way of redress.

As argued in earlier chapters, there has been a consistent shift in emphasis towards vocational knowledge and skills in the curriculum. However, closer examination suggests that the traditional humanist curriculum has remained remarkably intact, and the revised primary curriculum marks a renewed emphasis on individual subject disciplines rather than a more thematic, integrated approach, integration being consistently identified as one of the defining characteristics of the 1971 child-centred curriculum. Gleeson and Granville (Chapters Four and Three) have indicated the manner in which more integrated approaches in the junior post-primary sector have been successfully resisted and marginalised. It appears, therefore, that mainstream curricula in the secondary sector, not withstanding innovations such as LCA and Transition Year, have been largely inured from radical curriculum development. In so far as deep curriculum changes have been effected, they have been allowed to linger on the margins, thus perpetuating a two-tier system.

It is important to note, however, that there can be innovation and reform without deep and sustained change. Reform that is dictated from the top or centre is much more likely to fail due to the fact that teachers frequently have little ownership of the initiative (Sarason, 1996). Top-down reform is likely to result in a cosmetic and superficial exercise with minimum compliance by re-assembling the curriculum "tableau" differently. While being critical of top-down reform initiatives, it is important not to valorise local "bottom-up" reforms either, while they do increase the possibility of ownership and shared commitment (Sarason, 1990,

1996; Fullan, 1991). When terms such as reform, change and innovation are used interchangeably, it is much more difficult to know precisely the nature of what is planned and intended, let alone actually implemented and embedded in practice. When the tools of the trade of improving the quality of teaching and learning are blunted consistently, the substance and process of improvement are likely to lack clarity and precision. Efforts to bring about substantial and significant change may be sacrificed on the altar of pragmatism in an effort to allow partners or stakeholders to attach their preferred "meanings" to the latest initiative; cordial relations are maintained and there is frequent minimal "buy-in" that is designed to conform and appease rather than generate a collective and shared commitment that is systematic and sustained.

Persistence with traditional curricula is having a seriously alienating influence on middle-class students also, those who traditionally have been regarded as coming to school with "cultural capital" and poised to maximise their benefit from a largely culturally congruent curriculum. Recent research conducted in England suggests that "70 per cent of kids at secondary level say they are bored" (Hopkins, 2003, p. *xi*). As an increasing proportion of middle-class students take on part-time employment during schooling to fund their expensive lifestyles, they are inclined more to resist the imposition of "school rules" which, to them, appear outmoded and petty, while their disposable income frequently changes the nature of relationships between them and their teachers. More traditional secondary schools sometimes respond by seeking to implement and enforce such rules with greater vigour and determination while failing to recognise the changing sociocultural dynamics at play within and beyond the immediate school community. Some of those who can afford it seek a kind of refuge in so called "grind" schools, where there are trade-offs such as being on first-name terms with teachers and where wearing designer clothes may be substituted for a conformist school uniform, and a "promise" by the institution to maximise "points" for the student "clients" when they sit the Leaving Certificate. Such shifts are manifestations of a "competitive individualism", already evident in the system (Lynch, 1989). We agree with Hopkins's analysis when he states:

> There is a fundamental mismatch between what we know "turns on" the interest of young people and how we teach. If we do not fire the imagination of our young people and give them enjoyment in learning, then we will not only fail . . . we will also violate the aims of education. (2003, p. *xi*)

Greater prescription of curricula combined with the high-stakes testing of public examinations is likely to exacerbate rather than alleviate this growing trend. However, such criticisms should not be understood as a pandering to a lowest common denominator of consumerist idiosyncrasy, but an appeal for food for the soul, beyond the knowledge economy where personal meaning within a cosmopolitan identity in an interdependent world are weighted appropriately and integrated with cognitive challenge and success. We concur with the conclusion that: "state education . . . must deal with the human consequences of the knowledge economy — teaching beyond as well as for it, adding values to the agenda of reform that build community, develop social capital and forge cosmopolitan identity" (Hargreaves, 2003, p. 160). The issue of "social capital" must sit squarely on the table beside concerns for "economic capital".

We have tried to indicate also that, in the Irish context, this poses a considerable challenge due to a "values vacuum" engineered by a confluence of socio-historical and economic forces. There is an urgent need therefore to re-inscribe society and community into the dominant discourse of the knowledge economy. As Waldron (Chapter Seven) indicates, the revised primary curriculum has potential to re-introduce more communitarian considerations that will enable learners to develop character and citizenship and identities sufficiently robust to compete in as well as to transform and transcend the knowledge economy into the kind of society they wish to shape for themselves and their children. If this ambition is to succeed, it will be necessary to move beyond the "civic" education of manners and politeness, a kind of "domestication" typical of earlier efforts and more traditional schooling and curricula, to more systematic and sustained engagement with issues of structure and agency. This is unlikely to happen without adequate support and professional development for teachers. Teachers in particular, as the orchestrators of this more encompassing conversation, have a crucial leadership role, and policy-makers need to inscribe this broader vision into discourses of reform beyond instrumentalist and pragmatic thinking and tinkering.

Coffield's (2000, pp. 240–2) comments resonate with those of Sennett (1998) and Putnam (2000) when he argues that the generation of social capital through education is worthwhile because it helps create social cohesion. But the dominant technocratic version of society being promoted by government policies is "moving us into the performative society, where the true goal of the system is the optimisation of the global relationship between input and output [and the fostering of] conformity, compliance and control rather than emancipation, empowerment or the enhancement of learning". Writing in an Irish context, Healy (2000) provides evidence that senior politicians are keenly aware of the international debate on social capital and issues a warning that "an excessive reliance on top-down approaches to levering social capital may rob it of its essential value" (p. 92). The absence of any serious or sustained debate on the balance between economic and cultural capital within mainstream education almost constitutes an additional silence in the setting.

Signpost Three: Standards

Educators, and others, in the Irish context, frequently attribute recent economic success to the quality of our education system, its promotion of high standards and the achievements of its students. Prominent individuals within the education community have sometimes proclaimed that "we have the best education system in the world". More cautious and considered views recognise that, in general, the system does well when compared with other OECD countries where teacher–pupil ratios are generally lower and expenditure per pupil considerably higher. FitzGerald summarises these circumstances in the following terms:

> ... primary and second-level education are under-resourced, to the tune of something like one-third. But the evidence suggests that the average standard reached by Irish students is at or slightly above the EU average, and that the proportion who complete education to age 18 is slightly higher than the EU average. Thus, in terms of what might be called "educational productivity" — output in qualitative and quantitative terms related to input of resources — Ireland seems to have been performing about 50% better than the rest of the EU. (2002, p. 130)

Such statistical evidence needs to be treated with caution as decontextualised "rank ordering" of countries in international league tables often conceal more than they reveal (Oldham, 2003; O'Leary, 2001). Accountability measures internationally, many of which have been born out of school effectiveness research and school improvement initiatives, have generated relentless pressure and preoccupation with raising standards, particularly during the past decade. Such efforts have led to a veritable "back to basics" movement where literacy and numeracy have been the major focus of "performance training sects" where professional support for teachers has been reduced to drill and practice routines to enable students to "beat the test" rather than improve comprehension or instill a love of reading, or increase students' capacity to solve problems (McNeil, 2000; Hargreaves, 2003). In a relentless effort to raise or improve standards, a combination of school inspection and other "incentives" have effectively increased standardisation where centralised "prescriptions" have been translated into homogenising tendencies in terms of both teaching and learning.

High-stakes testing of public examinations promote such standardisation, while the revised primary curriculum generally places much greater emphasis on the necessity for teachers to be "assessment-literate". This globalising, homogenising tendency towards standardisation has been refracted in the Irish context through efforts at whole school development planning at both primary and post-primary levels, while whole school evaluation continues to be championed by the Inspectorate. It would be difficult to argue against the merits of these initiatives but increasingly teachers are raising questions about competing demands on their time and the trade-offs between time to teach and the demands for paperwork. There is concern also that such paperwork may become an elaborate means of reducing their work to mere accountancy rather than more comprehensive accountability measures (Dunne, 2002). However, in comparison with the "naming and shaming" culture that has been associated with league tables and publication of school inspection reports in England and Wales, legal prohibition of such tables in Ireland has meant that the general climate in which educational reforms have been conducted continue to be more positive and less critical. Nevertheless, greater emphasis on planning and accountability generally are prominent dimensions of more global rhetorics of reform, and they may take on a significantly sharper tone in the Irish context if the economic outlook continues to decline; there will be increasing pressure on the education system to raise standards to maintain a competitive edge in the global economy. In such circumstances, "regimes of performance training may . . . improve results in basic skills in the short term but may imperil more complex knowledge society objectives in the long run" (Hargreaves, 2003, p. 141). The degree of emphasis on performance indicators in the latest Strategy Statement 2003–2005 (DES, 2003) is particularly worrying in this regard.

In terms of substantial curriculum change, policy-makers and teacher unions in particular are at a critical moment in the Irish context. As part of the postmodern condition where traditional authority and authority figures are being questioned and held to account, there has been a decline in morale among teachers too and a growing feeling that their individual and collective contributions are no longer appreciated to the same extent. Teachers have internalised the market forces ideology of bonuses and share options, and have come to the conclusion that the ground rules under which they became teachers and their commitment to "making a difference" have been altered irrevocably. They have sought "redress" through the benchmarking process in an effort to regain some of their economic status. Ranked seventh out of 27 countries in an OECD comparative study of teachers' salaries, Irish teachers are paid above the EU average, but this relative position, both nationally and internationally, has declined dramatically in the past decade (Coolahan, 2003, 3.2.10). While the importance of remuneration and general social standing of the teaching profession should not be underestimated in terms of attracting and retaining high calibre entrants to the profession, there is risk also in becoming preoccupied with these concerns only to the veritable exclusion of other big picture concerns such as emergent forms of new professionalism with all that teaching for the knowledge society entails (Hargreaves, 2000; 2003).

In an international context, the combination of new managerialism, school improvement measures and the imposition of a standards agenda with a narrowing of criteria to determine both accountability and improved results, has reduced teaching in many instances to a technical requirement of increasing test scores. Commitment to care, to social justice, to fostering creativity and individual talent have been sacrificed on the altar of standardisation and in a competitive context where those with cultural capital are always going to have the edge on their poorer peers. Hargreaves (2003, p. 126) summarises this confluence of forces in the following terms:

> The reduction of standards to soulless standardisation in many places has generated public dissatisfaction with teacher shortages in schools, and the loss of creativity and inspiration in the classroom. . . . If schools are to become real knowledge communities for all pupils, then teaching must be made into a real *learning profession* for all teachers. (p. 126)

Teachers themselves must resist the accountability standardisation agenda in favour of a much wider commitment to care, inclusion and the promotion of the highest standards without falling prey to homogenisation. More fundamentally, teachers themselves need to restore some of the lost trust in the profession by committing publicly to a vision of teaching and learning that embraces the knowledge society, and not merely the knowledge economy, to become public intellectuals that steadfastly defend and promote the public sphere as a means of building character and community in ways that provide an important buffer to the anarchic tendencies of market forces. More than ever before, teachers need to shape and influence the criteria by which their standards of stewardship are to be measured. Efforts at curriculum innovation must not be confined to content, delivery and preordained outcomes. They must engage also with identity, citizenship and the common good in ways that inform, influence and inspire the passions of students. The establishment of the Teaching Council (see Coolahan, 2003) provides an important context for addressing this agenda. However, the legislation already enacted to create this council seems much more preoccupied with structures and regulation rather than being a generative force for rethinking teaching and learning as well as fostering emergent forms of appropriate professionalism. In this regard also, as further evidence of global rhetorics taking hold, albeit so far with "shallow roots" (Cuban and Usdan, 2003), the most recent DES Strategy Statement (2003–2005) represents a significant "shift" in terminology (and thinking) as evidenced by its abundance of performance indicators.

SILENCES

As already indicated, there are significant silences surrounding curriculum change and educational debates in the Irish context, and these too deserve to be put on the agenda as a means of generating more inclusive educational dialogue. For example, there are silences or virtual silences surrounding issues such as the feminisation of the teaching profession as well as the degree of influence exerted by textbook publishers on a relatively small market and the manner in which the virtual monopoly of a few reduces risk-taking in the production of texts and materials; thus, paradoxically, experimentation is further limited by market forces! There is silence also regarding existing structures and their propensity to increase fragmentation. Lack of attention to transition from primary to post-primary schooling is a good example, while retention interventions deal with symptoms rather than underlying structures. However, in the interest of economy, comment is confined here to three issues only, all of which relate to structures.

Silence One: Education Structures

The historical origins of Irish primary and post-primary education must be seen in the context of the colonial days of the nineteenth century (Coolahan, 1981). Notwithstanding the smallness of the country (more school children in Greater Manchester), the exercise of power and control is complex and fragmented, reflecting the deep structures of Irish education. In the context of postcolonial Ireland, education was regarded as a most important and sensitive vehicle for the transmission of religious beliefs and values. As discussed by Gleeson above (Chapter Four), the Catholic Church had little interest in the school curriculum (apart from RE) as long as the arrangements for school management were satisfactory. The hierarchy, not renowned for its willingness to consult and listen, established a strong foothold on the management of schooling and teacher education at that time. There were other significant centres of power, all characterised by fragmentation. The Inspectorate was divided into three distinct groupings with little communication or collaboration between these "sectors" — primary, secondary and vocational (post-primary) — while recent integration and regionalisation have sought to address such institutional apartheid. Separate provision for primary and post-primary teacher education were established also in the nineteenth century. These "givens" of the system have been re-inscribed into contemporary structures regarding research, development and curriculum policy-making.

The deep fault-lines of the system contribute also to fragmentation of effort in the context of planned curriculum change. As indicated above, a key generative principle that underpinned the establishment of the Interim CEB was to ensure a more broadly based approach to the selection from culture (Logan and O'Reilly,

1985). The original Board was representative without being representational, and established three Committees to progress its work — a Senior Cycle Committee, an Assessment and Certification Committee and a Joint Committee. The selection of the term "joint" was very deliberate as it was intended to signal clearly the committee's remit to deal with education from junior infants to the end of compulsory schooling, and it was premised on the belief that the Council "had to take account of continuity in thinking and planning throughout first and second levels [of education]" (CEB, 1985). Ó Ceallaigh (1985, p. 11) intimated that the proposed frameworks in the consultative document from the Joint Committee, *Issues and Structures* (CEB, 1984), "correspond closely to the various aspects of the primary school curriculum, set out in the *Teacher's Handbook* (Department of Education, 1971). The "areas of experience" framework, internationally reputable in the 1980s, was to be the conduit for "breadth and balance" in the curriculum. The OECD (1991), rightly in our view, argued for a well-planned continuity of experience between primary and secondary schooling and this perspective endorsed the view espoused by the Interim CEB (1986). However, the recently revised primary curriculum places greater emphasis on individual subjects, particularly science as a major economic concern. The Board, however, conceded a great deal to subject-centred teaching by claiming that existing subjects should be the "starting point", and this is reflected in the current policy of a subject-based curriculum culminating in the new Junior Certificate (pp. 68–73). However, power relations and a fear of the unfamiliar determined otherwise. Mulcahy (1989, p. 85) subsequently expressed astonishment at what he describes as "the lengths which are gone to in order to demonstrate that [the] idea [of areas of experience] can be accommodated without any significant departure from the existing subjects on the curriculum". Gleeson recalls that the unrelenting message from the NCCA when the Junior Certificate was being launched as one of "there's nothing to fear; we have just updated subject content". Such minimalist approaches resonate with our comments above regarding the interchangeable use of terminology where shuffling the deck of existing curricula is identified as substantial change.

Despite, as much as because of, these internal disagreements, the principles of "breadth and balance" and "curriculum continuity" were both imported into the Junior Certificate, the first major development from the NCCA "stable". One of the underlying principles of that programme is "to reinforce and further develop in the young person the knowledge, understanding, skills and competencies acquired at primary level" (NCCA, 1989, p. 5). However, more recently Granville (interview) has suggested that, due to internal disputes, these principles were diluted to become "a guideline which schools would interpret at local level". Power relations and vested interests succeeded in maintaining existing compartmentalised thinking within established structures. Arguably, the continued lack of continuity of learning, both in terms of location, curriculum and pedagogy, for early adolescents as they relocate from primary to secondary schools, contributes significantly to alienation from learning that frequently results in attrition from schooling of the most vulnerable. Instead of dealing with discontinuities and the deep structures of the system, school retention programmes are put in place to address surface difficulties, to deal with symptoms not causes.

On a recent visit to a High School in Boston, where one of us compared notes about our respective systems with the principal, when he was informed that secondary schools in Ireland cater for students from the age of twelve to eighteen, he remarked: "What have 12- and 18-year-olds got in common?" Ironically, in the days of "Secondary Tops", typically an adjunct to an established primary school, arguably there was greater continuity between primary and secondary schooling in terms of location, familiarity and teachers, than currently exists in a much more "developed" system of education. The creation of middle schools at junior cycle, on the same campus as primary schools, or the creation of schools that cater for the period of compulsory schooling, are important possibilities. They could be founded and fostered as a means of moving beyond existing structures in ways that seek to re-inscribe breath, balance and continuity into curricula, teaching, learning and schooling in more meaningful ways, particularly where student attrition is acute. While the NCCA committee structure is currently redolent of existing divisions, altering these has potential to signal leadership in the system that is overdue.

The current Minister for Education and Science appears to be aware of the constraints imposed by a representational partnership approach. It may be a means of finding agreement on the "lowest common denominator" rather than effecting significant change. He is inclined to the view that this approach "might . . . ensure that the status quo thrives at the expense of radical change, because radical proposals are harder to agree, because the radical is no friend of the comfortable" (Dempsey, Address at Inaugural Meeting of the new NCCA, Mont Clare Hotel, Dublin, 26 March 2003). Altering these structures, however valuable symbolically and in terms of promoting greater continuity in learning, are likely to be relatively ineffective without altering existing structures of schooling.

The perpetuation of existing structures within the NCCA, DES and the Inspectorate, as well as the separate provision of primary and secondary schooling, contribute significantly to and perpetuate discontinuities, fragmentation, existing power relations, suspicion and lack of trust in the system, with the needs of learners being relegated to secondary consideration. Such existing scenarios continue to privilege curriculum subject content over more generic cross-curricular considerations such as critical thinking, creativity, imagination, problem-solving, social and emotional learning, all of which are vitally important as contributions to, as well as for participation in, a knowledge society. Towards this end, Stoll, Fink and Earl (2003, p. 187) recommend a more radical move also towards greater curriculum autonomy at local level when they say that it is necessary to:

> Define curriculum in terms of learnings, not subjects, and empower schools to address these learnings across the school. We recommend that the organization and at least 30 per cent of the curriculum be designed locally to respond to the contextual needs of different communities.

Existing structures at national and local levels, as well as the power relations that are derived from and perpetuate these structures, are unlikely to achieve such ends. Teacher education is another structured systemic silence that also perpetuates these structures.

Silence Two: Teacher Education

Nineteenth-century power relations between the Churches and the colonial government have left a legacy of fragmented provision in teacher education both north and south of the border. The border itself as well as its positioning is a manifestation of the emergence of nationalism as a dominant nineteenth-century ideology and the attendant power struggles that accompanied it on this island. These "forces" continue to be played out in particular ways, internally refracted by competing trajectories of history and culture that are repeatedly re-inscribed into political and educational discourses. Consequently, there is a double apartheid in teacher education. Until very recently, there was little or no contact beyond personal relationships between teacher education institutions and personnel north and south. On both sides of the border, too, teacher education is distinctly patterned and structured in a fragmented manner due to these competing and conflicting versions of our collective past. Due to the influence of "big brother" on the "mainland", teacher education in Northern Ireland has state and denominational (Catholic) institutions but with less fracturing between primary and secondary sectors. By comparison in the Republic, denominational development is the key to understanding contemporary arrangements. There are five teacher education institutions that prepare students to work in the primary sector only,[1] and all of these are denominational, privately owned by the Churches, while being publicly funded (though not all on the same basis). Programmes in these five colleges are primarily premised on a concurrent model of teacher education, while recent teacher shortages in the primary sector have resulted in the resuscitation of the dormant consecutive postgraduate Diploma that is of eighteen months duration.

By contrast, the dominant location of teacher education programmes for the secondary sector is within Education Departments in five of the Universities. The dominant model is
consecutive, a one-year postgraduate Diploma, except for a minority of programmes such as PE, Technology, Home Economics
and Religious Studies that provide four-year concurrent degree
programmes and for the most part in institutions that are
denominational. In a small system, these provisions represent
considerable fragmentation of institutions, personnel and programmes. However, in the present context, the focus is on structures and their attendant implications for curriculum policy and
development as well as on the delivery and quality of teaching
and learning for primary and secondary pupils and students.

In 1999, the then Minister for Education and Science established
two "working groups" to "review current arrangements for the
preparation of teachers in light of the many changes occurring . . ."
(DES, 2002, p. 3). Current separation of the primary and secondary sectors appear to be so institutionalised and internalised that
having two separate reviews has been accepted without question.
It has already been pointed out above that the NCCA has replicated these structural divisions in terms of its committee structure, thus perpetuating primary and secondary mindsets in ways
that tend to generate mistrust and suspicion, as well as perpetuating distinctly different professional identities among primary and
secondary teachers. These differing identities tend to underestimate respective roles and responsibilities, and are used in negative and partial ways that seek to shape identities by exaggerating
difference rather than celebrating commonalities. This is a regrettable consequence of existing structures of separation. More than
fifty years ago, admittedly in a context where primary teachers
did not enjoy access to a degree programme like most of their secondary colleagues, the INTO advocated in *A Plan for Education*
(1947, p. 26) that "there should be a common basis training for all
teachers", and this "training course should extend over four years
. . . leading to a university degree and entailing attendance at university lectures". However, participation in university life should

not be confined to mere attendance at lectures. Rather, students "should have academic contact . . . with young people preparing for other professions and should play their part in the social, athletic and cultural activities of the student body". There was recognition then that segregation between student teachers and between primary student teachers and other university students was unhealthy, and tends to continue to perpetuate a cultural myth of the "born" teacher (Sugrue, 1997, 1998; Britzman, 1989, 1991), a myth that appeals to essentialist tendencies in our culture, and is inimical to more research-based approaches to teaching, learning and professional formation.

The manner in which inherited teacher education structures have been institutionalised systemically, and internalised by those who work within it, has serious ongoing consequences for teachers and learners. Disruption, divisions and discontinuity at the end of primary schooling are exaggerated and exacerbated to the point where the period of compulsory schooling is rendered relatively meaningless. This fragmentation within the system has been largely ignored despite the OECD (1991, p. 96) comment that "transition arrangements between primary and secondary schools need to be improved and . . . steps need to be taken to foster greater continuity in curriculum and pedagogy from the beginning to the end of schooling. This report also recommends that: "basic education should be affirmed in organisational terms as continuity throughout the whole period of compulsory schooling" (p. 62). Existing structures perpetuate thinking that belongs to a period when the vast majority completed formal "learning" at the end of primary schooling. In a context of lifelong learning, as well as greater competition for scarce resources, the necessity for economies of scale and efficient use of resources, the deep structures of education that sustain fragmentation, mistrust and suspicion, are anathema to quality curriculum planning and development. With greater awareness of and commitment to Early Childhood Education (Ireland, Government of, 1999), current fresh ferment provides an excellent opportunity to question and to alter nineteenth-century structures and to address issues of specialisation at primary level — for example, the possibility that primary teachers could teach to the end of compulsory schooling, and that secondary teachers could experience teaching in the senior classes of primary schools. In terms of learners' needs, curriculum reforms and espoused pedagogies at Junior Cycle level, primary teachers appear to be eminently suited to sustaining continuity, particularly for some of the most vulnerable students.

A more strategic approach to teaching and learning for the knowledge society is likely also to necessitate greater attention to Curriculum Studies as a "field" of study. Serious and sustained interrogation of the field of curriculum tends to be entirely marginal or ignored in favour of subject "specialisation" or fragmentation, depending on perspective, with a focus on content and pedagogy. Such arrangements indicate the extent to which separate subjects dominate policy, process and practice. Current structures, therefore, appear to be wasteful of resources and are poorly positioned to serve existing and emerging needs. Addressing root causes rather than surface realities pushes the system and its leadership towards deeper structural change. At a systemic level, we have to choose between tinkering and transformation (Fullan, 2003). Similar challenges are apparent in the areas of research and evaluation and the OECD (1991, p. 76) identified "piecemeal" efforts as problematic and inadequate:

> . . . the basic goals and values of the education system have tended to be tacit rather than explicit during a period when major transformations in the society, economy and culture have been occurring; curriculum, assessment and examination changes have been continual but piecemeal.

When attention is focused on research and evaluation, there is additional evidence of piecemeal initiatives but with less continuity.

Silence Three: Educational Research and Evaluation

One of the necessities that emerges from a more rapidly altering educational landscape is greater need for and urgency to create evidence about what is actually happening in the system. Additionally, as various innovations are introduced, piloted and implemented, there is increased need also for evaluation. Both ongoing research and evaluation therefore need to be embedded as fundamental routines of the educational system. In the Irish context this has never been nor is it currently the case. This is a major systemic silence and weakness that occasionally becomes a whisper or a whimper. From a policy practice and reform perspective (and argued in Chapter Six in particular), the absence of evidence in the system has important consequences for power relations. This lack of evidence tends to facilitate major players' reinvention of the status quo rather than lead to more systemic reforms. Significantly, where action research has been completed and put into the public domain, it is worth noting that it is almost exclusively located in primary and further education settings, sufficiently distant from the levers of power to dilute its transformative potential at a systemic level (see McNiff, McNamara and Leonard, 2000).

More than a decade ago, the OECD (1991, p. 42) visiting committee remarked:

> Although the universities and teacher training colleges complain that they are starved of funds for educational research, and although there have been relatively few empirical studies, the current overall output of pedagogically oriented research is impressive for a small country.

However, the report continues: "what might be regarded as unsatisfactory is the dearth of policy-related research as distinct from a growing body of policy discussion literature" (p. 42). What these comments fail to acknowledge is that due to the absence of adequate, significant and sustained funding for educational research, of either a policy- or pedagogy-related kind, even the "impressive" pedagogical output is achieved most frequently by individual commitment and effort rather than being fostered and funded by the system. In the absence of an appropriate and adequate career structure in the Colleges of Education,[2] as well as inadequate funding, sustaining a research culture is rendered doubly difficult. In the university sector, where faculty numbers in education for the most part barely rise to double digits, sustaining a research culture is also a major challenge. The existence of the Educational Research Centre (ERC) as a "free-standing" institution on the St Patrick's College Drumcondra campus, has tended also to contribute to a separation between teacher education as primarily if not exclusively a teaching function, and the conduct of educational research. Due to the fact also that for the vast majority of years since the ERC was established in the mid-1960s, its funding has been part of primary estimates and budgets, the primary inspectorate was enabled to "commission" research of particular interest to its remit, while the secondary sector had to forage for funding to investigate concerns of relevance and importance to it. There has been "suppression" of research reports and findings also that might give rise to embarrassment or a questioning of policy and practice. Consequently, research, at best, has frequently been deployed as a vehicle for good news if positive findings on a particular issue or topic could be garnered. Conversely, such investigations were sometimes "sat on" and kept from the public domain if the evidence they contained was likely to lead to questions being raised. The piecemeal evaluation that has been conducted sporadically in the system has tended to be functionalist in orientation with an emphasis on what works rather than any critique or questioning of assumptions or approach. The purpose and process of evaluation appears as a sporadic extra that is occasionally useful, while commitment to dissemination of "findings" is often determined by its good news potential rather than through any commitment to informing debate and policy decision-making.

There is evidence too that the absence of adequate funding has serious consequences for the nature of the research conducted (see Sugrue and Uí Thuama, 1994). There has been an over-emphasis on survey and library-based investigations and a notable absence of observational fieldwork that cannot be undertaken or sustained without adequate funding. For somewhat different reasons, primary and secondary classrooms and schools continue to be veritable "secret gardens", which is all the more surprising and disturbing given the rhetoric of reform and its unrelenting pace during the past decade. Arising out of existing structures, the fragmentation of effort and the difficulties posed to building and sustaining both research capacity and culture, despite the intervening decade, the questions posed by the OECD continue to resonate with contemporary realities, and have relevance to the present discussion. The report posits the following questions:

> Is it that the authorities in Ireland . . . have become disenchanted with the whole process of educational planning and, perhaps, dubious of the utility of the research findings brought to their attention, or is it that they have difficulty in identifying clear-cut priorities? Or does the daily pressure of their jobs preclude a systematic review of literature on policy issues? (1991, p. 42)

Within the confines of the present discussion, the answer to the above questions continues to be yes, while there are other considerations also that are exacerbated by existing structures. For example, research on the period of compulsory schooling is generally avoided as studies tend towards an exclusive focus on primary or secondary. More importantly, there is a lack of transparency regarding the generation of a research agenda and such priorities as exist tend to be reactive, the recent investigation of "Exploring Masculinities" within transition year programmes being a good example (see Mac An Ghaill, Hanafin and Conway, 2003). A very definite policy commitment to the identification of research priorities is necessary and vital, and this needs to be conducted in a manner that provides much greater evidence that "partnership" applies in this important area also. In addition, such a policy commitment requires much greater commitment to the funding of educational research with an identifiable and dedicated annual budget. More adequate and transparent funding should be accompanied also by commitment to publication of research reports and greater transparency regarding adjudication on research proposals and the awarding of funding. Educational research and evaluation needs to be elevated to a more prominent and central role in educational policy and practice beyond being a useful tool periodically deployed as a reactive response to a "problem" or personal interest of systemic "insiders" or powerful "players". To do otherwise is to continue to neglect a crucially important aspect of curriculum reform and policy-making, while failing also to build research capacity within the system in a manner that raises the general level of educational debate, thus leading to more sophisticated and better-informed reforms for more complex and diverse needs among learners.

FINAL COMMENTS: NEW DEPARTURES

We are conscious that issues addressed in this concluding chapter are partial only. A comprehensive agenda would extend well beyond just three signposts and as many silences. For example, we have not touched on the contested issue of language and culture, nor the more recent challenges posed to established orthodoxies by diversity and multiculturalism. Rather, we have tried to do three things: to stay close to the evidence and argument in the earlier chapters, to provide a contrapuntal reading of the educational landscape by identifying some major systemic signposts and silences, and to situate these contemporary currents and subterranean structures within international discourses; to identify and locate national reform trajectories and refracted discourses within a global/local nexus. We made clear also at the beginning of this chapter that we did not wish to circumscribe debate or to predetermine outcomes. With these caveats in place, we bring our contribution to this chapter and text to a close by identifying items for a new debate. Our hope is that the "tenets" described will provide the basis for and point of entry to educational debate with potential for curriculum transformation. In this manner, bringing the curtain down on this text also heralds a new beginning in the Irish chapter of curriculum contestation and transformation.

- Curriculum policy, design, development and diffusion can never be reduced to a technical matter. It is always ideological. In the Irish context, it is necessary to articulate in a much more conscious and transparent manner the values, beliefs and "stance" being espoused in any reform endeavour. As part of this approach, it is necessary also to be conscious of, and committed to, preparing students for the knowledge society and not merely for the knowledge economy. Recognition of and resistance to the global forces that buffet and shape such scenarios needs also to re-inscribe the notion of vocation into teaching, to recognise its essential moral enterprise. However, teaching as a moral enterprise necessitates a commitment to social justice and inclusion rather than a condescending "charitable" stance towards the most vulnerable and marginalised. Teachers in the knowledge society need to be public intellectuals with a passionate commitment to teaching and learning. In the absence of such commitments, curriculum is essentially moribund.

- There is an increasing necessity and urgency to question the taken-for-granted structures of the education system and their attendant processes; to recognise that "partnership" is flawed and contested, requiring constant interrogation and vigilance. Seeking to change in fundamental ways the deep structures that are a historical legacy and a contemporary anachronism within the system may release proscribed agency in ways that disrupt the status quo and dominant if not entirely hegemonic power relations.

- The relative neglect of research and evaluation and their optional status within the educational system has been a persistent dilemma that requires immediate redress by identification of research priorities in a consultative manner, by making annual funding provision to support the generation of evidence about the system, and by greater commitment to publication and critical debate of the evidence provided as a means of informing policy and practice.

- Due to the pace of change and the seemingly relentless demand for curriculum innovation and other aspects of teaching and learning, there is an increasing tendency also towards more hyper-rational demands for planning and accountability that encroaches on the autonomy and professional judgement of teachers. When such centralised prescriptions reach a critical mass, which differs for individuals depending on career stage and school context, there is a growing tendency towards "early retirement" in an attempt to regain control of one's personal life and to seek calmer waters. Global forces must be harnessed for creative and imaginative ingenuity rather than more homogenisation. Designing curricula, pedagogies and attendant evaluation mechanisms must leave room for professional autonomy and judgement as a means of protecting and promoting quality learning. Differentiated and sustained professional support in various formal and informal ways helps to sustain passionate commitment, while further surveillance and accountability increases uniformity, kills initiative and forces teachers into early retirement. Enlightened responses rather than futile resistance to global forces are the most sure-footed means of preparing the rising generation to have the confidence, creativity and competencies to create their own future.

- At a time when evidence abounds of increasing social fragmentation due to the influences of market forces and their tendency to create an anarchic individualism, there is an overwhelming need to continue to invest in the public sector. This should not be construed as special pleading. Rather, there is a greater necessity than ever to build cultural and social capital for all while promoting and advocating an appropriate version of the common good through revitalising and supporting community. The economic imperative of global capitalism needs to be leavened by sustained commitment to inclusive and sustained attempts to build social capital so that there is real substance to the rhetoric of "no child left behind", and participatory citizenship as well as lifelong learning become the "cosmic soup" from which appropriate versions of the common good are created and sustained in an interdependent world.

This is the broad canvas on which curriculum and its ideology in the Irish context will "play" in the immediate future. Apart from specific items on that agenda that await our individual and collective attention, there is need also, as part of a wider debate on "the world we want" (Kingswell, 2000), to devote more attention to education as a major area of public interest. In the "infotainment" "imagineered" (Barber, 1996) world that we inhabit, where the "soundbite" is king (or should that be queen!), there is a noticeable and regrettable absence of sustained interest in major educational issues. It is notable that, in comparison with other countries and their political leaders, prominent Irish politicians rarely make public statements on education. Rather, the media sensationalises particular and immediate stories of rat-infested schools, suspensions and expulsions and thus avoids more in-depth discussion of more enduring significance. It is often asserted in a self-congratulatory manner that "the Irish people" have an abiding interest in and respect for education. If this is the case, it is time to bring that interest to "market". If this consideration, in addition to the signposts and silences raised above, can be inscribed into a national educational discourse on curriculum teaching and learning in ways that begin to refashion and transform the educational topography as well as some of its underlying structures, then our efforts will have been worthwhile.

References

Allen, K. (2000), *The Celtic Tiger: The Myth of Social Partnership in Ireland*, Manchester: University Press.

Ball, S. (1994), *Educational Reform: A Critical and Post-Structural Approach*, Buckingham: Open University Press.

Barber, B.R. (1996), *Jihad vs. McWorld*, New York: Balantine Books.

Beck, U. (2000), *What Is Globalization?* Cambridge: Polity Press.

Bourdieu, P. and Wacquant, L J.D. (1992), *An Invitation to Reflexive Sociology*, Chicago: University of Chicago Press.

Britzman, D. (1989), "Who has the Floor: Curriculum Teaching and the English Teachers Struggle for Voice", *Curriculum Inquiry*, Vol. 19, pp. 143–62.

Britzman, D. (1991), *Practice Makes Practice A Critical Study of Learning to Teach (with a foreword by Maxine Greene)*, New York: SUNY.

Coffield, F. (2000), "Lifelong Learning as a Lever on Structural Change? Evaluation of White Paper: Learning to Succeed: A New Framework for Post-16 Learning", *Journal of Education Policy*, Vol. 15, No. 2, pp. 237–46.

Coolahan, J. (1981), *A History of Irish Education*, Dublin: IPA.

Coolahan, J. (2003), *Attracting, Developing and Retaining Effective Teachers: Country Background Report for Ireland*, Paris: OECD.

Coolahan, J. (ed.) (1994), *Report on The National Education Convention*, Dublin: The National Education Convention Secretariat.

Corcoran, M.P. and Peillon, M. (2002), *Ireland Unbound: A Turn of the Century Chronicle,* Dublin: Institute of Public Administration.

Cuban, L., Usdan, M. (ed.) (2003), *Powerful Reforms with Shallow Roots Improving America's Urban Schools* (with a foreword by Elizabeth Hale), New York & London: Teachers College Press.

Curriculum and Examinations Board (1984), *Issues and Structures in Education: A Consultative Document*, CEB: Dublin.

Curriculum and Examinations Board (1985), *Information Bulletin*, No. 3, September, CEB: Dublin.

Curriculum and Examinations Board (1986), *In Our Schools, A Framework for Curriculum and Assessment. Report of the Interim Curriculum and Examinations Board to the Minister for Education*, CEB: Dublin.

Dempsey, N. (2003), Address at Inaugural Meeting of the New NCCA, Mont Clare Hotel, 26 March.

Department of Education (1971), *Primary School Curriculum, Teacher's Handbooks Parts 1 & 2*, Dublin: Government Publications.

Department of Education and Science (2003), *Statement of Strategy 2003–2005*, Dublin: DES.

Dunne, J. (2002), "Citizenship and Education", in Kirby, P., Gibbons L. and Cronin, M. (eds.), *Reinventing Ireland: Culture, Society and the Global Economy*, London: Pluto, pp. 69–88.

European Commission (2001), "Report of the Eurostat Task Force on Measuring Lifelong Learning", Brussels: Eurostat.

FitzGerald, G. (2002), *Reflections on the Irish State*, Dublin: Irish Academic Press.

Fullan, M. (1991), *The New Meaning Of Educational Change*, London: Cassell.

Fullan, M. (2003), *Change Forces with a Vengeance*, New York & London: Routledge/Falmer.

Galbraith, J.K. (1992), *The Culture of Contentment*, London: Sinclair-Stevenson.

Gleeson, J. (2003), "Flexibility, Transferability and Mobility in Initial Vocational Education and Training — An Irish Perspective on COST Action A11", *International Journal of Vocational Education*, Vol. 11, No. 1, pp. 5–24.

Goodson, I.F. (1994), *Studying Curriculum*, New York and London: Teachers College, Columbia University.

Hargreaves, A. (1994), *Changing Teachers, Changing Times*, London: Cassell.

Hargreaves, A. (2000), "Four Ages of Professionalism and Professional Learning", *Teachers and Teaching: Theory and Practice*, Vol. 6, No. 2, pp. 151–82.

Hargreaves, A. (2003), *Teaching in the Knowledge Society*, Buckingham: Open University Press.

Healy, T. (2002), "In Each Other's Shadow", in Bohan, H. and Kennedy, G. (eds.), *Is the Future my Responsibility? Our Society in the New Millennium*, Dublin: Veritas, pp. 78–96.

Heaney, S. (1995), *The Redress of Poetry: Oxford Lectures*, London: Faber & Faber.

Homer-Dixon, T. (2001), *The Ingenuity Gap*, Toronto: Vintage Canada.

Hopkins, D. (2003), Foreword, in Hargreaves, A. (ed.), *Teaching in the Knowledge Society: Education in the Age of Insecurity*, Buckingham: Open University, pp. viii-xii.

INTO (1947), *A Plan for Education*, Dublin: INTO (Cahill Printers).

Ireland, Government of (1995), *Charting Our Education Future: White Paper on Education*, Dublin: Government Publications.

Ireland, Government of (1998), Education (No. 2) Bill, Dublin: Stationery Office.

Ireland, Government of (1999), *Ready To Learn: White Paper on Early Childhood Education*, Dublin: Stationery Office.

Ireland, Government of (2000), *Learning for Life: White Paper on Adult Education*, Dublin: The Stationery Office.

Kingwell, M. (2000), *The World We Want: Virtue, Vice and the Good Citizen*, Toronto: Penguin.

Logan, J. and O'Reilly, B. (1985), "Educational Decision Making: The Case of the Curriculum and Examinations Board", *Administration*, Vol. 33, No. 4, IPA.

Lynch, K. (1989), *The Hidden Curriculum: Reproduction in Education, A Reappraisal*, London: Falmer Press.

Lynch, K. (1992), "Education and the Paid Labour Market", *Irish Educational Studies*, Vol.11, Spring.

Lynch, K. and Lodge, A. (2002), *Equality and Power in Schools*, London and New York: Routledge/Falmer.

Mac An Ghaill, M., Hanafin, J. and Conway, P. (2003), "An Evaluation of the Exploring Masculinities Module in Transition Year", an evaluation report commissioned by the DES, Dublin: DES, unpublished.

McDonald, B (1976), "Evaluation and the Control of Education", in Tawney, D. (ed.), *Curriculum Evaluation Today*, London: Macmillan.

McLaren, P. (1993), *Schooling as a Ritual Performance* (2nd ed.), London and New York: Routledge.

McNamara, B. (1918), *The Valley of the Squinting Windows*, Tralee: Anvil Books.

McNeil, L. (2000), *Contradictions of School Reform: Educational Costs of Standardisation*, NY: Routledge.

McNiff, J., McNamara, G. and Leonard, D. (eds.) (2000), "Action Research in Ireland", Poole: September Books.

Mulcahy, D.G. (1989), "Official Perceptions of Curriculum in Irish Second-Level Schools", in Mulcahy, D.G. and O'Sullivan, D. (eds.), *Irish Educational Policy, Process and Substance*, Dublin, IPA, pp. 77–98.

NCCA (1989), *A Guide to the Junior Certificate*, Dublin: NCCA.

O'Carroll, J.P. (2002), "A Century of Change", in Corcoran, M.P. and Peillon, M. (eds.), *Ireland Unbound: A Turn of the Century Chronicle*, Dublin: IPA, pp. 133–48.

Ó Ceallaigh, A. (1985), The Work of the Curriculum and Examinations Board, *Compass*, Vol. 14, No. 2, pp. 7–18.

O'Donoghue, F. (2002), "Civic Expression: The Value of Volunteering", in Bohan, H., and Kennedy, G. (eds.), *Is the Future my Responsibility? Our Society in the New Millennium*, Dublin: Veritas, pp. 60–77.

OECD (1991), *Reviews of National Education Policies for Education: Ireland*, Paris: OECD.

OECD (2001), *The Well-Being of Nations: The Role of Human and Social Capital*, Paris: OECD.

Oldham, E. (2003), "From FIMS to PISA to our Classrooms: Can Large-Scale Cross-national Studies Help us to Teacher and Learn Differently?" *Irish Educational Studies*, Vol. 22, No. 1, pp. 1–28.

O'Leary, M. (2001), "Item Format as a Factor Affecting the Relative Standing of Countries in the Third International Mathematics and Science Study (TIMMS)", *Irish Educational Studies*, Vol. 20, pp. 153–76.

O'Sullivan, D. (1992), "Cultural Strangers and Educational Change: The OECD Report Investment in Education and Irish Educational Policy", *Journal of Education Policy*, Vol. 7, No. 5, pp. 445–69.

Putnam, R.D. (2000), *Bowling Alone: The Collapse and Revival of American Community*, New York: Simon and Schuster.

Said, E.W. (1993), *Culture and Imperialism*, London: Chatto and Windus.

Sarason, S. (1990), *The Predictable Failure of Educational Reform*, San Francisco: Jossey-Bass.

Sarason, S. (1996), *Revisiting the Culture of the School and the Problem of Change*, New York: Teachers College Press.

Scheper-Hughes, N. (2001), *Saints, Scholars and Schizophrenics: Mental Illness in Rural Ireland* (Twentieth Anniversary Edition, updated and expanded), Berkeley, Los Angeles & London: University of California Press.

Sennett, R. (1998), *The Corrosion of Character: The Personal Consequences of Work in the New Capitalism*, New York: Norton.

Stoll, L., Fink, D., and Earl, L. (2003), *It's About Learning (And It's About Time) What's in it for Schools?* London & New York: Routledge/Falmer.

Stone, D. (2002), *Policy Paradox. The Art of Political Decision Making* (rev. ed.), New York and London: W.W. Norton and Company.

Sugrue, C. (1997), "Student Teachers' Lay Theories and Identities: Implications for Professional Development", *European Journal of Teacher Education*, Vol. 20, pp. 213–26.

Sugrue, C. (1998), *Teaching, Curriculum and Educational Research*, Dublin: St Patrick's College.

Sugrue, C. and Uí Thuama, C. (1994), "Substance and Method in Postgraduate Educational Research", *Irish Educational Studies*, Vol. 13, pp. 26–41.

Endnotes

---

[1] The two major Catholic teacher education institutions are Mary Immaculate College, which has its programmes validated by the University of Limerick, and St Patrick's College, Drumcondra, which is a College of Dublin City University. The other three colleges are Froebel (Blackrock, Dominican) and St Mary's Marino (Christian Brothers) and the Church of Ireland College of Education (Rathmines). All three of these colleges have their Degree accredited and awarded by Trinity College, Dublin University.

[2] The legacy of the nineteenth century is evident in the restricted career structure afforded teacher educators who work in the Colleges of Education when compared with their colleagues in the university sector. There are no professors of primary education in the system, and neither is the promotional post of Associate Professor available in the Colleges. This historical legacy is discriminatory and one that the teaching profession as a whole, and particularly the INTO, should seek to eliminate since its membership has been the main beneficiary of primary teaching becoming a graduate profession from the 1970s onwards.

Also Available from The Liffey Press . . .

Childhood and Its Discontents

The First Seamus Heaney Lectures

Edited by Joseph Dunne
and James Kelly

Today there is heightened sensitivity to the needs and rights of children. At the same time, strong pressures tend toward the creation of a less child-friendly society. Greater appreciation of ambivalence and contradiction in attitudes towards, and treatment of, children points to the need for more searching inquiry into the nature of childhood and the complex dynamics through which different childhoods are constructed by adults.

Childhood and its Discontents aims to advance this inquiry and will be of particular interest to parents, educators and policy-makers. By bringing together perspectives from psychology, sociology, history and philosophy, the book is intended as a contribution to greater understanding of children themselves and of adults' imaginative and emotional investments in them. Such understanding, not least of adult failure and neglect, may provide a basis for more enlightened policies towards childhood and greater wellbeing for children.

The essays collected here were first delivered as lectures in the inaugural Seamus Heaney Lectures Series at St Patrick's College, Dublin. This is a biennial series, in which distinguished scholars in education and the humanities, from Ireland and abroad, address topics of central concern to the general public.

€19.50 paperback / December 2002 / 240 pages / ISBN 1-904148-17-4

To order, telephone The Liffey Press at (01) 8511458. Visa and Mastercard accepted, or send a cheque to The Liffey Press, Ashbrook House, 10 Main Street, Raheny, Dublin 5.

www.theliffeypress.com

Also Available from The Liffey Press . . .

Who Chooses Science?

Subject Take-up in Second-Level Schools

Emer Smyth and Carmel Hannan
The Economic and Social Research Institute

The proportion of students taking science subjects for the Leaving Certificate has declined in recent years. This has led to policy concern about a potential shortage of scientific skills within the workforce. However, little is known about the factors which influence subject choice within second-level education and beyond.

Who Chooses Science? draws on a national survey of over 4,000 students along with detailed case-studies of science teaching within eight schools. It highlights best practice in science education and identifies the factors which affect the take-up of Chemistry, Physics, Biology and higher Maths at senior cycle. It also indicates the student and school characteristics which influence the choice of course on entry to higher education. The book indicates the way in which schools can facilitate or constrain the choices made by students and discusses the implications for educational policy.

Who Chooses Science? will be of interest to policymakers, academics, school management, guidance counsellors, teachers, parents and the broader scientific community.

€22.50 paperback / December 2002 / 264 pages / ISBN 1-904148-24-7

To order, telephone The Liffey Press at (01) 8511458. Visa and Mastercard accepted, or send a cheque to The Liffey Press, Ashbrook House, 10 Main Street, Raheny, Dublin 5.

www.theliffeypress.com